mud

rocky

15′

73   74   75   76

ồng

mud
rocky

17°00′   sand
                          mud   sand   sand
là Lợi Trung   gravel
                                    sand
                                    gravel
Hà Lợi
rung   mud
Dunes   Hà Lợi Trung
Ha Loc
Cồn Tổng
ảnh   Ⓗ CỬA VIỆT
Tương Vận   Hà Tây
Xa Thi /12   Vình
    Dương Xuân   Hòa
Fy   Lương Kim   Phương
Giao Liem   Thanh Hồi
ộc Lê   560   Lê Xuyên   Bình An
                                mud
Thôn Dương Lệ Văn Thôn   Thôn Ba Lăng
                Linh An   10   10
Thôn Trà Liên Tây Cem   ·8   Thôn Gia Đẳng   rocky
        Thôn Thương   Thôn Gia Đẳng   sand
Tân Định Thôn Đạo Đầu Trạch   Thôn Tân An   rocky
                Thôn Văn Phòng   sand   10
Triệu Phong   Thôn Linh Chiều Thôn Mỹ Thủy   sand
    Ⓗ   Thôn Xuân Dương
    TRIỆU PHONG Xuân Kinh Thôn Phương Lang Đông
NG TRI   555   Thôn Trung An   sand
12 QUẢNG TRI   Xóm Thương An Xóm Thương Hòa   Thôn Thâm Khê   10
    557 Thôn An Thái Cem   Thôn Đơn Quế
3   Lăng La Vang Tả   Thôn Hội Yên ·19   Phường Giáp Đông
n Bieu QUẢNG TRI/LA VANG   Thôn Cu Hoan   Thôn Xán Viên   Thôn Tân Hối
Như Lệ Cem 18   Ⓗ   Thôn   Thôn Thanh Hương Thôn Mỹ Hòa
    Thôn Mai Đạng   HẢI LĂNG Phước Điền
    Thôn Phú Long ·15 Hải Lăng Thôn Diên Trường 555 Ấp Vân Trinh Thôn Kế Môn Thôn Thế
Thôn Trương Phước   Thôn Thôn Phú Kinh Ấp Siêu Quần △24 Thôn Thế
    Thôn Trương Thọ   Giáp Thôn Văn Qui   Chí Tây
                Hậu Trường Sanh Thôn Hưng Nhơn Ấp Lương Mai
            Thôn Xóm Bờ   Ấp Phố Trạch Ấp Mỹ Phổ
ÔNG ĐỒ]   Trương Thôn Cầu Nhi   Ấp Tây Hoàng Hương Điền
·275   ·118   Thọ   Ấp Mỹ Xuyên Ấp Tây Hoàng Cem
    Thôn Xuân Lộc MỸ CHÁNH Ấp Đông Hồ
·61   Thôn Văn Phong
                Gare de Phổ Trạch Xóm Đức Tích
            Thôn Mỹ Chánh
NG TRI   PHO TRACH Ấp Thủy Lập
ỪA THIÊN △84 15 Ấp Vĩnh Nãy
    NÚI CAI MƯƠNG Thôn Vân Trạch Hòa Phong Điền Ấp Bạch Thạnh
                Ấp Khánh Mỹ Quảng
    Đinh Điền ·69 QL Ấp Cổ Tháp
    Hòa Mỹ   50   Ấp Thương An Ấp Phú U
            Thôn Hà Lạng

D1572157

Yesterdays Are Forever

Yesterdays Are Forever

A Memoir

A Rite of Passage
Through the Marine Corps
and Vietnam War

Richard D. Jackson, Major USMCR

Yesterdays Are Forever. A Rite of Passage Through the Marine Corps and Vietnam War. A Memoir

ISBN 1-883707-42-0
First Edition, January, 2000

U.S. Marine Corps photographs pages,
115, 116, 117, 118, 120, 121, 125, 126

To order contact:

Protea Publishing
2920 Peachtree Industrial Blvd
Suite B
Norcross, Georgia 30071
USA

770-242-9891
770-242-6468 fax

kaolink@msn.com

www.proteapublishing.com

In Remembrance of my parents,
Vivian and Harry
and for my children,
Kimberly and Christopher.

"Write this above my head in some forgotten grave.
Here lies no hero listed with the brave.
Beyond the score he only loved the game,
and when the bell gave out it's final call,
he had not much to give, but gave it all."

Grantland Rice

A Sporting Epitaph

CONTENTS

The Author, Okinawa 1967

AUTHOR'S NOTE

Everybody should write a book. Fact or fiction it matters not. The experience is stimulating, educational, insightful, and absorbing. Once the story begins to unfold, your interest grows as you work your way through the tale. You become driven, moving recklessly, but with a mission. Consumed in your own writing, everything else seems to take on lesser importance. You must finish and you must get it right.

After returning from South Vietnam 32 years ago, I had wanted to write about the combat activities of my rifle company. We had won our little war, with minimum human expense, and the men in my command had performed, as a team, in a commendable manner.

I started writing in 1968 and did complete some material, which is included in this memoir, but I didn't have the staying power, in those days, to maintain the course.

In early 1998 I began writing again, somewhat haphazardly and sketchily, and by the end of the year I had gained the motivation I needed. The story was beginning to take on dimension and finally my objective took focus. I concluded, the only possible way to convey the significance of my story was to include the entire eight years I spent in the U. S. Marine Corps, with some orientation on how I got there.

As I wrote, unearthing incidents and people, I discovered many overlapping and leading events, unfolding, one to the next, all taking me on this written road to my destination.

Unfortunately, I can no longer recall all the names of the people, or the exact dates and locations of each incident. But, my pulse beats faster as I press on with my memories and few scattered notes from my experiences in the Corps. Fragments crystallize and form a larger and clearer image. I have worked diligently to put these images into words that tell a credible story.

This Memoir is based only on my personal recollections and information contained in a few documents within my possession. The observations, interpretations and conclusions are my views unilaterally, and in no way represent the policy or position of any persons, organizations, or historical records.

I have crafted this story from a young man's perspective, which was reality as I lived and witnessed these events. Others may have seen them differently, and from their perspectives might have reached different conclusions. That is to be expected, as the scattered observation points in life, present many angles of view and individual personal realities.

Most importantly, to me, these years would have a significant impact on my life, affecting the style, choices, and decisions I would make as a consequence of these experiences.

As this is my first and probably only literary effort on this period of time, I will acknowledge that this document is far from perfect. You might well conclude that it is a bit "rough around the edges", as I have been all my life, in both design and content. However, I am hopeful it presents a factual and interesting record of events while respectfully acknowledging the people and organizations that played a dominant role in my personal growth, and Rite of Passage through the United States Marine Corps.

PREFACE

It was early 1966 and the Vietnam War was raging endlessly and it was raging without me. What was a dedicated and determined Marine Officer to do to hasten his involvement in the war? Wait your turn? It was certain to come eventually. Or, initiate a process, which would provide the opportunity sooner? In mid-1966, I mailed a letter to Headquarters, Marine Corps, Washington, DC. In it, I requested assignment to Vietnam. This letter was answered positively. After six and a half years of military service, my objective as a 29-year-old Captain, was nothing less than to be a Rifle Company Commander in the Southeast Asian War.

*   *   *   *

In January 1967 the NVA wake-up call and welcome came to the new Commanding Officer of Mike Company, 3rd Battalion, 4th Marines.

At 0230 hours all hell broke loose. The sky lit up like Times Square on New Years Eve. The gunny was screaming, "Skipper, Skipper, Incoming"; I shot from the cot in a roll and hit the deck with the impact of a bag of wet sand. Gunny was clinging to the floor as I tried desperately to pull on my jungle boots. What a night to sleep without my boots on! I vowed it would be the last.

Mortar fragments slammed into the back of my head causing a sensation similar to the sting of a yellow jacket. My body pressed even flatter against the makeshift wooden floor, still wrestling with my damn boots. Double rows of sand bags circled our tent, standing about 3 1/2 feet high. I could feel the vibrations as shrapnel crashed deep into the bags. The enemy

82mm rounds kept peppering the company position. I knew I had to get to the command bunker and coordinate the counter mortar fire and defense against a possible ground attack.

As I rushed from the tent, the exploding mortar rounds continued to rain down on our position. I was scared, really scared as I skirted across the barren ground. But, I forced myself to reach the safety of the tiny opening in the ground that lead into the protected bunker.

I made it through the small orifice and immediately began receiving compass azimuths. These came over the company command radio net from points within our position to the muzzle flashes of the enemy mortars.

During the confusion we somehow managed to get a fix, or approximate location, on the enemy mortars and relayed the fire mission over the Battalion Tactical Net. It was only minutes before we received an "On the Way" from the artillery gun position. However, much to our surprise, the first six rounds did not drop on the enemy position, but fell well short puncturing our own perimeter. The concussions were so close to my CP that I though the enemy had stepped up the attack. Realizing what was happening lead to an instant scream into the radio to cease fire. We were to find out later someone transposed numbers in the coordinates we transmitted, causing a 3,000 meter error. It's one thing to be killed by the enemy in battle, but to "buy it" from "friendly's" makes it a futile ball game, indeed.

EPILOGUE FOR A PROLOGUE

We had been engaged with the enemy for about two months in the Cua Viet River area. During this time we had developed a new method of war fighting in our zone of action. We were winning and winning big without taking significant casualties. We operated almost on an independent basis, and this was significant, since we organized and developed each combat plan based on the fluidity of the situation. Our reaction time was as good or better than the enemy. We played their game our way and won.

On February 18, 1967 we received the enclosed message from Major General Kyle, Commanding General of the Third Marine Division. As far as we were concerned it said everything that needed saying about our operations and our results.

On April 1, 1967 the attached Third Marine Division bulletin was published on our company activities in the Cua Viet area. This document along with General Kyle's Message, were the crowning achievements of what Mike Company had accomplished and was more or less a fitting beginning of the end for me. We still had a few battles to fight; however I would be transferred from Mike Company in May 1967, while on an operation in the DMZ. I would spend my remaining months in the Marine Corps, at the Third Marine Division Headquarters in PHU BAI, Vietnam and later become a civilian in January 1968. My life as a Marine had been a good run.

In December 1967, I returned home from a thirteen-month tour in Vietnam. The war was still raging in Southeast Asia, but for me it was over.

*   *   *   *

I had joined the Marine Corps in March 1960, when I entered the Officer Candidate Course at Marine Corps Schools, Quantico, Virginia. Upon graduation, three months later, I was commissioned a Second Lieutenant in the Marine Corps Reserves. After two years of military service I requested, and was granted, a Regular Officer's Commission and was seriously considering a career in the Marines.

*   *   *   *

I arrived home a Captain, with nearly eight years of military experience, and had been selected for promotion to Major, which would have probably happened in two or three months. But, something had occurred that caused me to reconsider my career choice of the Marines. Several months prior to departing Vietnam, I had proffered my resignation and it had been accepted. Consequently, I had only one month of service obligation remaining when I returned to the United States.

To this day, thirty-two years later, I cannot recall the exact reasons for my change of mind. I liked the Marine Corps, the traditions, and my eight years had provided me with interesting and fulfilling experiences.

I made the decision to leave the Corps while on a search and destroy operation near the DMZ. At that time, I was commanding a rifle company, Mike Company, 3d Battalion, 4th Marines, Third Marine Division and we had been attached to an Infantry Battalion that was engaged in a critical operation, with the enemy. We spent a couple weeks pursuing a large NVA force that was finally retreating steadily toward their base in North Vietnam.

Unfortunately, my relationship with the Lieutenant Colonel commanding the Battalion was highly unsatisfactory, to say the least. Frankly, I thought he demonstrated little personal regard for his troops. He seemed only interested in making a name for himself. Maybe I was fatigued, overwhelmed, disenchanted, or perhaps I had a higher calling of some kind. All or part of which must have had some influence on my decision. It matters little after all these years, but at the time, when the operation was over, I had resolved to resign my commission and change my life's destiny.

Ever since leaving the Corps in January 1968, I have wanted to document my experiences as a Rifle Company Commander in Vietnam. I actually started this text thirty years ago, but too many things interfered. I couldn't commit the time, mental energy, or effort. I was unable to construct a format which would present in logical sequence, the events I wanted to describe. Initially, I wanted to only chronicle the combat actions of my unit, Mike Company. It was to be a review of our tactics, how we deployed them, and the results. Just a kind of historical report on a Marine rifle company in combat.

But, as time passed, many of those events faded from my memory, and my ability to recall specific actions began to wane. I nearly abandoned the idea, but since semi-retirement, I now have the time and internal commitment to focus on my story -- which has become a labor of love and an awakening of memories from an exciting past. Now, when I write, images from those days cascade from my mind with clarity -- each occurrence forming the foundation for the next sequence of events.

The "Epilogue for a Prologue" contains documents I found buried in an old footlocker stored in my basement, along with other war memorabilia and field equipment. This discovery stimulated me to begin writing once again. And has been a catalyst for recalling the memories around which this memoir is organized. My entry in the Marine Corps seems the proper starting point to review an eight year career that shaped my thinking forever and favorably impacted my personal value system.

Marine Corps Correspondence

Enclosure: Message from Commanding General
Wood B. Kyle, Third Marine Division.

Attachment: Third Marine Division Bulletin lessons
learned in sweep techniques.

CONFIDENTIAL

AND NR 25.....25..

R 180621Z FEB 67
FM CG THIRD MARDIV
TO THIRD MARDIV FWD
INFO THIRD MARDIV
BT
C O N F I D E N T I A L
1. THE EXCELLENT RESULTS OBTAINED BY CO M 3/4 IN AGGRESSIVE SEARCH
OPERATIONS IN THE VICINITY OF THE CUA VIET AREA HAVE BEEN NOTED
WITH PLEASURE. INDICTIVE OF EXCELLENT COMBAT LEADERSHIP, HIGH
LEVEL TROOP PROFICIENCY AND EVVECTIVENESS HAS BEEN THE CAPTURE/

KILL OF NUMEROUS VC, THE CAPTURE OF ARMS AND EQUIPMENT AND THE
UNCOVERING OF TUNNELS AND CACHES.
2. KEEP UP THE GOOD WORK. MAJOR GENERAL KYLE SENDS.
GP-4

BT

CONFIDENTIAL

HEADQUARTERS
3d Marine Division (Rein), FMF
FPO, San Francisco 96602

DivBul 3120
3/JHG/das
1 April 1967

DIVISION BULLETIN 3120

From: Commanding General
To: Distribution List

Subj: Lesson's Learned as a result of sweep techniques employed during
        operations within the 3d Marine Division

Encl: (1) Report of methods employed by Company M, 3d Battalion, 4th
            Marine Regiment in conducting search operations in the Cua Viet
            area

1. Purpose. To disseminate information regarding sweep operations conducted
in the area of the Cua Viet river.

2. Background. Company M, 3d Battalion, 4th Marines, operating in the
area near the mouth of the Cua Viet river, developed and successfully
employed techniques and special equipment which could prove benefical to
other units conducting similar type operations.

3. Action. Attention of leaders at all echelons is invited to the methods
and procedures described in the enclosure.

4. Self-Cancellation. 24 September 1967.

A. D. CEREGHINO
Chief of Staff

DISTRIBUTION: "B" & "C"

1. The following is a report on the method employed by Mike Company, 3d Battalion, 4th Marine Regiment in conducting search operations within its assigned TAOR in the Cua Viet area.

   a. Background:

       (1) Mike Company occupied a unique position. The circumstances surrounding the conduct of operations have had considerable bearing upon the success achieved and therefore should be disclosed at the outset of this report.

           (a) The company had available to it on a continuing basis the mobility and fire power of an Amphibious Tractor Company. Consequently, more time was spent in searching an area and less time in moving to that area. The LVTH-6 provided immediate and direct artillery fire support for Mike units. The problems of coordinating transportation were minimal.

           (b) The Cua Viet coastal area is characterized by soft, sandy soil. Consequently the "Special Probing Device", described later in this report, works extremely well. The soil can be easily probed to a depth of three feet in most parts of the area. The flat terrain provides excellent fields of observation and fire.

           (c) Continuous movement throughout the assigned area, facilitated by supporting AmTracs, enabled Mike Company to familiarize itself thoroughly with the terrain. The Company's knowledge of the terrain equals that of the enemy, an unusual situation in guerrilla warfare.

   b. Formations/Organization:

       (1) In conducting a company size sweep, Company M was organized into four elements and a CP group. The elements were: forward security, company on line, rear security, and a blocking force.

           (a) The forward security for the company consisted of two fire teams deployed on line across the company front.

           (b) The main body, company on line, followed the forward element at an interval of fifty meters. The company CP group and 60mm mortars moved in trace of the main body in a position from which they could best control and observe the progress of the sweep.

           (c) The rear security, consisting of 2 fire teams, followed fifty meters behind the CP group. This element was deployed in the same manner as the forward security except that it was oriented toward the rear.

           (d) The blocking element consisted of the LVTP-5's mounted with .30 cal machine guns and protected by an adequate force of infantry. LVTH-6's were positioned where they could best support the company.

ENCLOSURE (1)

c. Technique/Equipment:

(1) Each member of the main body was provided with a "Special Probing Device". This device consisted of the rod from a 105mm ammunition box, sharpened at one end and fixed with a handle at the other. As the line moved out in sweeping, each man probed the ground at his front and flanks to a depth of about three to six inches in an effort to locate hidden punji traps, spider holes and buried caches. In probing knolls or mounds the device was sunk deeper into the soil. The sweep was slow but exceptionally thorough. Ammunition caches were discovered at a depth of three feet below the surface using this probing device. It must, however, be understood that the value of this device decreased as the consistency of the soil increased.

(2) In addition to the "Special Probing Device", the company employed the "Special J Hook". It consisted of a metal hook in the shape of a "J" secured to a thirty meter length of line. One "J" hook was carried per squad. The hook was used to remove the lids covering spider holes and buried containers when a possibility of booby trapping existed

(3) It was noted that the employment of RCA met with poor results in forcing the V.C. from their spider holes. The CS grenades allowed the enemy sufficient time to throw fragmentation grenades at the Marines who uncovered the positions. The M-26 fragmentation grenade was far more effective when the enemy refused to abandon his hole and continued to fight and or throw grenades.

d. Results:

(1) It was observed that the men of the company carried out their probing with unusual enthusiasm which was heightened with each new discovery.

(2) The following is a list of arms, ammunition and rice uncovered, and enemy personnel killed and captured during the period 1 Feb - 28 Feb 1967 utilizing the methods described above.

(a) Weapons - 25	(h) Spider traps - 40
(b) Grenades - 90	(i) Small arms ammo - 6000
(c) VCC - 10	(j) 3.5 rocket rds - 4
(d) VC KIA - 20	(k) 57mm rocket rds - 6
(e) Mortar rds - 26	(l) Booby traps with explosive devices - 30
(f) Rice - 180 lbs	(m) Communications equipment - complete set
(g) Punji pits - 400	

ENCLOSURE (1)

Starting Out

"I shall be telling this with a sigh
somewhere ages and ages hence:
two roads diverged in a wood,
and I,
I took the one less traveled by,
and that has made all the difference."

Robert Frost

The Road not Taken

HUNTINGTON, WEST VIRGINIA

My birthplace, Huntington, West Virginia, is located on the Ohio River, just a few miles from Ashland, Kentucky. At that time, it was a city of about ninety thousand people, the largest in the Mountain State, full of heavy industry, and a big supplier of war material and goods during the Second World War.

I was born 30 days after the flood of '37, on February 15. Sometime after the waters receded a sixty-foot floodwall was built along the city riverbanks to keep the flooding waters of the Ohio from ever entering again. As a small boy I played on parts of this mound of earth, that protected the city, and it was part of the simple life that we enjoyed as children.

In those days, many families lived together in order to make ends meet, and I was happy to be the only child in a household consisting of my parents, grandparents, uncle, aunt, and cousin.

My mother's parents, my grandparents, Bert and Della, whom I loved very much, owned a 35-acre farm located near Point Pheasant, West Virginia. I spent many weeks living with them, enjoying the loving pleasure of their company, and their simple life style, with absolutely no frills. Their farm was located well back in the hills, where the whippoorwill's nightly song ricocheted through those hollows. The nearest dirt road was over three miles away, and their farm was accessible only by foot, or horse drawn carriage. We had no electricity, running water, or plumbing. It was a real frontier life, and I loved every moment I spent there. The memories of this hard scrabble way of life would remain with me forever.

Unfortunately, while serving in Vietnam a quarter century later, I did not receive a property tax notice, probably not uncommon due to the circumstances and the difficulty of forwarding mail to Vietnam, and as a consequence of not paying the taxes, the property was auctioned and sold on the court house steps in Point Pheasant. It had been willed to me from my grandparents, and when I lost it, a part of my youth went with it, but those wonderful memories will always be with me.

My grandfather, Bert Lockhart, had served under Teddy Roosevelt in Cuba as a nineteen-year-old private, and charged up San Juan Hill as a member of his Rough-Riders. He filled my young ears with tales of that war and the exploits of he and his comrades later in the Philippine Islands, during the Spanish American War. He was a great storyteller and musician. He had played the fiddle and banjo in Roosevelt's band along with his older brother. Undoubtedly, his military service was the highlight of his mostly agrarian life.

I attended Saint Joseph, the only Catholic school in the city, and early on, developed a vivid interest in sports. My young mind reveled with the thoughts that some day I would be an All American in every sport I played. I was initially drawn to athletics because there was little else available to young people in our social class. I loved the competition, how my body felt from the strain of exercise, the public recognition for a good performance, and of course the developing desire to be an athlete the rest of my life.

Sports were all I had at that time in my life, but it was enough for me. In the 1950's, living in a basic blue-collar city with minimum financial means available, the simple joys of living evolved around friends, movies, parties, sporting events, and all the heroes were athletes. I longed to be one of those heroes.

We owned no cars; our thumb, feet and an occasional bus, provided our mode of transportation. It was elementary; we didn't have much and didn't need much. We didn't have a clue about life in the rich fast lane. It didn't matter, because we were happy most of the time with our simple pleasures.

My last two years in Junior High school were in Huntington, living with my Mother, Vivian, who worked in a drug store to support us, while we lived in a four-room apartment. She was my biggest fan, loved me dearly and provided for us the very best she could. She had a wonderful personality and everyone admired her.

My first year in High School was at A. L. Brown in Kannapolis, North Carolina, living with my father Harry, as my parents were then divorced. We shared a bedroom and a double bed, and were part of the household of his brother and wife. The year with my dad was difficult because we lived in cramped quarters, but I was welcomed to the house, as my Uncle and Aunt had no children and they enjoyed having a young person around.

My Father was a small man, but had played football in high school. I was told he was a very good halfback and had been tendered a college scholarship which he didn't accept. He worked in odd jobs all his life, took good care of my needs while I lived with him, and imbued a quality of courtesy and politeness in my character.

In North Carolina I was introduced to football, after playing basketball and baseball through junior high. I made the team, barely, as a one hundred and forty five-pound guard, but didn't play much except on the junior varsity. However, the seed of enjoyment for the game was planted inside me and would blossom over the next several years.

During the summer months of those teenage years, I would visit with my Dad's Parents, Hugh and Mamie on their farm in Mt. Croghan, South Carolina. Grandpa was a man's man, small in stature, strong willed, a hard-nosed Baptist with absolutely perfect manners. He made certain all his children and grandchildren behaved appropriately and displayed the proper courtesies, especially to their elders.

He worked his grandchildren hard when they visited the farm, clearing fields, raising cattle, turkeys or whatever was his fancy at the time. I learned how to milk cows, raise chickens, cut a mean axe, drive a car, pick blackberries, trim hedges, drive a tractor, and about a thousand other farming tasks during the summers I spent with him.

He had a significant influence on my life, gave me no material gifts, but taught me about pride of doing a good job and earning the respect of others. He was a stern, demanding, hard-nosed, God fearing man, and at age sixteen, when I learned of his death, I cried like a baby. I loved and respected him deeply.

I tried all the sports my sophomore year, including football, baseball, basketball, and track, and did moderately well as a skinny five foot ten inch kid, but I doubt I raised anyone's eyebrows with my performance or demonstrated much potential worth noting. My greatest achievement was that I tried every sport and gave my best. Athletics, constant training and the thrill of the game continued to absorb me as I grew older. It was my only outlet, the only thing I had to differentiate me from other people and to satiate my need to be recognized and accepted in a world where I had little to bring to the table economically or intellectually.

At the start of my junior year, I moved back to Huntington having packed on an additional twenty pounds on my otherwise skinny frame. I was now a 160 pound first team defensive end for the Huntington High School Pony Express. By my senior year I had gained both speed and weight, was moved to a halfback position, and was fortunate enough to be selected to the All-State Football Team, in West Virginia as well as win a 2nd place and a 5th place in the 220 and 100 yard dashes in the State track meet. These final years of high school were devoted to athletics and I was one of the last jocks to play four sports for the Pony Express, graduating in 1955.

Athletics was much different in those days and a small fast man could participate. These were the days before both speed and size became a dominant prerequisite for sports. Football was now my primary game. After several scholarships offers I accepted one from Marshall College in Huntington, which become a University in 1961.

Marshall was a Liberal Arts and Teaching college of about forty five hundred students, a member of the Mid-American conference, and I thought it's size would provide more opportunity to play football regularly. It was also my home where I had already received recognition as a good athlete, consequently, my transition to college sports would be easier.

I played football, basketball, and track there, belonged to the varsity club, the Pi Kappa Alpha Fraternity, and graduated with a Marketing/Retailing degree in 1959 with a C+ average. Not a great scholastic achievement and therefore, no significant job opportunities waited at my doorstep.

In those days, young single men were required to enter the military service and fulfill there obligation with either six months active duty followed by six and a half years of reserves, or three years active duty. It was difficult to locate a promising job until the military responsibility was satisfied in one form or another. Although, I had been offered a professional football try-out with the 1958 World Champions Baltimore Colts. I decided that I should put my military responsibilities behind me. I believed I could play ball in the service, grow a bit more, gain some additional experience and maturity and then try professional football after the military. It made rational sense, but that was probably a pipe dream, because deep inside I didn't have the confidence in my abilities, the talent or the physical attributes to be a professional athlete.

The only military organization that looked exciting to me at that time, was the U. S. Marines, so I applied for the Officer Candidate Program. After two testing attempts, I passed the qualifying exam and was notified in January 1960 that I had been accepted and was to report for the next class starting in March. My grandfather Bert, had provided me with his legacy of military service and perhaps in doing so had aroused my spirit to seek out the same kind of excitement and experience he had found in his life, sixty years past. I heard the siren call and would soon be on a similar path.

When I recall my formative years in school, what I remember are the influences driving me toward the military or, more specifically, to the Marine Corps. There were those recruiting posters on the street corners and on our campus bulletin boards. TV commercials, the Victory at Sea series, and stories of World War II and Korea were shown weekly on our black and white television set. The marketing theme presented by the Corps promoted top of mind awareness for specific types of hardy men. Men, willing to face the physical challenge and the so-called test of courage embodied in the slogan "The Marine Corps Builds Men". Even after years of high school and college athletics, working in a steel factory and the coal fields of West Virginia, I must have believed that there was still some character building needed, some moral fiber and mental toughness lacking to finally grow into the person I wanted to be. If this were not the case, surely, I would have chosen a less challenging path after college. But the call of the Marines sounded in my ears and echoed through my bones. I responded, accepting the challenges they promised. In return, I made the commitment to become a Man and a Marine - in their mold.

It was then March 1960. I was out of college some nine months, and on my way to Marine Corps Schools as a member of the 26th Officer Candidate Class (OCC), at Training and Testing Regiment. At midnight, I boarded the Chesapeake and Ohio Railway sleeper car, and departed Huntington, en route to an abrupt change of lifestyle and a new destiny. Not certain what my future would bring, I still looked forward to this new opportunity with a mixture of anticipation and regret, for the rigorous life I was entering and the comfortable life I was leaving. After sleepless hours listening to the clatter and rumble of the tracks beneath the train, I arrived at the sprawling Marine Corps base south of Washington, DC. It was in a place called Quantico.

Learning The Trade

*"The more you sweat in peace,
The less you bleed in war."*

General George S. Patton

QUANTICO, VIRGINIA

The train clattered into the small station at Quantico, Virginia, about mid-morning. Carrying my luggage, I casually debarked from the sleeper car, where I had spent a restless night. On the landing, a big, strapping Marine Sergeant greeted me and several others from my class - future friends and companions, I had yet to meet. In a voice that would stop a crowd, the sergeant not so casually suggested that we all get our asses in motion, fall in single file and double-time our worthless selves to the bus which was waiting for us. We had work to do and should not waste his valuable time in asking stupid ass questions, because, we lacked the intelligence to understand his answers anyway. Just keep our mouths shut and do as we were told.

The Officer Candidate course is the would-be Marine Officer's equivalent of the famous or infamous Boot Camp endured by non-officer enlisted recruits. Enlisted men go to Paris Island, S. C. , or Marine Corps Recruitment Depot, San Diego, California. Officer recruits go to OCC at Quantico. Same hell, different names and places but the intent and effect are the same.

Before the day ended, I was sheared of my long black hair, wrapped in Marine Corps Green utilities of blouse, trousers, hat and boots. Also, I had learned to keep my eyes to the front after being screamed at by a First Lieutenant who caught me trying to observe some minor incident while waiting for my orders to be processed by the Administration Clerks. On the wall behind them was this huge banner saying, "Welcome to the United States Marine Corps," in large, maroon and gold letters. No kidding.

During the next three months, we literally ran the gauntlet as we learned about the Corps, its History and our future responsibilities as a Marine. Our Platoon Leaders tested us, both mentally and physically, to determine whether we truly possessed the commitment and mettle to become: Marine Officers.

Initially, I thought the prime mandate of the Corps was to mutate us into long distance runners, because they ran us constantly wherever we went, frequently in full battle gear with our weapons dangling from our shoulders. What became etched into our minds forever, were the appropriately named: "The Hill", "Power Line", and "The Chopsowamsik" trails. These were a few of the more topography challenging hiking trails introduced to us. All of the trails claimed a lion's share of our time and attention as we traveled them on countless forced marches, most of the time on the run.

The Obstacle Course adjacent to the Parade Field, also loomed large in our lives as we negotiated its confidence building challenges with still more running, accented with jumping and climbing. The obstacles were arranged in a line about fifty meters long and we were required to pass through, around and over them at our top speed, while our platoon Sergeants screamed at us with reinforcing, "expletives deleted" encouragement. All of these trails and obstacles courses were designed into the curriculum to challenge and condition both body and mind, while removing self-imposed limits that existed prior to joining this new breed of men.

The training put high demands on our young bodies, extracting the essence of both our physical and mental strength. However, in a few short weeks we grew stronger and began to adapt to the rigorous life.

When we weren't running or otherwise engaged in exercise or classroom instructions, we were found on the Parade Field marching and learning close order drill. Our beloved Platoon Sergeants ensured that we learned to march in the appropriate Marine Corps manner, and provided constant encouragement like "Keep in step Dip Shit," or, "your other left foot, Pisshead" as they marched us around for endless hours or so it seemed at the time. Commands flew at us like bullets, barked by our bull-throated Platoon Sergeants.

Frequent inspections were conducted to ensure we knew how to keep our personal selves "squared away and shipshape", our squad bays spic and span, and our gear cleaned and in flawless working order. We used an oily, grayish substance called "Brasso" to polish our belt buckles so they glistened in the sunlight; and we learned how to "spit shine" out boondocks, boots, so we could nearly see our own reflections in their curved surfaces when we looked at our feet. What was mandatory, at all costs, was exact neatness and impeccable appearance. We could not "be" Marines unless we learned how to "look" like Marines. When speaking, whatever else we had to say, the first and last words, uttered from our mouths when speaking to an Officer or Non-Commissioned Officer was always "SIR". To forget this was to draw the wrath and fire of God upon our heads, soon followed by our practicing a few dozen pushups on the spot to reinforce our memories. The training staff knew exactly how to get our attention and keep it; and if we didn't tow the line of their methods early in training, it had to be because we were stupid or simply loved pain.

The culture shock and training I experienced at Training and Test Regiment, the unit that conducted basic officer training at Marine Corps Schools, began to change me and my mindset in many ways.

The indoctrination training tears you down, strips away bias, removes your identity and dignity, humbles you to the lowest level, and then, step-by-step rebuilds you with a much higher level of self-confidence, determination, commitment, and *Esprit de Corps*. These traits are intended to remain with you for the rest of your life. The training is tough, instruction long, and your total attention demanded. When you graduate, if you do make it all the way through, you feel and believe you've been through Hell. And you have. However, the sense of accomplishment is overwhelming for the young men who pin on those hard-earned, golden, Second Lieutenants' bars.

At that time I believed this was the most significant achievement in my life, and I was proud to be an Officer in this elite military force. But, I was also saddened by the thought that the candidate brotherhood, established over the past three months by Trial and Test, was now ending and we were to go our separate ways. But, duty calls, time goes on, and so must we.

The basic precepts of the Corps are founded on sound leadership principles developed over two hundred years of duty, service and tradition. The published goal is to accomplish the mission and maintain the welfare of your people. These principles were taught to us early in our training. Not bad concepts, all and all. They have lived within me in all my endeavors during, and after, the years in the Corps. I was to learn very early in my new career that the application of good leadership in accomplishing your mission or objective, centered on your ability to motivate people by earning their confidence through positive example and a genuine interest in their personal well being. These principles, I found, not only worked in the military, but also in my later civilian career, where I discovered their importance in the business world.

Mnemonics was a pathway to success throughout our classroom instruction. These were catchwords and phrases driven into us by the rote method. We learned, through endless repetition, and learned how not to forget what we were taught. Mnemonics were our talismans for remembering such things as the operation of our rifle, the principles of war, various tactical considerations, and immediate action drills. We were introduced to the "Five Paragraph Order" through the word SMEAC (pronounced "Smee Ack"). It stands for "Situation, Mission, Execution, Administration, Logistics, and Communication" -- which define the essence in the development of any operational plan. Interestingly, all plans or orders, regardless of size or significance followed the basic format. The M-1 Grand rifle, which was still in service in 1960, and issued to us for our training, required a more complicated catch phrase to help us remember it's operation. The word IAMUWECAT (pronounced "I am you we cat"), describes the complete function of the weapon: (**I**gnition of the shell, **A**ction of the gas for the shell, **M**ovement of the bolt to the rear, **U**nlocking of the bolt, **W**ithdrawal of the firing pin, **E**xtraction of the shell from the weapon, **C**ompletion of the movement to the rear, **A**ction of the recoil spring to send the mechanism forward, and finally, **T**ermination of the movement forward.)

The M-1 rifle, weighing nearly ten pounds, was a grand old sturdy weapon that had seen action in both WWII and Korea. It was replaced about 1962 with the M-14 rifle and by the time Vietnam was underway, the controversial M-16 was put into action. Each of these weapons was lighter than it's counterpart and possessed much greater firepower. The M-16 caused a controversy, because it could malfunction under heavy usage. Some enhancements were made as the result of this claim, and the weapon survived the Vietnam war.

These teaching techniques ruled and marked our lives. We had much to learn in a short time, and our instructors demanded we know it all to the last detail. We had to retain it for sure and certain future use. So we practiced, recited, and studied until there was no question the knowledge was in our heads forever. After 30 years I can still remember most of these catch phrases, and after a few thoughtful moments, usually recite them verbatim. This was not rocket-science kind of learning, but the techniques worked. The objective, of course, was to ensure pre-conditional actions in emergency situations, like combat, where lives depended on immediate and automatic responses, which could possibly save your life or the lives of those around you. We were taught how to act and react when there was no time to think or plan. Just do it!

It was conditioning and training like this on enemy booby traps, which saved the lives of myself and my radioman later in Vietnam. While on patrol in the jungle, I stepped on a tiny wire crossing the trail. My learned and preconditioned instantaneous response, without need for any intellectual processing, kept both of us from being killed. The moment I stepped on that monofilament line stretched across the path, I knew without thinking it was attached to the trigger of an explosive meant to kill. I heard the click of the arming device, and looked down to see the nearly invisible line beneath the toe of my boot. I grabbed and pushed my radioman, screaming "Run!" All of this happened in the briefest moment possible, maybe two seconds. But we acted quickly enough to get ourselves out of the killing range of the explosion. My radioman was slightly wounded by a tiny particle of white phosphorous that struck his knee. My canteen and flak jacket was spattered with the burning material. But we were alive, and that was the only thing that mattered. We had run like hell gaining a distance of about ten yards in seconds, wearing full combat gear. Thank goodness I had been alert and responded so quickly. Otherwise my radioman and I would have been seriously wounded or even killed. No doubt about it.

I graduated from the Officer Candidate Course in June 1960, received my commission, and was ordered to report to Basic School Class 3-60, which was adjacent to Quantico, for Advanced Military Instruction. This was a kind of finishing school for newly commissioned officers like myself. The new officers would spend six months attending classes on various military subjects, and conduct field tactical exercises to prepare them for their responsibilities in a Marine Corps command somewhere in the world.

By the time I departed Training and Testing Regiment, en route to Basic School, I was beginning to think in terms of building a career in the Marines. I was totally indoctrinated, propagandized, and believed I wanted to be a Marine for the rest of my life. In reality, I have been in many ways as the phrase predicts, "Once a Marine, Always a Marine" - an effective slogan used by the Corps. The idea plants its roots deep in your mind and they grow forever. The thoughts are nourished by people like Marine General "Chesty" Puller, immortalized in Marine Corps history as a great leader and hero, who was awarded five navy crosses - our Nation's second highest commendation for valor in combat. Only, the Congressional Medal of Honor stands above the Navy Cross. He was a truly colorful person in almost every conceivable way. I was told that General Puller was to the Marine Corps, what Babe Ruth was to Baseball. He was a real walking, talking, living, legend.

General Puller spoke to our class one spring day during training and summarized the significance of our decision to become Marines. He told us the Corps should be the most important thing in our lives. He said the Marine Corps takes precedence over everything else, and used the cliché "to die a Marine is to live forever. " After his inspiring speech, as we stood on the Parade Field with our rifles hanging on our shoulders, our youth and enthusiasm was so incensed by his remarks, we would have offered our lives in any endeavor for God, Country, and especially for the Corps.

Upon graduation, I immediately took thirty days leave, badly needed after the past three months ordeal, bought a secondhand car in Quantico, and drove home to marry my college sweetheart, Mary Elizabeth (Libby) McLean. She had just graduated from Marshall.

We were married in Strafford, Virginia, a little town near Quantico, in a simple ceremony by a local Justice of the Peace. We were assigned base housing at Quantico and proceeded to set up living quarters. A Commission in the Marines, a used car costing $2,000 dollars, marriage, and the purchase of $400 dollars of furniture was a huge undertaking in those days, especially when it was all done in a two week period by someone having a salary of $360 dollars per month. Somehow we survived the financial gauntlet and a few weeks later I picked back up with my responsibilities.

With my head filled with the traditions and history of the Corps, all properly embellished, and my personal motivation at its' highest apex, I reported to the Basic School in August 1960 along with 200 other young wet-behind-the-ears Second Lieutenants. We were more than ready for additional military training and grooming to fill our individual roles as a Professional Military Officer and a Gentleman - decreed by congress when we were appointed officers by Legislative fiat. We proceeded through the demanding six-month course, attending classes, conducting field exercises, practicing weaponry, learning more history and traditions, participating in amphibious exercises, until finally, toward the end, we participated in the dreaded Five Day War.

This was a "simulated battle", or war games exercise in which we were expected to professionally utilize our recently learned military prowess. We were to apply our tactics and skills against an "enemy" force, primarily Marine enlisted troops, to demonstrate our ability and knowledge and, if assigned a leadership role, our potential to competently lead men. In this "war" we were graded on our capabilities and knowledge. Our grade would become part of our overall score in the course, which would in turn determine our standing among our peers in the class. This final evaluation could also influence our promotion potential in the Corps and our climb up the career ladder. These scores would be part of our personal files as long as we were in the Marines.

During the run of these war games, we were issued blank ammunition and a special adapter for our rifles that allowed us to simulate, as much as possible, the live fire of real battle conditions.

In war games, there are always humorous events that occur when least expected. One such incident happened in our group when we overran a fortified position as part of a field test problem. The Second Lieutenant assigned as leader for this particular exercise was extremely zealous and more than a little over-enthusiastic, as he attempted to demonstrate his superior capability and knowledge to the Officer in Charge of the exercise. We called these officers "spring butts", because every time an instructor asked a question in class, they would jump from their seats volunteering an answer, clamoring for recognition and a high grade score.

At the time, we had been in the field for four days, the weather was cold, and a few inches of snow had fallen the previous night. We were weary, wet, and our motivation was ebbing quickly, as was the enthusiasm of the enlisted men, aggressors. We had used all our blank ammo and were now resorting to screaming our heads off, yelling "Bang! Bang!" as we played our role in this simulated war. As planned, by our designated leader, the "spring butt" Lieutenant, we attacked the position screaming at the top of our lungs, overwhelming the enemy force. We were beginning to consolidate our position and place the captured forces under restriction, just as the book prescribed, except for one young tired Private, who was leisurely walking away from the battle, smoking a cigarette while his rifle dangled casually from his shoulder. The over-zealous Lieutenant, "Spring Butt," seeing this escaping aggressor, ran to catch him and screamed, "Bang! Bang!" you're dead" in the face of the slowly retiring trooper. But this enlisted man, without paying the slightest attention, kept puffing on his cigarette as he continued his stroll. Nonplused, the Lieutenant again shouted "Bang! Bang! You're dead!" When the Private still didn't respond in any fashion, our fearless leader screamed "Don't you know how to play the game? The young Private first class, who could have cared less about the Lieutenant, and much of anything else, (it is debated that PFC, Private First Class, really stands for Praying for Civilian), faced his foe with the words "Yeah, like man, Clank, Clank, I'm a tank!" It appeared from his retort that he had attained the highest level of simulated weapons in any tactical exercise. We all burst into laughter while the no longer over zealous Lieutenant slunk away with an expression of total defeat and despair on his once imperious face.

I don't know what score he received from the instructor that day, but the PFC received high marks, in our minds, for his repartee, deflating our comrade-in-arms, a fellow who had definitely been a pain in the ass to all of us.

We graduated from Basic School a few weeks later, in January 1961. I received my MOS or Military Occupational Specialty, Infantry Officer type 0302. This was exactly what I wanted. I also received orders to remain at Quantico and report to Special Services, Marine Corps Schools for assignment as the Assistant to the Marine Corps Schools Track and Field Relays Director. This assignment came as a complete surprise to me, but I suppose occurred because of my background in college athletics. Although, I was interested in gaining command of a rifle platoon, I looked forward to my new responsibilities and the opportunity to meet some of the finest athletes in America.

In those days, the Marine Corps Schools Relays were one of the largest track and field events conducted, and included both military and college athletes. There were more than 750 athletes participating in the Quantico track meet from 75 colleges, universities, and military bases. Marine Corps Schools hosted this event, providing all lodging, meals, facilities and logistical support for the athletes, coaches, judges, and VIPs. It was a first class event, and the Corps received outstanding publicity and kudos from all the participants.

This track and field event was normally scheduled in mid-April. After joining Special Services in early January, I discovered we had a lot of work to complete to make it happen on time. The track meet was a wonderful public relations and recruiting opportunity to attract officer candidates to the Marine Corps. Many of the young men competing in college sports, who wanted to continue with their athletic careers after graduation, were made aware they could do so in the Marine Corps. As officers they would be given this opportunity while they completed their military obligations. There were numerous great college athletes who joined the Corps, received a commission, and continued with their athletic specialty for another three years, while also gaining valuable experience and training as an officer in the Marines. As I had run track in college, I too, was drawn to the potential of continuing my athletic career in the Marines. When my duties permitted, I participated in a few meets. My specialty was Sprints, the 100 and 200-yard dashes. But I soon discovered I was out of my league attempting to compete against some of those nationally ranked trackmen.

When we ran Villanova, I had the opportunity to compete against Frank Budd, who held the world record for the 100-yard dash, and several other highly talented runners. There were eight runners in that race, Budd ran a 9.2 second hundred, equaling his own world record. I ran a respectable 9.9 second hundred finishing a distant last. I seem to recall, I was so far in the rear, when I crossed the finish line, the officials were already installing the hurdles for the next race. My form and effort was good, I was told, but good form and effort doesn't win races against world class athletes. Only talent can do that.

I don't know who started the MCS Relays, or if they exist today, but during the 1960's. It was one of the finest track meets in the country.

After both the Relays and the track season were behind me, I reported back to Training and Testing Regiment to assume my responsibilities for the summer months. I was to be a Company Executive Officer for two separate six week Platoon Leader Courses. This was a program designed for college students. They attended sessions on active duty during two summers, and if they successfully completed the program they were commissioned Marine Second Lieutenants upon graduation from college. This was my first command position in the Corps, and with it came the challenge of practicing the recently learned traits of a leader. Even though these students knew less than I did about the Marines, they were intelligent young men, and it was necessary that I do extensive homework before conducting classes. My demeanor, presence and bearing had to be professional in every way.

The physical part was also important, as we led the candidates on hikes and through the obstacle courses. A Marine Officer did not want to lag behind his candidates in these activities, as it might reflect poorly on him in their eyes. We were expected to be "beyond reproach" and set the standards for them to emulate. Consequently, we did our damnedest to stay in front, for our own self-esteem and for the approving and admiring eyes of our students. There were many young Lieutenants who pushed themselves to their physical limits in order to impress the candidates. But they did it, and that is what determination and leadership is all about. Do what it takes to accomplish the mission - that's the Marine Corps way.

While at Training and Testing Regiment, I was routinely assigned as Officer of the Day, as are most officers in their respective organizations. During this twenty-four hour duty period, the "OD" as he is called, is responsible round the clock for handling security and general order of the designated post. This requires routine inspections of the buildings and other areas of the base during the night and early morning hours. The OD is also required to ensure the effectiveness of the guards on their various posts, by checking them every few hours. He is required to maintain a written log of all actions taken, posts inspected, and any unusual events that transpired during his watch. Most of the time, this is a routine assignment, but it does carry significant responsibility. The instructions are documented, and any special orders of the day, are detailed in writing. All the OD has to do is follow the instructions. But if he doesn't, his ass will ache for several days, following the chewing it gets from his superiors.

On my first assignment as OD, I had an inauspicious beginning by receiving an ass chewing before actually assuming the responsibility.

My family and I were living in historic Fredericksburg, Virginia, which was normally a 45-minute drive to Quantico. The night before I was to assume the duty as OD, we had a heavy snow of 8-10 inches. The next morning the highway was an abomination. Even though I had left home much earlier than usual, I was thirty minutes late reporting to the Regimental Executive Officer. I offered my excuses, relating to the bad weather as cause of my tardiness, but it didn't take long for the ass chewing to commence. In a strident and vociferous voice, he informed me he didn't give a damn about the weather. I had been assigned a responsibility, and subject only to my own death, it was demanded and I was expected to meet my obligations in a timely manner. He continued, stating I should always anticipate problems by having a contingency plan ready. After his berating concluded he asked, "Do you understand fully Lieutenant?" In a very demoralized and weakened state of mind I replied, "Yes Sir. " There was nothing else to be said.

He had made his point, and I had learned a valuable lesson. I don't believe I was ever late again for anything. There are many ways to get things done, but in the Corps there is only one way: The Marine Corps Way. And you don't ever forget it.

In the fall, I was assigned as a Platoon Leader for an Officer Candidate Course - the identical type program from which I had graduated only a year and a half earlier. The men in the program, just like myself, had graduated from college and were in many cases close to my own age. Assuming they survived the course, they would be commissioned Second Lieutenants in three months.

This class assignment was more challenging for me than the Summer Platoon Leaders course, because these men were already college graduates. They were older, more mature, and very capable of taking the measure of those supervising them. Even though they were in a controlled environment, placed under continual duress, as was the nature of the training, it was important and necessary to make an extra effort to gain and maintain their confidence and respect. They didn't have much opportunity to express themselves, unless called upon. But with a little effort, a discerning person could tell what they were thinking by their responses to the stress imposed on them by our instructors.

I enjoyed training candidates for the officer program, because it presented a tremendous learning experience. Constant study, course preparation, and lecturing were mandates critical to success with the students. Consequently, my military knowledge base was substantially reinforced in this job, as I was required to present material I had only recently learned myself.

After completing this assignment, I was confident with my ability to handle the responsibilities of an Infantry Platoon Leader and was looking forward to the opportunity to prove myself in that capacity. However, Marine Corps Schools had other plans for me and in December decided I should again assume the responsibility as Assistant Relays Director with the new duties as Head Track Coach.

The six months from December 1961 to May 1962 provided me with greater organization responsibilities than I previously experienced and presented me with the opportunity to associate with some of the finest track and field athletes and coaches in the world. I went to work immediately and by mid-

December had selected people for the team from all corners of the Quantico base. Many of the officers, while in college, had participated in previous Relays, and had joined the Corps to continue their athletic careers. The emphasis on sports and physical training, hallmarks of the Marines, worked wonders in helping to fill their manpower needs.

Although I had participated in collegiate sports, I was a dilettante when it came to coaching. I knew the basics but not the finer points so critical in training and conditioning - the ultimate difference between winning and losing. I decided my job as Track Coach, should focus on recruiting the best athletes I could find, motivate them to train diligently, provide good facilities and equipment, and schedule the finest competition I could find. Knowing they would compete against some of the best athletes in their events, provided our team the incentive they needed to work hard and ultimately produce a winning season.

The other part of the job was to market and expose the Marine Corps Schools team on every college campus possible and to enter the team in most meets held on the East Coast. Obviously, this exposure would help recruiting and if we performed well, bring credit and recognition to the Marine Corps. I took the team to every major indoor track and field meet possible during January and February. In March as the outdoor season began, we participated in meets against schools such as North Carolina University, Villanova, West Virginia University, Maryland, Penn State and of course both military academies, West Point and the Naval Academy.

This was a fabulous opportunity, coaching the Marine Corps Schools track team, and I began to think I might locate a good coaching position if I chose to leave the military, but that was to be just wishful thinking on my part.

As Coach Jackson, I recruited a team which consisted primarily of Second Lieutenants and a few talented Non-Commissioned Officers. Although, I was the coach and the senior officer of the group, a First Lieutenant in charge of Second Lieutenants; I reminded myself of the adage, "seniority among Lieutenants is like virginity among whores. " - it does not exist to any appreciable degree. I tried to manage and lead by issuing few orders and instead, appealed to the competitive spirit of the men. I never tried to "pull rank" on the men, as this would have made me a pariah, and eliminated any possibility of gaining and maintaining their respect and cooperation. It was really simple, explain what we were going to do, define the constraints, do your share, and expect everyone else to do their part and don't be a demi-god. Somehow, we made it work on our team - most of the time. I will admit that I had to turn my head a few times to overlook minor infractions, but that's life.   Don't try to control everything, that's impossible. All of this was a part of learning how to get from your people what you wanted without destroying their personal motivation and cooperative spirit.

We had a number of world class athletes on our team and the most renown, at the time, was Lance Corporal John Uelses, who in February 1962, became the first man in history to pole vault over sixteen feet. He established a New World record when he jumped 16 feet and 1/4 inches in the Millrose games in New York City at Madison Square Garden.   Uelses had pioneered the use of a new fiber glass vaulting pole, which was lighter and more flexible than the metal or bamboo poles used by most vaulters.

After establishing a New World record, John's picture appeared on the cover of Sports Illustrated, which included a story on his tremendous accomplishment. John had worked hard on his own to gain this achievement. He established a world record, fostered a new method for Pole Vaulting, and eliminated the mind barriers that had precluded other great jumpers from gaining this record.

By summer, his record had been broken several times. Vaulters now realized the impossible was possible. His record did not stand long, but he was the first, and I think he made it possible for the others with his dedication and willingness to innovate a new technique.

After John set the world record, his notoriety soared and I joked to my friends that I was the only Lieutenant in Marine Corps History to become an aid to a Lance Corporal. It was a wonderful experience for everyone on the team to be a part of his accomplishment.

We had several other great athletes on the team, champions from their respective schools and conferences with national reputations. Consequently, we enjoyed a successful season competing against some of the best talent in America, and perhaps the world.

We ran in meets weekly to stay in good condition, wore colorful maroon and gold uniforms, which made our runners stand out among the crowd of competitors. I can remember announcers, during some races, when our men sprinted to a lead, bellowing out over a loudspeaker, "Here come the Marines". Our team got the crowd's attention and performed well doing it. We had a mission, and those athletes on the MCS 1962 track team acquitted themselves extremely well.

The Relay's were again held in April, and a record number of teams participated. We worked to make it a successful event, and the accolades for this event were again overwhelming. The Marine Corps had scored high marks with its sport program and I was pleased to have played a small part during my two years at Quantico.

A highlight at the 1962 Relays was the surprise attendance by Colonel John Glenn. He had only recently completed The Friendship Seven Space Flight. He was introduced, and of course, received a standing ovation. Now as I write, 36 years later he has again, at the youthful age of 77, made another successful flight into space, becoming the first man and the oldest man to orbit the earth. Quite an interesting combination of achievements.

Never again in my life would I be "Coach Jackson", as my job came to an end in May 1962 and my orders directed me to report for duty to the Commanding General, Second Marine Division, at Camp Lejeune, North Carolina. A new destiny was on the horizon and I was finally going to join an infantry Battalion.

The two years at Quantico had provided great experiences and imbedded in me a level of confidence that I could handle anything that came my way. And so, my wife Libby, two-year-old daughter Kimberly (born December 20, 1961 at the Naval Hospital), and I, departed from Quantico en route to our new duty station, leaving behind many wonderful memories and formative experiences. We looked forward with both anticipation and anxiety to the challenges and opportunities ahead. The future would demonstrate that our feelings, at that time, were right on target.

CAMP LEJEUNE,
NORTH CAROLINA

It was a typical hot, muggy day in June 1962, when I reported to the Second Marine Division at Camp Lejeune, which is adjacent to Jacksonville, N. C. After the normal delays and confusion, I was finally assigned to the 1st Battalion, 8th Marine Regiment. After more processing and introductions to the Commanding and Executive Officers, I was assigned to Charley Company, which was commanded by Captain Harry Field. Finally, after 2 years and three months in the Marines, I was in an Infantry Rifle Company. The Battalion was in the process of re-manning, and most of the summer months were spent going through reorganization and equipment refitting. Since the Battalion was short of officers, I was given the dual responsibility as Executive officer and First Platoon Commander of Charley Company. Most of the next two months were spent in limited training, conducting company marches, and performing administrative duties relative to reorganization of the Battalion.

Since our time was not fully utilized and I still had a strong interest in sports, I decided to try out for the base football team, which played a 10 game schedule, mostly against other military teams. I was given permission by my Commanding Officer to play and over the next three months spent half my time playing ball and the other part administering my responsibilities in the rifle company.

While engaged in sports, either in college or the military, most athletes receive certain dispensations during the season to help compensate for all the time practicing and playing. If the jock is not prudent and mature, it is easy to develop an attitudinal indifference and become convinced that they are

60

more deserving and should be held less accountable then their non-playing contemporaries. This happened to me after a few weeks, and I began to take some liberties with my responsibilities. Then the axe fell. What I did specifically, I don't remember after all these years. But I do remember the chewing out very well.

Captain Field, my Company Commander, was a big burley type of guy, with a booming voice and the most penetrating eyes I have ever seen. He was not, and did not resemble an athlete in any form or fashion. Fact is, he was not overly impressed with athlete types. He was a family man with 5 children, I seem to recall, and was a professional officer in every aspect. I grew to like him very much. But, at this particular time he took the measure of me and dropped my ego to a level that it deserved. He devastated me, pointing out all my inadequacies over the past several weeks, and explained to me in no uncertain terms, that I had better get myself and my attitude squared away, as well as my life in general. He left nothing out of his ass chewing. The fact is, I deserved what I got, and to this day I believe it had a positive impact on my life.

He touched a cord inside of me that made me take a look at myself a little differently and I didn't like what I saw. This had to be one of those turning points in person's life. Unfortunately, there would be many. After this little discussion, our relationship began to improve, probably because I changed my approach and performed my duties with a much-improved attitude and diligence. The lesson learned by me: accept responsibility and accountability for your actions. In other words, do what you are supposed to do when you are supposed to do it.

In the sixties, the Marine Corps total personnel was about 200,000 men and women spread out over the globe. But it was always interesting how the lives of those in the Corps would cross throughout the years. In 1966, I would again come into contact with Major Field, who at that time was the Battalion Executive Officer of the unit I joined in Vietnam. He

Commander of a rifle company. Destiny has a unique way of developing future events.

In the Second Marine Division, there was always a Battalion on alert status. This was a state of combat readiness requiring all troops, equipment, and supplies to be maintained for immediate deployment, if or when an emergency situation arose. During the alert phase, which I recall lasted about two weeks, all troops were required to remain in close proximity to the base and our personal combat gear was to be packed and ready to go. We were required to check in frequently and had Troop formations each morning, including the weekend.

It was Saturday Oct. 20, 1962, and the Base Football team was playing an army team, in our third game. It was a rout in our favor and I was fortunate enough to play and score a sixty-yard touchdown run on a punt return. This would be the last touchdown I would ever score as well as the last football game of that season, or any other season for me.

I left home early Sunday morning to report in, not knowing that it would be two months before I saw my family again. The Cuban Missile Crisis was unfolding rapidly and it appeared that unless something could be done, Russia and American were headed toward a nuclear war. Of course, at that time, we had no knowledge of this tenuous situation, but on that Sunday morning, we were told to embark all troops and equipment on trucks and to drive immediately to the Marine Corps Air Station at Cherry Point, N. C. We thought this was a drill to test our readiness status. Consequently, some of us did not take the situation seriously, and were unprepared for the unfolding events. Always assume the worse, plan for it and be surprised when something better happens. This is the way to anticipate events in the Marines.

We arrived at Cherry Point, which was in a state of confusion, as were we, and were assigned aircraft to board parked on the airstrip awaiting our arrival. Logistical supplies, ammo and rations were brought out on the airstrip from the storage stockpile, and we were instructed to load them ASAP on our transport planes. Minutes before we began the process of loading men and equipment, our assigned aircraft were changed. We were told to adjust our embarkation plans, which I had only recently completed en route to the airfield. We were to load our equipment and board aircraft requiring a completely different set of loading criteria. Another lesson learned, be flexible. So I loaded our newly designated aircraft by the seat of my pants, I had no experience, had never done this before, but as the embarkation officer it was my job and I did the best I could. There is nothing like "on the job" training.

Somehow, I got all the equipment loaded, mixed up, but on board. As we departed Cherry Point we began to realize it was not a drill but the real thing. While loading the supplies and ammo, which had been in storage bunkers, from all appearances for quite sometime, I discovered that the .30 cal ammo would not work in our weapons as we had been issued M14 rifles, which required different ammo. This change had occurred after the storage dumps had been established and the old ammo had not been replaced. I brought this to the attention of a Major, who was the loading coordinator for the air base. He was an aviator type, and his response was to load it anyway. In somewhat of a simplistic manner, I attempted to explain to the belligerent Major the bullets would not go down our rifle barrels, and why the hell were we loading them? He did not like my sophomoric lecture, especially coming from a brash First Lieutenant and informed me in no uncertain terms, "to load the goddamn stuff, get my ass on the plane, and to get the hell out of there. " I did as I was told, with obvious disdain showing in my facial expression.

When we arrived in Cuba, we had the ammo we required, and probably my outburst was uncalled for, but to me, at the time, this looked like a FUBAR (Fucked up beyond absolute recognition) situation. I experienced lots of FUBARS over the years.

We flew all night, trying to sleep laying on top of the equipment that was stored with us in the cargo department. Throughout the night, unable to sleep, one thought seemed to penetrate my consciousness as I worried about the events ahead. I silently reflected to myself and wished I had studied harder and knew more about my job. My confidence level was being challenged and I needed to overcome the fear that is probably normal when you face a critical uncertainty.

We landed in Guantanamo Bay, Cuba, which was an inlet off the Caribbean on the Southeast Coast. A U. S. Naval station was located here, manned by a Marine detachment, which was a reinforced Rifle Company. We spent the day issuing ammo and other supplies. Late in the evening we listened to President Kennedy's Address to the Nation about the Missile Crisis, and the navel blockade he was enforcing to keep Russian ships from transporting additional nuclear arms and weapons into Cuba. This was the first time we knew what was actually happening, and it was frightening, to say the least.

After the broadcast, under the cover of darkness, our company moved out in single file up a steep ridge to occupy our defensive position on the perimeter of the base. We had no idea what developing events would bring that night or the next day. But we set up our position, as had been directed, assigned fields of fire, laid in machine guns, tried to do it by the book and then settled in for the night. It was then about midnight. I was dead on my feet, no sleep for over 40 hours, beat- up from the football game I had played two days prior, and mentally exhausted from all the activity. I found a spot with my radio operator to the rear of our front line, laid down on the ground, took off my helmet, pistol belt, and other gear, removed the hand grenades from my suspender straps, placed then under my helmet, put my head on my helmet using it for a pillow, and went to sleep. I remember thinking that the grenades should be someplace else, but I was too weary to care. I never did that again. In the future, I would put both my head and grenades in a safer location, meaning not next to one-another.

The night passed without incident and the next morning, greatly refreshed, I conducted a reconnaissance of our location, since we did not get the opportunity the previous day. One of our squads reported activity a few hundred yards away from our position, over a small hill leading into a draw. After some analysis, we concluded that it was friendly troops, and we ventured forward for further investigation.   It was an artillery battery consisting of 105mm howitzers, dug in, and prepared to handle fire support missions when requested. Upon arriving at the position I introduced myself to one of the Sergeants in the battery. He told me who they were, how long they had been in that position, and that everything had been quiet around there until we moved in the night before.   I believe he muttered something like we sounded like a "Chinese fire drill". His descriptive term was not flattery and denotes total confusion in the military repertoire.

I was surprised and embarrassed. We had received no information about any gun positions or troops being in proximately to our location. Furthermore, we had set our position, troops and weapons facing our own friendly troops with our ass totally exposed to the enemy. This is not the way the book tells you how to do it. Either we didn't get the correct instructions or they were garbled. At the time, I was just thankful that neither unit mistakenly shot at the other during the night. But, according to the Battery Sergeant, we had made enough noise so that they knew we were friendly Marines.

There is an old military adage that runs, "10% never get the word. " On that night, I can speculate we were in that 10%. The next day we were moved to another location which was a hill overlooking no-man's land. This was a strip of terrain about 100 meters wide, heavily mined, covered by fire mission plans and fenced on both sides. This piece of land separated the naval air station property from the Cuban owned property and was the delimiting point between the two armed forces. As we dug our foxholes along the ridgeline, we could see the Cubans digging their holes across the fenced area. This was an interesting paradox; each of the opposing forces observing the other as they prepared to fight. This did not occur in Vietnam four years later.

The volcanic rock terrain made digging with entrenching tools almost impossible. We actually had our small steel shovels, entrenching tools, bend and split as we labored to dig gun pits and trench lines in the hard igneous rock. Most of us believed that if a war started and we could survive the first 30 minutes of artillery bombardment, non-nuclear of course, we had a chance of living. We thought our artillery and ships immediately off shore would silence the enemy's guns in short order. Our theory, dig deep and stay close to your foxhole when you could. This was also a wise tactic later in Vietnam. The maxim was, "Dig a hole whenever you stopped," they provided good protection from both artillery and mortar incoming fire.

After a few day of digging, we were ordered to move to another location, a hillock located adjacent to a Seabee camp, Mobile Construction Battalion-4, located along the edge of the sea. Their mission was to provide construction assistance to the forces at Gitmo - building airfields, roads, temporary facilities of all kinds, and anything else that was needed. They were hell raisers, but very capable and did their job without complaint. Our platoon position was close to their base and our defense was supposed to be coordinated with their position. So, I decided to visit them. Besides making contact for our defensive plans, I needed to obtain some essential clothing for myself.

When we were on alert status at Camp Lejeune, we were required to have our packs and gear ready to go if an emergency arose. Our field marching packs were displayed for inspection. Unfortunately, I chose to put two half gallon milk cartons in my pack instead of clothing because of the ease of packing and they made the pack look very neat. Actually, in parades and inspection many of the troops did this as it gave a "squared away" appearance. Obviously, it saved time packing, and made the pack, less cumbersome. Officer's packs were not inspected, and since some of us believed this was only a drill on readiness, we were not worried about our packs containing all the normal gear, like socks, T-shirts, under shorts, shaving gear etc.

So I went to Cuba, and possible war, with two empty half gallon milk cartons in my pack, and as we left quickly, I didn't have a chance to replace them. But I'm certain I had the neatest, most squared away pack on the entire island of Cuba when we arrived, for whatever that was worth. Since I had no supply of extra clothes, when I had a chance to bathe, I had to wash everything, put it back on, and hope it dried in the sun before night- time.

And so, I visited the Seabee Camp in hopes of obtaining some gear, as there were no Marine clothing facilities on the island. I was to embarrassed to tell anyone about my stupid stunt, and I didn't want to explain to anyone the reason I needed personal supplies so quickly after out arrival.

When I tried to talk them out of clothing, I learned quickly what great traders they were. After some discourse about my needs, I was told that they would help me, but in return they needed hand grenades, and two cases, about 50 grenades, would do. I asked if they needed them for the defense of their base perimeter and was told politely that they were to be used for fishing. It seems they would spot a school of fish close to the shore, arm a grenade, drop it in the water near the fish and after it exploded underwater, quickly retrieve all of the stunned fish for their dinner. I was greatly amused about their resourcefulness and initiative.

They got their grenades. I got some clothes. Over the next few days I thought I heard muffled explosions at high tide and wondered what kind of seafood dinner the Seabees were enjoying that evening. Whatever they were eating it was certainly better than c-rations.

"Rueben the Cuban" provided excitement during the early weeks of our deployment, and we needed it. After a while static situations can become quite boring when all you do is dig holes, clean weapons, man security posts and sit around and wait for something to happen day after day. We began to experience, what we thought initially, were nightly probes by the Cubans against our defensive positions. On several occasions, after we thought we heard or saw someone in front of our positions, we gave chase through the brush in hopes of capturing the errant trespassers. We never caught anyone, but we called our so-called infiltrator, Rueben the Cuban, but in reality, I think that it was probably a small deer walking around our position, searching for food. It didn't matter; we needed the excitement and the adrenaline surge to keep us motivated and alert. These events helped fight the boredom and we looked forward to the "enemy" incursions and the resultant chase, which we never won.

Sometime later, I was relieved of my duties as First Platoon Commander and Executive officer of Charley Company and assigned responsibilities as Headquarters Commandant of our Battalion Command Post. My new job was to involve security, administration, training, logistics and the general well being of all of the staff at that location, principally the senior officers. This was not an easy task because, more or less, you were required to work under a microscope of the senior staff officers including the Battalion commander, Lt. Colonel Jim Wilson. I survived this test somehow, and learned about the politics and bureaucracy associated with a headquarters staff.

I was to gain valuable insight into leadership during this time while training some of the enlisted headquarters staff. I would take them on field exercises for conditioning purposes and tactical skills enhancement. The Marine Corps believes and teaches that regardless of your military occupational specialty (the job which you are trained for), every Marine is in reality, a rifleman. This belief necessitates that all Marines qualify by annually firing their weapon on the rifle or pistol range, and receiving a limited amount of infantry refresher training. Of course, all Marines receive infantry training when they initially join the Corps as a part of their basic training.

Our Battalion Commander ordered all enlisted troops not on the front lines with combat units, to receive field training on a regular basis while in Cuba - and I got the mission. I was happy with these duties. I enjoyed field-training exercises and was particularly enthusiastic for the opportunity to escape from the Battalion command post bureaucracy for a few hours each week.

During one of the training sessions, I had scheduled a forced march of 5 miles, followed by small unit tactics. I had taken them through some strenuous training all morning, participating fully myself because I enjoyed the activity. I must admit, I could get carried away with all of the military stuff from time to time. However, I didn't realize the significance of my participation. The men were tired and we stopped for a break and to eat some chow. As I sat there ruminating about the morning, I called the sergeants over to get their views on how the training was going and how they thought the men were doing.

The "rear area" administrative Sergeants responded almost unanimously, "we don't like it worth a damn Lieutenant, but as long as you are here with us doing the same dirty stuff that we are, we'll do whatever you want us to do. "I was struck by their honesty and didn't know how to reply. I thanked them for their forthrightness and we did another forced march back to the command post.

Afterwards, I reflected on that conversation and the wisdom of the three Non-Commissioned Officers. They told me in a simplistic way what leadership was all about. Don't ask your people to do what you wouldn't do. You lead from the front by doing, not from the rear by watching - set the example. This tenant of leadership and management has remained with me throughout my career, both in the Marines and business. I will never forget their advice and counsel in the important area of human relations and command.

Finally, the Missile Crisis in Cuba began to abate and we enjoyed a more relaxed atmosphere as the prospect of war diminished by the day. One evening my First Sergeant and I concluded that a hot shower and a cold beer would be good for our personal morale. We decided that a short jeep trip to the Seabee camp would be in order. They had great showers and a small pub within their confines. At dark, we quietly slipped out of the command post and drove to the base in our jeep with our lights dimmed for security reasons. As we drove into their base entrance, a voice from the darkness cried out stridently, "Holdup, who are you? Where do you think you are going?" We slammed the jeep to a halt as a lone figure emerged from the dark and began questioning us in a most unmilitary manner. Somewhat surprised and under-whelmed, we explained who we were, where we were going, and the totality of our mission - a shower and a beer. After some rather uncaring remarks and expression of total disregard for us, our rank, or our lives in general, this young eighteen year old told us to go on and not to delay.

After our shower and libation, greatly refreshed and a new outlook, we headed back to our base. Again, as we passed though the entry gate, the young sentry appeared out of the night at the side of road, bellowing the vehicle to a stop. Again, we informed him of our identities. After more discussion I told him politely that he was not handling his sentry duties in a military manner, not using the proper challenging techniques, and if his superiors were to witness his performance they would probably rip him a new asshole. I thought he could probably understand the significance of the last part of my concern for him. I then told him in a solicitous way, that I would be happy to review the proper military procedures and perhaps help him stay out of trouble. He listened to me carefully and I was certain I had struck a cord of understanding in his young mind - and he would welcome my unsolicited assistance. But then, looking at me deeply with his cocksure eyes and devil-may-care attitude, he responded simply, "no thanks Lieutenant, I don't want to get too military about all this bullshit". It was a wonderful putdown. I could get carried away sometimes with my responsibilities by being a little "gung ho". I laughed aloud, while glancing at my amused First Sergeant who was enjoying the folly of my efforts and told him resolutely, "drive on". The possibility of war was dissolving rapidly in the minds of the troops and most of the military personnel were obviously ready to hang-it-up and go home.

In early December we were notified that we were going stateside, the missile crisis was officially over, and I guess our side won. Although, years later it was determined that the Kennedy administration closed some critical missile sites in Turkey as a quid pro quo with Russia, for the dismantling of the missile sites in Cuba.

After digging foxholes and preparing defensive positions for nearly two months in that hard volcanic rock, we joked among ourselves that the official word from headquarters was "fill 'em up and you can go home". We cleaned up our areas - "policed" is the proper Marine terminology for removal of debris and trash - filled in our foxholes with the same dirt we had shoveled out weeks before, and boarded our transport ships.

Three seasick days aboard ship in awful weather and rough seas, provided an appropriate conclusion for our Cuban Adventure. We arrived in Moorhead City, N. C. in mid-December just in time for the Christmas holidays. Our Expedition to Cuba had spanned two months and we arrived home almost to the day we departed in October. We enjoyed the Christmas season and quickly resumed our normal garrison duties at Camp Lejeune.

In January 1963 I was to take command of an Infantry rifle company. The Commanding Officer of our Battalion I assume, had been satisfied with my efforts during our stay in Cuba. It probably helped that a few of our senior officers were transferred and that by date of rank, I was the senior First Lieutenant in the Battalion and thought to be ready for command of a rifle company. Then again, perhaps I was the only available candidate, the last man standing after the Indian attack, so to speak. Whatever the case, I was elated and certainly felt ready for the job.

In retrospect, I hadn't screwed up too badly as Headquarters Commandant in Cuba and I had completed numerous correspondence courses on various Military Subjects during my first years of service. This, Lt. Colonel Wilson thought, was a positive enabler to my qualifications for command. Besides, I was a senior Lieutenant and finally, they needed a body to fill the position. My body got it, and I was overjoyed with the opportunity so early in my career.

The Marine Corps was a relatively small organization compared to the other U.S. Armed Forces. The Corps consisting of only about 200,000 people, including three Marine Infantry Divisions, containing 36 rifle companies, three Air Wings and miscellaneous support units. So, there weren't many opportunities for Rifle Company Command positions. Yet, a lot of candidates were available to fill them. These were primarily captains, and senior ranked Captains at that. And, these jobs, highly revered by all career infantry officers, were by the tables of organization, commanded by Captains. Successful Command of one of these units was very important in the selection and evaluation process for promotion to Major. A Rifle Company Command in the early sixties, particularly since we were not at war and so few such opportunities existed, was a significant stepping-stone to future advancement.

I was thrilled with my assignment, regardless of the rationale behind it, and I undertook the new responsibilities with great vigor and enthusiasm. I was to command Bravo Company for seven months. At age twenty-six, this was one of the most challenging times I had ever experienced.

I liked the outdoors, and I enjoyed field training, war games, forced marches, and sleeping under the stars. That's exactly where we spent most of our time, unless Battalion Headquarters had a job for us, like marching in a parade, guard duties, or some other less interesting duties. We departed every Tuesday morning and returned Friday at midday to give the troops an early liberty call after our weapons and equipment were cleaned. The troops liked the routine. It kept us out of trouble, out of sight, and away from menial tasks that distracts from being a well-oiled combat unit. That was my belief and it worked for us.

Bravo Company had a seasoned group of Staff Non-Commissioned Officers and enthusiastic Platoon Commanders who were hard chargers. This combination of people, skills and experience worked great. We learned from each other and everybody bought into the hard field training approach, which produced excellent teamwork and positive results.

The company acquired a fine reputation for itself within the Second Division and in several war games exercises, was noted for its success in achieving objectives in the maneuver exercises. We also had one of the best combat rifle quads in the Marine Corps, determined through competition. I believed we were the best company in the Battalion. I credit our staff for their combined efforts and dedication.

As the old adage runs, "All good things finally come to an end. " In late summer of 1963, I was relieved of my position as a result of the infusion of new captains transferring into the Battalion, hungry for command and the opportunity to enhance their careers - just as I had been fortunate to do as a First Lieutenant.

When the new Commanding Officer, a senior captain, was assigned to Bravo Company, I was reassigned as the Executive Officer of the Company. This was my third assignment in this capacity since joining the Corps. It was not an easy adjustment for me after enjoying, and I believe, succeeding with, the responsibility of command and the opportunity to run the show my way. It was discomforting to play a lessor role. I did not feel totally pleased with our new leader or his methods - a natural reaction to whomever replaces you. But you are taught and trained to do the best you can with what you have and to make the best of the situation. That's the way it was in the Corps, love it or leave it.

I undertook my new role with as much enthusiasm as I could muster at the time. The new Commanding Officer was a radical, uncontrolled, hard living, hard drinking, profane person with unusual views on most things. I believe he tried to imitate General George Patton and was always in some kind of trouble with his superiors. He kept the Bible and the Manual of Courts Martial on the top of his desk. I assume this was to demonstrate to the men that he could be a stern disciplinarian, or God fearing, whichever was appropriate at the time. He did not like complainers, and explained his philosophy of leadership as follows: "If a Marine came to me complaining about a sore knee, I'd kick the SOB in the balls so that he forgets about his knee. I like to give them a different problem to think about, even more severe than the problem they thought they had." I never saw this leadership principle in execution. He certainly was a character, an unusual personality. I did develop a friendship with him finally, even though he was nutty, and I did my best to help keep him out of trouble - a full time job.

In late summer, Base Special Services was looking for a football coach and I applied for the job, and nearly got it, except that my Battalion commander would not release me for this temporary assignment. Interestingly, another Lieutenant in our Battalion who had played at Ohio State got the position, with the Old Man's approval. The CO had developed a professional fondness for me and believed my efforts should be fully directed towards a military career. We didn't agree on that issue at the time.

Two weeks later, the Battalion Commander was transferred, to late for the coaching job, but the new CO, Lieutenant Colonel Herb Ing, did give me permission to try out for the team as a player. That is, if I could continue with my duties as Executive Officer of the Company. My Company Commander agreed with the decision and it was worked out to everyone's satisfaction. The entire affair produced an unusual set of events for me. Had I gotten the coaching position, along with my track coach experience, I might have decided upon a career in athletics. However, the two-week hiatus between the change of Battalion Commanders kept me from getting the job. This desire to play, a competitive athletic fire still burning in me then, turned out to be a bad call on my part. I ended up tearing the cartilage in my right knee during practice and after a recovery period it was clear that I could no longer run with the requisite speed or power. I had played my last football and was summarily retired from the game for life. The knee held up okay for 22 years before it needed an operation to remove cartilage debris.

Since I could no longer play football, I went back to full time status on the job. Shortly thereafter, Lt. Colonel Ing, a dynamic and charismatic leader, assigned me as an assistant S-3 in our operations section. When one door closes another opens, and this was a great opportunity. Our Battalion was due to depart for a six month Mediterranean Cruise that

January and the experience to be gained in this position would serve me very well in the future.

Prior to assuming my new job, while still EXO of Bravo Company, our unit had just returned from the field after several days of tactical training and as we walked into the barracks, we heard the announcement, President Kennedy had been assassinated in Dallas, Texas. It was November 11, 1963. I'll never forget.

I recall our entire base was put on alert. All liberty was cancelled, and we were required to check in regularly over the next several days.

During this time, my wife and I sat glued to the television, watched every report on the incident and the tear evoking funeral proceedings as the Nation grieved over the death of this young President, killed in his prime, leaving behind a beautiful wife and adorable children. I will never forget the scene of his young son John-John, as he was called at the time, saluting as he, his sister, and mother stood at his father's burial site. (And now, as this manuscript goes to press, comes the news of the fate of "John-John" and his wife, and sister-in-law; forever resting in a watery grave.)

We couldn't imagine how this could happen, in our country, to and American President. Like many people we wondered if the incident would be the prelude to a war - all sorts of rumors flying about a possible Cuban or Russian instigated plot.

Our country would loose other prominent men in the sixties also killed in their prime of life, Martin Luther King and John Kennedy's brother, Robert. It was a terrible time for our nation and the events would make a negative contribution to our history.

In late November I assumed responsibilities as an assistant S-3 operations and training officer and became deeply involved in the preparation of our plans for deployment to the Mediterranean. As part of our readiness preparations, our Battalion conducted numerous tactical field exercises prior to our departure.

As I enjoyed being in the field "playing games", I was full of piss and vinegar. I was always assigned to lead the aggressor forces. My job was to take one platoon of about forty men and act as the enemy force throughout the exercise. We were involved in attacking, harassing, probing, and staying on the move around the clock to inject as much realism and excitement into the maneuvers as possible. I loved it. We didn't take orders from anybody, acted on our own, totally independent, whenever, and however we chose, day or night. We did a good job of keeping the entire Battalion on their feet playing our role relentlessly and vigorously. This was Guerrilla warfare and we were the guerrillas' and the methods learned would travel with me later to Vietnam and serve me well. It was during one of these exercises when, after having gone for over forty hours without sleep, that I received a radio message informing me my wife was beginning labor pains and I was needed at home. Rushing to our house by jeep from some 30 miles in the "boonies", I picked her up at our duplex at Tarawa Terrace and took her to the naval hospital arriving only minutes before my son Christopher was born. Overjoyed, dead tired, ready to collapse from all the physical and mental anxieties, nearly incoherent, I finally made it home and did my thing - I slept peacefully and happily, enjoying the thoughts of my new son.

In mid January 1964, Battalion Landing team (BLT 1/8) composed of about 1,800 men, supporting arms, and equipment, sailed from Morehead City, N. C. for deployment to the Mediterranean. It took nearly two weeks to cross the stormy, wintry Atlantic Ocean, on the five ships carrying our group. The Naval designation was Phibron. Because of the substantial number of ships in the group the Senior Navy Captain commanding our fleet was designated a Commodore. It was rough sailing. The North Atlantic can be terrible in the winter. We experienced some serious bunk time, attempting to keep our food down from all the tossing and heaving of these slow moving amphibious ships. We sailed through the straits of Gibraltar and into the more peaceful Mediterranean waters. There, we joined up with the waiting force in-readiness, another Battalion landing team from Camp Lejeune. After conducting an official relief at sea, we assumed our responsibilities as the Alert Force for this part of the European Theater. The departing landing force sailed back to the U. S. We were on station for the next four months before conducting a similar relief upon our departure in mid May.

During this time, our mission was to stay prepared for deployment in the event of an unexpected crisis in that part of the world, to conduct practice landing operations throughout the Med. , and to further enhance our combat readiness. We didn't get much training time because we were immediately dispatched toward the Island of Cyprus, as hostilities erupted between the local populace.

Cyprus, a small Island in the Central part of the Mediterranean, had U.S. Nationalists and several U.S. companies with business interests living and operating on the island. Our mission was to stay within 10 hours sailing time, and to be prepared to execute amphibious landings at designated locations. We would evacuate U.S. Personnel or protect U.S. property if threatened as a result of the war. Over the next four weeks we sailed, and sailed, and sailed as we remained in a continuing state of alert to land on Cyprus. I was deeply involved in the development of five separate landing plans that would direct our amphibious operations to meet tactical objectives. It was a busy time and we worked around the clock.

We were supported by the U. S. Enterprise, which was the largest nuclear aircraft carrier in existence with over 100 aircraft aboard. The Enterprise was a magnificent ship, having a super structure 30 stories high with a ship's complement of about 5,000 men.

Over the six weeks we were given liberty on one occasion only, to visit the Enterprise. All the Marine Troops from the five transports in our BLT, were ferried over during the day in small boats to this huge carrier. It gave us the opportunity to stretch our legs and visit the ship stores. There were eleven or so stores on the ship, where the troops could purchase essential items like candy, personal maintenance items and also luxury goods like tape recorders, cameras and so on. A lot of this merchandise was not readily available on our ships and I'm confident, after all the time at sea, we made a huge dent in their store's inventory.

The flight deck was over 1000 feet long and we were able to get some much needed walking around exercise, impossible on our smaller and more crowded "amphibs". The Enterprise's speed was classified, at that time, but could make well over thirty knots at sea which was like a speed boat compared to our slow moving transports. They normally churned through the water at about six to eight knots per hour. Everybody enjoyed this experience, especially the troops who were required to live in cramped, uninviting sleeping quarters located in the depths of our floating metal tombs. Constrained in small living spaces with no privacy, little physical activity, no women or booze, Marines can become a little frustrated and unruly. Tempers flare, and arguments ensue. Shipboard life as a passenger can be very dull and to keep a sense of mental balance it was much better if you could find a way to stay occupied - that was the challenge.

Lt. Colonel Ing kept the S-3 operations shop busy developing plans and briefings for the proposed operations on Cyprus. We were involved around the clock, reworking, reorganizing, and revamping our plans to meet the changing situation on the island.

Living on a ship with no place to go and nothing to do manifests itself well in Parkinson's' Law: "Work expands to fill the time available". We filled our time with work and developed presentations that were made to the various commands supporting our operations. I learned to make effective chart and graph-accompanied briefings through long practice sessions. These were followed by hard-nosed critiques by our Commander Lt. Colonel Ing, who was a stickler for professional presentations and well documented plans. He pushed us toward perfection in these areas, and I think we came close to his goal. It was a great learning experience. When the timing was right to make the presentation, we visited the other ships by helicopter, or highline transport.

Being lowered by a hoist from a helicopter, hovering above a moving ship, was exciting and scary, and your gut tightened when the helicopter crew chief placed the harness around you and told you to step out of the chopper as it hovered over the ship. When you looked down, suspended in air by only a thin cable, all you could see were the ship's propeller's churning the water. Totally without any control of the situation, you could only pray the hoist lowering the line didn't give way, and would allow you to disembark at the proper location on the ship's deck. When my feet touched down I was always overjoyed.

"Highline" transport is a method of conveying people from one ship to another by a cable and chair as two ships proceed on a parallel coarse at identical speed, a short distance apart.

It is also a nerve-racking experience, perhaps more adrenaline pumping than the helicopter transfer. Placed in a chair, you were pulled across the water's waves, swinging, while suspended by cables. The chair would jump and plunge as the two vessels sped onward - only meters apart! If there was any slack in the lines you could get mighty wet if the seat fell to the water before the slack could be taken up. I probably picked up a few white streaks in my black hair during these "adventure trips."

Finally, after weeks of preparation and coordinating activities with our supporting arms, the Cypriots settled their differences and we were released from our Alert Status by the Joint Chiefs of Staff. It seemed that most of our communication had come directly from the Joint Chief's office while the crises prevailed.

Released from the readiness alert after a long six weeks at sea, we were told to proceed with our original mission and to conduct our routine landing exercises. But first, we were to select a liberty port anywhere we wanted in the Med. for a two-week sojourn on good old solid ground. The message was directed to the Naval Commander, our Commodore. I don't recall his name or much about him but I do remember him as a bit uptight and without personality. He seemed to have little interest in anything but his personal survival as Commander of our task force. Much to our amazement his reply to the message from the JCS was, he considered the USS Enterprise as the best liberty port in the Mediterranean. We couldn't believe this response. In our minds it was a gross demonstration of piss poor leadership and total lack of concern for the men in his command. How could a senior officer be so indifferent to the morale and well being of the people who were responsible for the ultimate performance of his organization? To us, the junior staff in particular (we were always ready to offer a candid and "unbiased" opinion among ourselves), it was obvious he wanted to make certain nothing went astray. I suppose he didn't relish the thought of allowing some eighteen hundred Marines and several hundred naval personnel embarking on liberty in a foreign country, particularly, after such a lengthy period of confinement. Aboard ship the Navy personnel were accustomed to this type of life but the high energy Marines were not. If he kept the ships at sea, little could go wrong and certainly there would be no incidents of misbehavior by the troops. More importantly it seemed he would have total control and ensure that no potential blemishes could possibly mar his personnel file.

Bless the Joint Chiefs of Staff because their answer was immediate and direct. "Proceed to Malta for liberty. " They obviously considered the response to their original message as inadequate. Thank goodness we finally disembarked our troops off those metal hulks and put them on liberty where they could raise some hell, get drunk, laid, or whatever else they do. They needed to expend some energy, have fun, and feel terra firma under their feet again. The days spent on Malta did a lot for all of our morale. By the time we departed, everyone's attitude had improved and we were ready to begin amphibious training exercises. Malta survived, and we probably enhanced their financial status without doing irreparable damage to the island-country.

It was back to the planning desk as we began developing new Amphibious landing plans for our practice operations. The first was to be on the island of Sardinia. The Secretary of the Navy visited us on shore and we were to alter our exercise to provide proper honors during his visit.

Our next landing operation was conducted on the French owned island of Corsica, Napoleon Bonaparte's birthplace. We were to conduct a bilateral operation with French De Phiba de la Marine, which was France's sea going equivalent to our U. S. Marine Corps. This operation was to be particularly instructive for me as I was to function as the S-3 operations officer, a Major's responsibility. Both the actual S-3, Major Phillips, and his assistant, Captain Daly were absent, planning a future operation. The French and US Marine Troops got along well and even shared rations in the field. Food and drink always has a way of breaking language barriers. The French were interested in our C-Rations and our troops were really interested in their food stuffs as they contained a small bottle of cognac. The French also carried loaves of bread and bottles of wine strapped to their packs while on maneuvers. They knew how to rough it in the field. I believe our troops out traded them because I saw a lot of silly grins on the faces of some of our men, which I am certain was alcohol induced.

All was going well, but then I undertook a foolish mission during these maneuvers with the French. That mission was brilliantly executed, there was no doubt, even the French agreed, but that I undertook it personally is what was foolish about it. I had the responsibilities as the Senior Operations Officer, and I did it because there was no one at Headquarters to stop me and I enjoyed the adrenaline pumping situation and challenge.

This exciting opportunity arose after we had been ashore a couple of days. We were playing our games with the French, and all had gone well. With spirits high and a cooperative attitude prevailing with the French, we decided to conduct a nighttime raid on their headquarters. After some deliberations and planning, I put together a squad size unit of about 14 men to conduct the surprise attack. Unfortunately, there was no officer available to head the unit, so I seized the opportunity without hesitation. Since there were no other senior staff around, I thought I could pull it off, undetected, so I left my

Senior Non-Commission officer and a Second Lieutenant in charge at the Command Post operations center - foolish.

Anyway, I was excited about this clandestine operation, of getting some time in the field and being away from my desk and the Administration that had consumed me over the past several months. I don't recall how we obtained the approval for the raid, I'm sure the Battalion Commander approved the concept, but I'm also certain that he didn't know I was going. I had a habit of leaving out minor details from time to time, especially if it was something I personally wanted to do. This was not a good trait and could get you into serious trouble, which always seemed to happened to me. My ass had been chewed out so many times during my short career that it was pock marked with teeth imprints. I guess I was a slow learner or enjoyed pain, otherwise I would have exercised more prudence with some of my crazy schemes.

We developed our plan which involved the use of two speedboats obtained from the Navy, at my direction. Under the cover of darkness we would load our assault team on one boat and use the other boat for diversion. The diverting boat was to run at full throttle about a mile or so off shore from our landing site while our speedboat would silently drop us off one a quarter mile from shore and we would then paddle the rest of the way in rubber rafts to a small draw between two hills that would conceal our approach. We hoped the noise and commotion created by the diversionary boat would mask our landing and prevent detection by the French. It worked, we landed without incident, concealed our rafts under some bushes, and stealthily made our way about a mile up the draw in a column formation. Emerging on a small hillock overlooking the camp, we were provided with good observation and could easily determine the disposition of their troops and headquarters.

Locating a narrow passage through a defile into the camp, three of us worked our way into the confines of their perimeter and located the command post. We proceeded into the bunker and found the entire group asleep with their radios blustering out incoherent messages from various outposts. Deciding that we shouldn't raise a lot of hell, discretion being the better part of valor, we found a piece of cardboard and wrote an inscription on it: "BLT 1/8 was here". Laying it at the foot of the Commanding Officer's cot, where he slept soundly, we made our way out of the camp, joined our troops and proceeded back down the ravine to our rafts. After calling our pick-up boat on the radio, we paddled our rafts out to sea and were retrieved by our speed boat and returned to our camp around daybreak. We felt good about a successful mission but wondered what would happen when our "clandestine" message was discovered by the French.

After numerous congratulations and pats on our back, I released the troops for some well earned sleep, but I had to get back to work with my responsibilities at the command post. The excitement, long night with no sleep, and adrenaline surge, took its toll on me and by midday I was exhausted.

Later that morning, our Battalion Commander had received a message from the French Commander, acknowledging our incursion into their camp and offered his congratulations for our successful "raid". He then extended an invitation to our CO and staff to join him and his staff for dinner that evening to celebrate the success of the joint French and American exercise. He also requested that the leader of the patrol attend the dinner as his special guest. Then all hell broke loose as Major John Phillips, our S-3 arrived in camp, and learned of the patrol while viewing me in my state of stupor. He ask me who had led the patrol and sheepishly I responded I had, but he knew before he inquired. Both my past record for similar activities and obvious incoherent state provided the answer before he asked.

To describe him as being distressed or pissed-off would be an understatement. He immediately went into a verbal harangue, telling me in no uncertain terms I had abandoned my responsibilities as the operations head of the Battalion and I had let him down personally, since I was supposed to be acting for him in his absence. Furthermore, I was now obviously tired and ineffective. He asked how I could be so stupid to engage in some frivolous operation for my own personal gratification without regard for my more important responsibilities. I had been aggressive, but had acted irresponsibly, and these characteristics were not compatible with my leadership responsibilities. He informed me if I ever did anything even remotely like that again while under his command, he would personally ensure that my life was made as uncomfortable as possible. I got the message and he was 100% right. What else can I say?

Major Phillips was a super officer; I really liked him, he taught me a lot as did his assistant Captain Daly. He was later to become a General and a damn good one.

That night, the French hosted a dinner for us, and I attended as requested by the French Commander. As we dined, under a tent at the French camp, wine was poured and the French toasted and presented me with a small medal as a token of our patrol's accomplishment. The acclamation was somewhat bittersweet because of my irresponsible actions, but in due course, Major Phillips forgot about the incident and I worked hard to get back into his good graces. The senior staff was pleased that we had been successful and our efforts were noted with praise from our Commanding Officer. That was the good side of the incident.

We boarded our ships after the Corsican operation and headed back to sea continuing our training exercises. We had liberty in Barcelona and then conducted our turnover meeting with the Battalion Landing team that was reliving us of our Mediterranean responsibilities.

Lt. Colonel Ing made certain that we had a perfect set of turnover files - impeccable and totally professional, would better describe these documents - typical hallmarks of his approach to command. He knew how he wanted things done and demanded that his staff meet his expectations. We did, and actually, were very proud of our efforts, especially after the long tedious hours of preparations. His motto "On Top", was adapted into an insignia displaying a combat Marine, weapon at ready astride the globe, and the motto inscribed across the front. It was made into a cloth badge and we used this insignia to identify our Battalion while in the Med. I was to meet Colonel Ing again in Vietnam, three years later at a briefing in Phu Bai. He was commanding an infantry regiment, and as I recall, his unit had been successful in combat against the enemy. He always did a good job and had an admirable reputation. I would have been pleased to serve under his leadership again.

After the turnover with the new landing team, we sailed West across the Atlantic arriving in Morhead City, NC in late May 1964. With our return to Camp Lejeune, our Med. Cruise Experience concluded. We began dismantling the Battalion landing team, and back with our families, settled into a normal routine.

Recalling the initial contact with my family after five months absence, I remember the shock when I realized that my small children, Kim and Chris, didn't recognize me. It took some time to become reacquainted with them. Returning home after a lengthy period was always a bittersweet experience when children are young, but it was terrible when you left your family unsure *if* you would return. Such were my feelings when I went to Vietnam two and a half years later.

At this time however, my four years of required military service as a regular officer were ending and I was strongly considering returning to civilian life. I had no idea of where we might live or what occupation to undertake. Fate has an unusual way of either interrupting your plans or forging a new direction at the most illogical time. Before I could finalize my decision, orders arrived directing me to Honolulu, Hawaii, for assignment at Camp H. M. Smith.

There it was, I could resign from the Corps, go back to a civilian lifestyle doing who knows what, or, if I chose, relocate to Hawaii and spend at least two more years in the Marines. The idea of living in Hawaii was compelling. I had never been there and probably would never have the opportunity to go again. After some discussion with my wife we concluded that no practical alternative was available. I had little financial resources, no specific job qualifications, and a wife and two small children to support. We chose Hawaii.

Happy and content with our decision, we departed Camp Lejeune and spent the next three weeks visiting family while driving across country to San Francisco. We boarded a naval ship of the type adapted to carry military personnel and their families. After six days at sea we arrived in Honolulu on the island of Oahu. This was an exciting time and we looked forward to living in the beautiful Hawaiian Islands.

We did not have an auspicious entry into Hawaii. I departed the transport with my family, sweating in the warm weather, dressed in a heavy gabardine uniform, carrying my young son in one arm and a "filled" white plastic diaper pail in the other. We descended the gangplank from the ship to the awaiting greeters and were accosted by a lovely Hawaiian girl dressed in the traditional Hula skirt, who placed a lei over my perspiring head.

Between the commotion and confusion of our arrival, a crying baby in one hand, a diaper container in the other, smothering in a wrinkled sweat stained shirt and coat, weighted down with a huge flower lei around my neck, trying to keep up with my daughter running around the pier, I did not look or feel like the paragon of a professional Marine Officer in any sense of the word. But, we were excited to be in Hawaii although, we were bewildered with all the welcoming parties. Finally, we made our way to our temporary quarters on Waikiki beach where we would live for the next sixty days.

It was a wonderful experience, the trip across country, the ship board travel and finally the extended time living in the resort section of Honolulu, while awaiting permanent housing.

Fortunately, in those halcyon days, we did not suspect that our tour in Hawaii would be interrupted by the events unfolding in Southeast Asia, and that America would soon be involved in a long war with shattering consequences for many people and the Nation as a whole. There were both opportunities and challenges ahead. We would have to sort through them and make decisions and sacrifices that would affect the rest of our lives.

CAMP H. M. SMITH, HONALULU, HAWAII

Camp H. M. Smith was a small headquarters facility located on Aeia Heights, a hillside overlooking Pearl Harbor. It was named for General "Howling Mad" Smith, a feisty Marine General, who played a major combat leadership role in the South Pacific islands campaign fought against the Japanese, in WWII. The camp was used as a hospital during the second world war and later became a Marine base that housed two major Naval and Marine Corps Commands: CINCPAC, Commander-In-Chief of Pacific Forces, Commanding all Naval Forces in the Pacific Theater; and, FMFPAC, Fleet Marine Forces Pacific Command, in charge of all Marine Corps units located in the Pacific Area.

Both of these large, significant headquarters, were overflowing with senior ranking officers, as was common with most major commands. It was not unusual to see "Bird" Colonels or even Generals rushing around the base facilities in pursuit of their administrative responsibilities. Encounters with these high ranking officers were frequent and kept junior officers like myself, on their toes to ensure that we accorded proper recognition and respect when we made contact with them. I was not accustomed to this environment and it took me a while to adapt to the constant "pomp and circumstance", after my time in a basic infantry Battalion, that spent most of it's time in the "boondocks. "

Upon reporting for duty at Camp Smith, I was assigned to the Headquarters Battalion which was responsible for operation of the base. The Battalion was to maintain all administrative and logical facets of the base while supporting the needs of the two headquarters. My new job was to be Camp Special Services Officer. I would be in charge of athletic and recreational activities, which included everything from sports intramural programs, and recreational facilities, theatre, bowling alley, riding stables, and other miscellaneous functions, all provided for military personnel and their dependents. I knew very little about management of these activities, but my sports background helped with some insight into their operation. I preferred this assignment over that of a junior staff officer, which was to be lost in the bowels of the Fleet headquarters, shuffling papers and running errands or getting coffee for a staff officer. In a short time, I settled into the routine of Camp Smith, learning all I could about Special Services, while availing myself and family of the benefits of the job and living in Hawaii.

As 1964 ended, the war in Southeast Asia was beginning to occupy significant space in the newspapers and Washington was sending more military personnel to support the South Vietnamese in their struggle with North Vietnam and the Viet Cong. The Commanding General of FMFPAC, Victor Krulak, who had the nickname, "The Brute," was a martinet around the headquarters and had everyone jumping. Greater numbers of Marines were being committed to the war efforts on a monthly basis.

In March 1965, the first Marine Forces in Hawaii, designated for Vietnam, were dispatched from Kaneohe Bay, the base of the Fourth Marine Regiment. Two months later a parade was conducted in Honolulu and I was directed to have a single Marine jeep in the parade displaying a bright maroon sign baring a message in gold lettering: "This vehicle represents the Fourth Marines now serving in Vietnam." It was simple and to the point. It was Krulak's idea. He was not only a brilliant taskmaster but also a magnificent marketer for the

Marine Corps. He was short, probably about five feet four with a stout voice that commanded respect - and he got it. He also had an admirable military record as both a warrior and staff officer. At the time of this writing, his son is Commandant of the Corps.

The reason I was involved in all these activities was because Special Services seemed to get every job that no one else wanted; and all the advice and criticism that came along with it from both military personnel and their dependents. Everyone had their idea of how the facilities and programs were to be operated. It all went with the territory and I took it as part of the job.

After six years of active duty I was promoted to Captain. The Commanding Officer of the base held a small ceremony in his office. He and my wife, Libby, attached the new "railroad tracks", the two parallel silver bars, on each side of my shirt collar. It was at that time I set my goal to become the base S-3 operations officer, a billet normally filled by a Senior Captain or a Major. I wanted the job because it was a senior position and coordinated training for all enlisted personnel stationed at Camp Smith. Being in that position would allow me to get back to the field again in a training capacity, which had become a labor of love, and to advance my military skills and knowledge considerably.

Good things happen to those who wait their turn, as the old adage runs, especially if you work like hell and do every conceivable thing you can to get what you want. I did, including lobbying with the Commanding and Executive Officers of the Battalion, and when the major, who was the S-3 was transferred, I got the job. It was a new day for me after a year as Special Services Officer; I would move to a higher level in the organization and have more responsibility and influence in our overall base operations. My world was expanding and I hoped that I was growing with it. Time and diligence would tell.

The nature of activities and work at Camp Smith, and particularly at CINPAC and FMFPAC, became noticeably more intense as the Vietnam War continued to escalate throughout 1965 and into 1966. Several Command Conferences were held at our base, hosting Senior Government Officials and Military Officers from South Vietnam and the United States.

When the first Honolulu Conference occurred, I was scheduled as Camp Officer of the day for this momentous meeting between the Heads of State and top military representatives. As the OD, I was put in proximity of the dignitaries and had the opportunity to observe them at close range. I was overwhelmed by both the significance of their position, and their appearance. President Lyndon Johnson and his cabinet members were dressed in dark suits, white shirts and most seemed to have flowing white hair with skin tones pasty in color. At the time they appeared to me as very large men and seemed to tower over me.

The South Vietnamese Leaders on the other hand, were small in stature, also dressed in dark suits, with a little hint of grin creasing their faces, but otherwise serious and deliberate.

As a young officer, or a young man for the matter, I was easily impressed by the facades that these high profile VIP's presented and it was interesting how much larger than life they appeared, when seen in public.

A case in point was General Westmorland, Commanding General of all U. S. military forces in South Vietnam. As Camp Smith housed the two Major Command Headquarters for the Pacific theater, it was logical that high level staff meetings would be coordinated at this midway location between Washington and Vietnam. On numerous occasions top-ranking officers visited from Vietnam for strategy and planning sessions. General Westmorland visited the headquarters at CINCPAC several times and on one visit I was in charge of providing a gun salute and parade in his honor. I remember his presence well, standing at attention while the troops passed in review, very dignified, tall, stately, certainly in his prime of life. He also seemed to tower above me.

Twelve years later I had the good fortune to meet him at a Young President's Organization meeting in Bermuda. He was retired and one of the keynote speakers for our conference. We were on a small sailing craft being transported across the harbor for dinner and I took that opportunity to introduce myself. I was then forty years old, he was in his sixties. I had gained experience with maturity and had more self-confidence than I had in those earlier years as a young Captain. While we conversed, standing on the bow of the leisure boat, it was interesting that we seemed to stand eye to eye. I didn't believe he had shrunk or I had grown taller, but as a young man, people in prominent leadership positions, regardless of physical size, always impressed me as being large men with great bearing. Both events and people take on more accurate proportions as one gains experience, age, and maturity. It is said that perception is reality, and in those early years, everything I witnessed seemed very real, and very large in scope. But, time alters your perception and reality presents new and more revealing impressions.

Marine General Lou Walt, the senior commander of all Marine Corps Forces in Vietnam was also a frequent visitor at Camp Smith, spending his time with General Krulak, planning and reporting on activities in the Marine sector. Walt's command in South Vietnam was the Third Marine Amphibious Force located in the northern sector of South Vietnam. General Walt was a big, broad shouldered man, well liked and a highly decorated officer from both WWII and the Korean

Conflict. I was appointed his aid on one of his visits. It was at this time that Krulak announced Walt's promotion to Lieutenant General and gave him his third star. I wanted to do a good job in my role as his aid-de-camp, but I was concerned because I didn't really know what to do or how to function in this position. Everything was done on the spur of the moment and required a lot of creativity and anticipation. One thing was certain; I didn't want to screw-up. Consequently, those three days were very stressful. Even though Walt didn't demand much personal attention, I had to be on call around the clock. He seemed down to earth, exuded confidence, personality and strong leadership qualities. Men obviously would follow him, and he appeared to be a caring person about his troops.

After he departed, and my role as aid was over, I received a complimentary thank you letter from him. It was a nice, polite gesture on his part which he didn't have to do. His thoughtfulness was much appreciated by this young officer who was very uneasy with his responsibilities the entire time. I presented the letter to the administrative section to be included in my personnel file and made part of my officer qualification record. The sagacious Sergeant advised against it, lest I become earmarked for assignment as an aid. I immediately withdrew the request and took the correspondence home never to be seen again. There was no way I wanted to be assigned that kind of position. It just wasn't my thing. I didn't possess the desire or nature to serve so closely in that capacity, regardless of the opportunity for advancement such a position might have offered. My service as Marine I felt most intensely towards the Corps as a whole, and not to superior officers.

Colonel A. D. Cereghino, who was to have much influence over my life, became the new Commanding Officer about the time I became Camp Smith's Operation Office. He had the reputation of being a professional type of staff officer and was well respected. With his encouragement and support I began to develop a training syllabus for the enlisted personnel at Camp Smith that would eventually receive high marks from most everyone, including General Krulak.

My staff and I enriched the program by including more field training and less classroom instruction. When we had lectures they were held outdoors whenever possible. They would be followed by application of the techniques under as much realism, or simulated combat conditions, as we could devise. With the Vietnam War gaining momentum, we believed that it was important to incorporate into the training, lessons learned from the battle operations in Southeast Asia. New tactics were always evolving and becoming part of the Marine Corps doctrine on counter insurgency - and more so, as the war efforts became ever more potent.

Search and destroy, hammer and anvil, anti-booby troop warfare; terms such as these were coming into use. They were either new terms or modifications applied to certain types of tactical actions and reactions that were becoming more frequently described in reports flowing from Vietnam.

Our small training shop at Camp Smith reviewed copies of everything from the war we could get in our hands. We built our training program around these reports and the lessons learned, by our troops in combat, with every new enemy encounter.

We developed good relationships with the Army and Air Force units on the island. We were able to borrow some of their weapons for our training program, even before they were issued to the Marines in Combat. Our training program was beginning to take on some sizzle.

An unique job enriching opportunity came my way in late 1965, when we received notice of a quota for two Marines from Hawaii, to attend the British Army Jungle Warfare School in Malaysia. It was a six week program and after a great deal of pleading, begging, and cajoling with Colonel Cereghino, I convinced him that I should attend so that after completion I would be more competent and capable of injecting greater realism into our Guerilla Warfare training program. He finally wore down from my constant harangue and agreed to allow me to take one of the quotas. The other quota went to a young Lieutenant from one of the remaining companies of the Fourth Marines on OAHU. Three U. S. Army Officers attended from Special Forces. The one caveat he attached to his permission was that I write to him while at the school and let him know what I was learning. Upon my return I was also to provide him with a detailed outline of the course and what I was going to do with my new revelations in our training program. Of course, I agreed and began writing while still en route to Malaysia. I don't believe I corresponded much. All the time was spent surviving the experience, which took all I had. I did present my analysis at the conclusion, but demands on everyone were becoming greater by the day, due to the war in Vietnam, and the Colonel had other fish to fry.

The British Army Jungle Warfare School was located in Johore Baru, about 30 miles north of Singapore on the Malayan peninsula. It was surrounded by secondary jungle vegetation, denser and even more difficult to navigate than primary vegetation. This happens when undergrowth, once cleared, is allowed to grow back. It creates a thick, green, tangled mess - a jungle hell.

The training courses were exceptionally good. Lots of instruction on patrolling, compass navigation, small unit tactics, anti-guerilla warfare, weapons instruction, and survival techniques. Most of our time was spent in the bush, and we learned to live with the leeches, bugs, snakes, monkeys, tigers and other inhabitants that makes that environment so formidable.

I had read somewhere that the Jungle is Neutral, it is neither for you or against you. You must learn how to live in it otherwise your life will be miserable and the options for survival limited. All of the instructors had spent considerable time in the bush and were extremely knowledgeable. We listened attentively, learned all that we could, as much for our own good then, and for future reference, if and when we went to Vietnam.

The first night spent in the bush, my group of four men were on a training compass march. While we bivouacked in the dense vegetation that night, our camp was circled by a tiger. It certainly kept our attention all night. We sat, huddled around the small fire cradling our weapons, watching and waiting for the attack. Finally when daylight broke our friend departed.

I had never before operated in an environment where you could not distinguish critical terrain features, nor see much daylight through the treetop canopy. Moving through the jungle, we had to weave around thick undergrowth or cut our way through with a machete. This effort alone was exhausting. We'd sweat buckets full as we meandered on under pelting rain showers several times a day, battling leeches as they affixed themselves to our precious body parts, lusting after a delicious blood meal.

The British patrol techniques were excellent. They depended on stealth movement and patrol base occupation and organization - but primarily oriented toward small units of platoon squad size or less. Later I adapted many of these techniques for our company of nearly 200 men while engaged in search and destroy operations in South Vietnam.

The British methods of counter-guerilla warfare had been tested and perfected in the early 1950's in the war against the Communist Terrorists in Malay. At that time, it was a British Colony and the enemy, CT's, as they were called, were attempting to overthrow the local government. The guerilla war waged for several years. After it was over the country became an independent member of the commonwealth in 1957. Since 1963 the country has been known as Malaysia.

According to Military history, the British utilized tactics developed during the war with Japan after they invaded Singapore. They left military units called, "stay behind parties" in Malay, to harass, interdict, and ambush the Japanese in jungle fighting. These tactics were then enhanced against the communist terrorists in the fifties as they struggled to eliminate the insurgency in the bush fighting.

The British were successful, and after a few years of fighting, completely eliminated the terrorists from Malay. Their war was quite different from battles fought in South Vietnam for several major reasons. The Malay Peninsula was bounded by water on three sides. Primary re-supply sources had to come through the narrow neck of the peninsula at the northern tip of the landmass. Some did came by sea but the British were able to minimize these incursions by controlling the seaward approaches. This also limited enemy troop reinforcements leaving the British forces consistently with a numerical troop advantage of 10:1, which grew to 30:1 by the end of the war. Their doctrine indicated that a Counter-Insurgency Force required this superiority of troop strength, in order to overthrow a guerilla insurrection.

We did not have this numerical troop advantage in Southeast Asia. The enemy was able to re-supply their forces and provide reinforcements regularly throughout the war using the Ho Chi Minh trail. The trail originated in North Vietnam and snaked through the jungles of Vietnam, Cambodia, and Laos. The enemy moved logistical supplies and troops into South Vietnam by truck, bicycle, and long foot marches. Consequently, the North Vietnamese and Viet Cong could engage in set piece battles, attacking established bases for extended periods of time. They massed troops and artillery; kept them re-supplied with arms, equipment, and ammunition, in quantities nearly equal to or greater than our own. So, while the British tactics and methods of operation were tested and sound as applied in Malay, they required adaptation to meet the realities of war in Vietnam.

I developed a great respect for the soldiers from the different countries attending the course. I was particularly impressed by the Australian staff and the Gurka troops, serving in the British Army. The Gurka, from the Mountains of Nepal, are small people, tough and resilient as any people I ever met. On long marches and patrols carrying heavy loads. They could keep going on long after the physically larger Americans would be on their knees.

The British bragged on the Gurka's toughness and related a story about their attempt to teach them to parachute from a helicopter. After several misdirected interpretations by the Gurkas, they finally told the instructors that they must fly the British chopper at a lower altitude, that they were flying much too high, better to fly at about tree top level, so they could leap from the chopper and grab at the tree branches as they plummeted to the ground. Communications between the Gurka's and British instructors finally connected when it was understood by the Gurka soldiers that they would have parachutes on. Imagine, those small tough soldiers were actually ready to jump out of a chopper flying about 150 feet above the ground at 60 miles per hour. They were certainly fearless fighters with obvious daring and courage.

The course lasted six weeks and after a short stay in both Singapore and Bangkok we made the long flight to Oahu. I arrived home with a moderate case of dysentery. But, after a few days of drinking good water and receiving treatment at the naval hospital, I was no worse for wear. I'll never forget however, those long busy 10 hours on the plane as I continuously worked my way back and forth down the isle to the john. It was not a pleasant trip home.

After a few days home I submitted my report on the Jungle Training Program to my Commanding Officer. With my head filled with exciting new ideas, the experience still fresh in my mind, my staff and I started reworking our training programs. Up to this time, we had been moderately successful in getting the enlisted personnel at the headquarters into our bimonthly training sessions. As we became more creative in building more challenging and realistic facilities, taking the troops on extended overnight field exercises, as we attempted to mirror situations in Southeast Asia, we began to get attention and support from the senior officers at Headquarters - a significant development, usually nearly impossible to accomplish.

Considering, that most senior Command Headquarters are concerned primarily with administration and staff related functions, creating paper work daily by the ton. Training of any kind is not considered a priority. Staff officers, have a legion of paper work to read, memos to write, orders and plans to disseminate and other miscellaneous tasks that requires dedication and long hours. In short, they needed all the administrative help they could get, and for us to take their clerks away from the office a couple of days a month just wasn't normal, especially since the war was escalating and putting greater demands on everyone at Headquarters.

We did our job with pride, providing the finest realistic combat training program available anywhere in the Marine Corps. I loved being in the field, away from my desk, and reveled in being able to test and apply new tactical ideas in simulated combat conditions. Our training staff became, monomaniacs with a mission, and I suppose I was the biggest.

In the hills above Camp Smith, which were heavily forested, in a small ravine shielded by ridges on both sides, we constructed our jungle-type live fire shooting range. Building trails through the thick underbrush, we positioned stationary as well as hand-pull pop- up targets that would suddenly appear as our Marine trainees passed through, practicing patrolling and quick fire techniques. These were high-energy skill tests, filled with excitement. The men enjoyed testing their ability to score hits on the targets. This shooting range was a successful addition to our training program and many of the senior staff non-commission officers, who normally attended only classroom type training, asked to test their shooting and reaction skills on our course.

We followed this success with construction of a jungle village. We perched it up on an open hilltop above Camp Smith with a view of Pearl Harbor. For over a month our troops were cutting bamboo and hauling it to our building site, from God knows where. Like a wise officer, I never inquired too closely. I guessed that somewhere on the island of Oahu there were bald patches hidden among Bamboo stands where my cutters had gone prowling.

We spent over two months in construction and when finished, we had several thatch huts, a false well, underground tunnels, several simulated booby trap contraptions and a large menacing bamboo fence, sharpened tips and all, circling our simulated fortified village.

Our manufactured jungle hamlet presented a good replica of what one might expect to see in the South Vietnam Theater. We included, in our training syllabus, instruction on sweeping and searching jungle villages. The training was enhanced when we introduced "aggressors" dressed up in black pajamas, hidden in the tunnels, the well, and huts. Simulated booby traps were also concealed throughout the village. This phase of our training was highly successful and realistic.

General Krulak visited our facilities and seemed impressed. Colonel Cereghino and I walked him around and we conducted a mock attack exercise for him and his staff. Afterwards, we were asked to perform similar demonstrations on the proper method of attacking a jungle-fortified village for both military personnel and civilian groups on Oahu. We had so many requests for these demos it was necessary to put up bleachers to accommodate our visiting VIP's.

We learned how to put on a good "Dog and Pony show". Each success gave more emphasis to our training efforts, and we initiated additional rigorous fieldwork in a remote mountain area on the westward side of the island.

While in the field, we kept the troops constantly on the go, often patrolling and playing war games all night. After each weekend program the staff went home thoroughly exhausted.

It was all good fun, but demanding, with realistic combat training that included sound and up-to-date military battle techniques. In my heart, I knew that we were teaching our Marines how to take care of themselves and perform their responsibilities if ever they found themselves in harm's way. Patton was correct when he said, "The more you sweat in peace the less you bleed in war." That's the bottom line, and that's what our efforts were all about.

As part of our training syllabus we published two manuals that dealt with survival and combat operations. My interest in jungle and guerilla warfare had reached a high plateau, and I researched everything I could find on those subjects. With the help of the printing section at FMFPAC, we were able to publish a small pocket sized reference manual titled " The Jungle and Survival. This book was a compendium of information and pictures on survival techniques I had come upon in my training in the Marine Corps and jungle warfare school. Later, we published another pocket book sized handbook, called the "Combat Leader's Handbook". It to was provided as training reference material and contained topical information and reference on operating in South Vietnam.

Copies were forwarded to the training section at Headquarters Marine Corps and I was later informed that these manuals had been distributed to various Marine Corps Commands.

In July 1966, prior to my departure from Camp Smith, the Commanding General, FMFPAC, General Krulak, presented me with a Letter of Commendation for the work done at Camp Smith in our training. Although it was addressed to me, I must give tribute to the men in our S-3 Operations and Training section for their diligent efforts in making our program successful. It was a team effort and everyone worked long hours to deliver an effective, realistic, and timely, training program. Krulak's letter noted the following:

"The imagination and thorough training program which you executed for Marines at Headquarters and Service Battalion has resulted in a dramatic improvement in the knowledge of these Marines in their general military subjects, and has significantly improved the combat readiness of every Marine in the Battalion. Your performance is a source of pride to me and your diligence is worthy of emulation for all. Well done, -
Lieutenant General Victor H. Krulak. "

The Vietnam War effort continued to accelerate, throughout 1966 and was to grow, in manpower deployment, to over one half million military personel, In Country during 1967. I decided that I should be part of that contingent. I had one more year remaining in my current assignment, but in April 1966 I requested through official channels, a transfer to South Vietnam. This was done without my wife's knowledge and was to cause me some grief later when she discovered what I had done. But I couldn't help myself. I had to go, to participate, to taste from the Cup of Combat. I couldn't' continue to teach warfare techniques without having personally experienced and participated in the smell of the battlefield.

Some internal drive inside my psychic told me I would never be a complete, professional Marine until I experienced this war. I had to prove to myself that I could handle the rigors of combat. The mountain stood before me. I had been trained to climb it. The test must now to be taken, and I had to pass.

Infantry Captains were apparently in demand, and within sixty days after submitting my request, I received orders to the Third Marine Division, Headquartered in Phu Bai, South Vietnam.

Moving my family from Honolulu to Charlotte, North Carolina, was the next challenge. We packed all our belongings, boarded a Commercial ship and headed toward my family's soon to be new home. In Charlotte, N. C., I bought a house for them, primarily because of the uncertainty ahead and for my peace of mind that they would be taken care of if something happened to me.

After they were settled I hopped a military flight and headed back across country, reporting into Camp Pendleton, California, home of the First Marine Division. Pendleton served as a jumping off point for most Marines going to South

Vietnam. I was assigned to a Transplacement Battalion for thirty days of training and orientation. Our time was spent firing weapons, reviewing small unit tactics, physical training, and general instruction on the Vietnam theater of operations.

There were some people critical of this training. It added another month to the time they would be away from their families thereby extending their tour. Others, believed it was too basic and not particularly relevant to the tasks ahead.

For me it was essential, because if I had not experienced the training on booby traps, I am confident I would have been severely wounded or killed while on a search and destroy operation later in Vietnam. The emphasis on this aspect of training instilled an awareness of the horrible effects from this type of weapon. Later, in Vietnam, it helped foster the development of the anti-booby trap techniques that my Rifle Company employed in the Qua Viet.

Both the Viet Cong and North Vietnamese Army soldiers used booby trap devices extensively. Their devices took on many variations in size, shape, and method of deployment. Frequently, they were concealed on trails or in and around areas likely to be traversed by U. S. Troops. They were normally triggered by a carefully hidden trip wire or by pressure when stepped on or driven over.

Many were crude in design such as the Punji pit - a construction from bamboo poles sharpened on one end. The enemy would dig a hole from a few inches deep to several feet. The pointed spikes were arranged vertically in a cluster in the pit with some natural covering over the top that blended in with the surroundings. When an unsuspecting Marine stepped on top of the trap, the camouflaged cover would give way and the momentum of the falling foot or body would drive the spikes into the exposed body part. The bamboo could easily pierce a boot. To make the trap even more lethal, metal tips would sometimes be placed on the spikes. The VC would go so far as to defecate on the tips of the spikes to help foster infection when the tip pierced the skin.

These devices were feared by the troops because of the unsuspecting way they were used, the difficulty in locating them, and the terrible injury or death that could result. There were many different types, some incorporating hand grenades to land mines with enough explosive power to destroy a small vehicle or even disable a tank. They served a dastardly purpose in the war and left many men maimed for life and countless killed. They created more terror and uncertainty in the minds of our men than any of the weapons in the war.

The fear and stress of war on most men is terrible, but booby traps created an additional dimension of chaos in the mind of the foot soldier, perhaps greater than in any previsions war. To face your enemy in a fire fight or in a hand to hand encounter is one thing, but to be maimed or killed by an unsuspecting, clandestine device that offers no warning can cause a mental concern that is without boundary.

The men who lived with the mental madness of booby traps on a daily basis, I'm confident, are among those that suffered from Delayed Stress Syndrome - the mental condition from the war that became apparent only after they returned home. Booby traps might be one of the most prevailing causes of the Syndrome, in spite of the many other terrible incidents the combat veteran had to internalize and put into perspective after the war.

Back at the Transplacement Battalion training class, a full day was devoted to booby trap warfare. Because of my recent training job, I had developed a strong interest in this method of warfare and particularly because it was so prevalent in Vietnam.

Part of the training included a mock course consisting of mines and booby traps with trip wires, hidden and arranged along a trail in a densely wooded area. These simulated booby trap devices were armed with a small bursting cap that would produce a loud sound when triggered by a patrolling Marine.

The trial was to locate the devices as you moved through the trail, disarm them using proper techniques and move on to the next opportunity. I don't know how many times I worked my way though the course, but I spent most of the day attempting to locate every booby trap, and trip wire. A few times I failed causing a "detonation", but I kept at it most of the day until I was confident of my ability to locate and disarm them. The worse thing that could happen, was to allow the bursting cap to go off in your hand as you attempted to disengage it from the device. It could leave you with a stinging sensation in your hand, but the experience was worth more than I realized at the time.

As mentioned before, this training was probably the reason my radio operator and I survived when I accidentally stepped on a booby trap device several months later while on patrol in Vietnam. The mock booby trap course raised my awareness level, consequently, the immediate action response to the arming sound, which I had experienced during the training, was almost subconscious. It served as the crucible in that life and death incident.

The life's lesson for me was to take advantage of every learning opportunity, regardless of how much you think you know or even if the quality of instruction is not up to your standard. It may provide some "pearls of wisdom" that give you the advantage when you need it.

While at Pendleton, I visited a doctor to have my ears checked because I was experiencing a terrible hissing sound in my right ear. It was very distracting and interfered with my hearing. I had apparently suffered a small, non-critical, rupture caused by shooting and explosions over the years. A tiny auditory nerve had been shattered and it was in a constant state of vibration creating inner ear noise. I asked the Doctor what I could do to mitigate the hissing sound, or at least keep it from becoming more severe. He advised that I should wear earplugs when around any shooting. I explained that I was en route to Vietnam and that solution did not appear to be practical, as I was very likely to be around a lot of explosions. He said to wear one plug only in the affected ear. That would only partially affect my hearing. If I had followed his advice I probably would not have heard the snap from the trigger of the booby trap grenade. Frankly, I never considered his remedy for my problem, regardless of the potential affect on my hearing.

Today, the hissing is still there in my ear as loud as ever, and it can be very disconcerting, especially if I focus on the sound. I try not to think about it, but when I am around shooting today, like quail hunting in South Georgia, I don't hesitate to use earplugs. Different situations migrate you to different solutions. The doctor's advice today is practical and his diagnosis was correct, but his prescription was insane for that time and pending duty assignment.

After I completed the training and orientation at Camp Pendleton, I was assigned as the officer in charge of approximately 200 replacements who had also undergone training. We boarded the "Big Bird with the Golden Tail", Continental Air Lines, who I believed owned the commercial contract for air transportation of Marine troops between the USA and South Vietnam. We were flown to the island of Okinawa, famous for one of the last amphibious assaults and battles during the Second World War with the Japanese, and home of the Third Marine Division. It housed several other military bases, including the large Cadena Air Force Base.

Okinawa, more or less served as the final jumping off point to South Vietnam. Units were also rotated back to this island base from Southeast Asia for short periods of time for Rest and Relaxation. My Battalion would eventually be rotated back in 1967 for the same reasons, prior to a major push into the DMZ.

During the short time I spent on Okinawa I had the opportunity to meet and befriend the future Commandant of the Marine Corps. Major Carl Mundy, then also en route to join an infantry Battalion, where he distinguished himself during his tour in Vietnam. We flew together on the same aircraft into Da Nang, South Vietnam, parted company, served our time, and interestingly left Vietnam together approximately 13 months later in December 1967.

I never saw Mundy again until 1995. He was visiting Atlanta as the Commandant of the Marine Corps, to attend a Reserve Marine Corps Officer function held at the Officers club at Fort McPherson. Over the years, living in Atlanta, I had been active and supportive of many events conducted by the various Marine organizations and naturally received an invitation to this special event. I looked forward to the opportunity to reintroduce myself to General Mundy after almost thirty years. As my wife and I entered the club, we joined the receiving line and proceeded toward our guest of honor for the appropriate introductions. When I came face to face with the General and began to introduce myself, he immediately recognized me, relating how we had traveled to Vietnam together, recalled what unit I joined and then reminded me that we had came home together on the same plane, a fact I had forgotten. It was incomprehensible how he could have remembered in such detail our insignificant liaison of nearly 30 years before. This demonstration of memory recall was absolutely uncanny, and I thought he had been briefed on the attendees, but even if he had, no one could have been that familiar with our short past history.

To achieve the rank of General in the Marine Corps is a significant accomplishment. Competition for the few available positions is keen, and the people selected must have absolutely impeccable records of performance, while also possessing the highest level of talent, ability and sharp intelligence.

To be selected Commandant of the Marine Corps, requires an even higher level of capability and achievement. General Mundy, obviously had proven himself and consequently, achieved the ultimate in his military career. Mundy made a tremendous impression on me and I held my head a little higher because of his sensitivity and attention.

I believe the record will clearly reflect that his tour as Commandant was highly successful and his performance and contributions, exceptional. In short, the Marine Corps benefited under his leadership.

After a short stay in Okinawa, we again boarded our plane and flew into DA NANG, South Vietnam. Interestingly, the same stewardess on the Continental jet that flew with us on the arriving flight would be on the returning aircraft the following year. They were great fun, but the next thirteen months would not provide the same joy.

1st Platoon, A Company 26th Officer Candidate Course First
Lieutenant Sweeny, Commander: May 1960 (Author directly behind Sweeny)

1st Platoon, A Company 29th Officer Candidate Course
First Lieutenant Jackson, Commander, December 1961

1962 MCS TRACK TEAM - Front row, left to right, Cary Weisiger, Kent Mills, Jim Hart, LtCol. G.W. McHenry Jr., Specail Services Officer; LtGen. E.W. Snedeker, CMCS; 1st Lt. Richard Jackson, track coach; Ken Jordan, Bill McCardle and Dale Marshall. In the second row, left to right, Manager Ron Nelson, Don Jeisy, Bill Mattel, John Prichard, Nick Kovalakides, Dave Emery, John Butler, Steve Paranya, John Uelses and Trainer Al Frankovich. In the back row, Dick Edmons, Barnie Frakes, Henry White, Ed Oleata, Jim Buckley, John River, Kya Courtney, John Spencer and Dick Coultrane.

Lieutenant Jackson and John Uelses viewing plaque from Mellrose Games Track Meet. Awarded for the first sixteen foot pole vault in history and a new World Record.

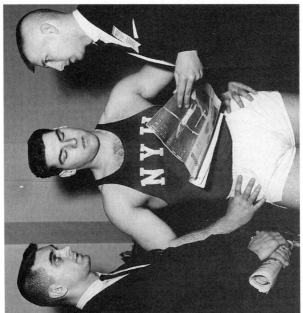

Gary Gubner, a New York University with Quantico track coach, Lt. Richard Jackson on the left and the SENTRY Sports Eidtor during a break at the National AAU Championship Track and Field Meet in Madison Square Garden. Gubner's 64' 11 1/2" effort is pending as the world's indoor record.

Commanding Officer & Company Commanders
1st Battalion, Eight Marines, 2nd Mar. Div.
Lt. Col. J. E. Wilson, Battalion Commander
Camp Lejeune, N. C. June, 1963
(Author on extreme right)

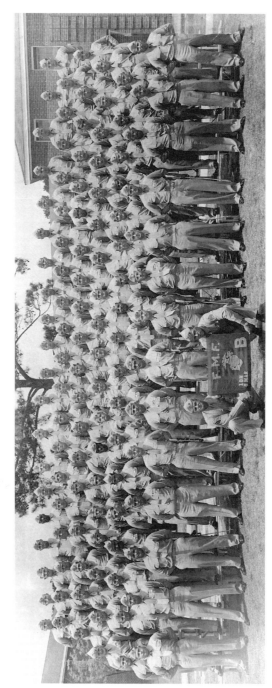

Company "B", 1st Battalion, 8th Marines, 2d Marine Division, FMF
Camp Lejuene, N.C. June, 1963

Kimberly and Christopher
on the beach in Hawaii 1966

Libby, Author, Kimberly, Christopher
Honolulu, Hawaii, August, 1964

Headquarters and Service Battalion Staff
Camp H.M. Smith, Honolulu, Hawaii
Colonel James F. McClanahan, Commanding
1965
Author 2nd from right, front row

NEW CAPTAIN - Colonel James F. McClanahan, Camp Commander, presents Captain Richard Jackson's new "railroad tracks" as the skipper's wife Libby observes. Captain Jackson serves as the Camp Special Services Officer.

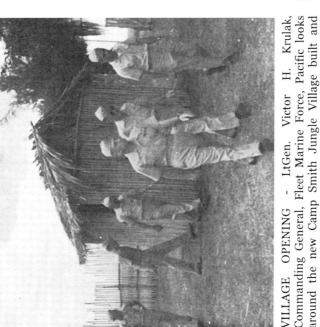

VILLAGE OPENING - LtGen. Victor H. Krulak, Commanding General, Fleet Marine Force, Pacific looks around the new Camp Smith Jungle Village built and operated by the H&S Battalion S-3 Office. Just prior to this the general officially opened the village. With Gen. Krulak are A.D. Cereghino, Commanding Officer, H&S Battalion, and Capt. R. D. Jackson, Battalion S-3 Officer.

Learning The Trade
Camp H.M. Smith. Field Training, 1966

123

Helicopter flight into the DMZ, May 18, 1967.

Captain Jackson, Lieutenants Gus Donnelley and Bill Curt at the Cua Viet, March 1967.

Admin Headquarters

Children in a village near the Qua Viet

124

Marine Interrogation Team with South Vietnam Popular Forces and former Viet Cong Soldiers

"On Patrol" - crossing river at Qua Viet

Mike Company Staff after Sarch and Destroy operation February 1967

3rd Battalion, 4th Marine – "The Thunder Mug"

Mike Company. 3rd Battalion, 4th Marines.   Okinawa, May 1967

And, He's Proud He Could Serve His Country

Major Glad His War Is Over

By SAM STANLEY

Richard Jackson — major, Marine Corps — is home.

He's home from Vietnam, and he's glad.

He's glad that for the first time in over a year he can spend some time with his wife and two children — a girl six and a boy four.

He's glad that within a month he'll leave the Marine Corps to pursue the life of a regular businessman, a career he went to college for, nearly 10 years ago.

He's glad that he'll do no more fighting in Vietnam.

But Richard Jackson — former Marshall University and Huntington High School athletic star — is also proud.

He's proud that he is a Marine.

He's proud that he had a chance to serve his country.

He's proud that he fought to give people in another land freedom.

And most ot all, the 30-year-old major is proud of the type of young men America is sending to Vietnam.

"I just can't say enough about the calibre of men America is sending over there. They're young, from 18 to 23, but the complete dedication and intelligence they possess is magnificent."

Richard Jackson — Vietnam frontline company commander — knows about these young Americans.

He spent six months, from last January to June, as leader of a rifle squad around the demilitarized zone that separates North Vietnam from South Vietnam and where today, the fighting is the heaviest.

His company of more than 200 men was among the first to enter the 'DMZ' and this phase of the fighting.

Maj. Jackson remembers a lot about Vietnam. But mostly he remembers the Vietnamese people.

"When you see little children and peasants, it creates a great deal of sympathy in the average fighting man. Each man feels that he is contributing to bring freedom to these people."

This is why Maj. Jackson believes we are in Vietnam.

"I can't say anything about the war politically," he says.

"But I can tell you a lot about what I actually saw and experienced."

"This is an entirely different situation for the American fighting man. He's not only fighting the enemy, but trying to gain the confidence of the people and win over their hearts and minds."

Author showing "Mike Spike" to Colonel Herzog at 6th Marine Corps District Headquarters in Atlanta at Awards Ceremony, July, 1968

Lt. Jim Conklin, 3rd Platoon, Author, and Lt. Rich Scolio
1st Platoon, Washington D.C., 1993

Paul Henning, Author, and John Woodson, "M" Co.
4th Marines Reunion, Washington D.C., 1993

The troops of 3/4 at the Marine Corps Monument, Washington D.C., 1993

Applying The Trade

*"There is nothing so exhilarating in life
as to be shot at without result."*

Winston Churchill

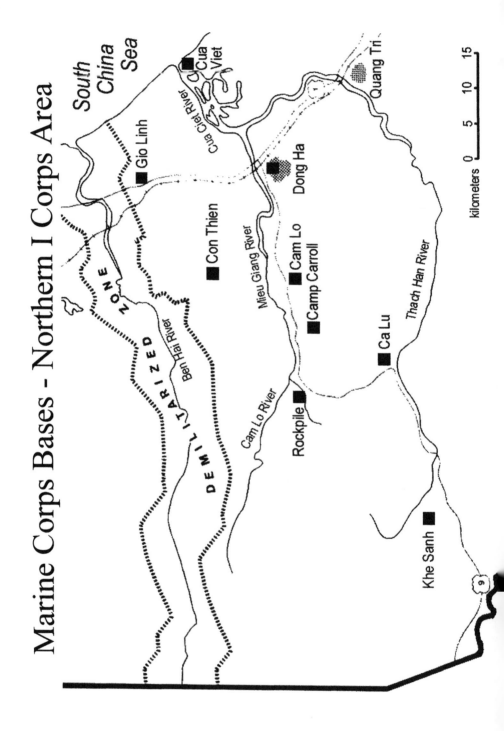

Marine Corps Bases - Northern I Corps Area

South China Sea

Cua Viet

Gio Linh

Cua Viet River

Quang Tri

DEMILITARIZED ZONE

Con Thien

Dong Ha

Ben Hai River

Mieu Giang River

Cam Lo

Camp Carroll

Thach Han River

Cam Lo River

Ca Lu

Rockpile

Khe Sanh

9

kilometers

0 5 10 15

DA NANG

In early November 1966, as a 29 year old Captain, I arrived in Da Nang, Vietnam to begin my thirteen-month tour of duty. I will never forget the smell, heat and general disorder that I sensed when I debarked from the big troop carrying, commercial jet. I grabbed my personal belongings, housed in a seabag and a military issue suitcase, lifted my seabag on my shoulder, and with my suitcase in the other hand struggled across the tarmac surface of the huge Marine Air Base.

Sweating profusely after only a few moments in the hot dusty climate, I finally reached my destination, a wooden building housing the administrative clerks that were to receive and check us in country.

I was assigned to the Third Marine Division, based in Phu Bai, and was told that I would fly out the next day on the first available aircraft. Although anxious to get to my final destination, wherever that was to be, and to find out what my next job would be, I was to spend my initial night in South Vietnam enjoying the pleasure of the Marine airbase facilities; which were few in my estimation.

Upon completion of the processing of my orders, I was dispatched to a mess hall for dinner and then assigned sleeping quarters. This was another wooden hut along the edge of the busy airfield. Provided a cot and blanket, which I used for a pillow, I attempted to settle in for the evening along with a few other officers. We spent the night listening to the constant roar of jet engines as they launched and landed throughout the long night. I recall that I slept very little, somewhat confused, startled by the frenzied activity, the constant noise of planes, and last but certainly not least, the anticipation of the unknown of what tomorrow would bring.

Many years later, after experiencing my introduction to Vietnam, I saw the movie "Platoon" which was to win the Academy Award as the best picture of the year. As I sat in the darkened theater on a cool winter night in Atlanta, I would vicariously experience the same sensations of the smell and heat of Vietnam; watching the troops on the big screen debark from their transports for their tour of duty - an imitation but realistic version of South Vietnam. Some experiences become indelibly etched in your memory and sensory facilities and are forever there as a constant reminder, called forth with only the slightest provocation.

Even today, after thirty odd years, when I hear the sound of a low flying helicopter and the "whop-whop" noise of the hovering engine, my recall springs into action. I'm reminded of choppers in the war and experience a momentary rush of adrenaline as I gaze into the sky, almost expecting them to execute a mission of some kind. The sensation passes quickly only to arise again with the next reminder.

At first light I hauled my body from the plain vanilla army cot where I had spent a restless night. I located the mess tent and forced down some hot coffee and dehydrated eggs. After checking with the Admin. Section, I was given a time and flight number for my trip to Phu Bai.

After gathering my gear, I found the transport plane. It was an "R4Q", nicknamed the flying Boxcar because of its ability and capacity to carry large loads of men and supplies in its cargo compartment. I hauled my seabag, suitcase, and ass on board, probably in that order.

I would visit Da Nang again a couple of times during my duty at Phu Bai with the Division Headquarters seven months later. My visits would be to the III Marine Amphibious Forces Headquarters where I would do some coordinating staff work as an Assistant Operations Officer for the Third Marine

Division. Unfortunately, I never had the opportunity to spend much time in and around Da Nang City or to explore any of the sights. I was always limited to the Marine Base. I did avail myself of the bar at the officer's club a few times, where the beer and air conditioning were always cold. Duty at that headquarters was very pleasant, good food, a comfortable bed, hot showers, and no one shooting at you. My final trip to Da Nang would be in December 1967, when I boarded a plane for Okinawa en route home.

The flight to Phu Bai was approximately one-hour from Da Nang - a real trip. As we boarded the transport, we sat on the floor of the cargo space, grasped a cargo belt that was stretched across our laps, and held on tight for the takeoff. We had some local Vietnamese on the plane interspersed between us. Some were holding children, others carrying foodstuffs, chickens, and other small animals including a pig. This trip did not resemble a military flight other than the fact that we were on a military aircraft. As we landed in Phu Bai, again we wrapped our arms again around the cargo belt, and held on as the plane came to a bumpy and abrupt stop at the end of the runway. It was not first class, but we arrived in one piece and everyone was happy to get off the aircraft.

These Vietnamese seemed to be moving everything they owned. Many locals were moved from time to time, to different villages or hamlet's (a series of small villages grouped together) when the Viet Cong threatened them. It was little wonder that the local peasant population didn't know whose side to be on in that war. Military Forces on both sides harassed them. Their lives turned upside down when Viet Cong conscripted troops from their villages; demanded logistical support; and attempted to turn them against the South Vietnam government. U. S. troops on the other hand, while trying to protect them, would out of necessity, continually search their villages for VC members, inspecting their hovels, uninvited, as they looked for hidden arms and supplies. We disrupted their lives as did the enemy, and they ended up fearing the VC and remained continually suspicious of the U. S. troops. While our forces were well intentioned in their activities as they tried to do their jobs, we didn't understand their mores, and they, sure as hell, didn't understand ours. All the local village and hamlet inhabitants wanted was to be left alone so they could grow their rice and live their lives in peace. They didn't give a damn about Hanoi or Saigon, the politics of the ensuing struggle, or the reunification of the north and south as a single nation under a single government - albeit, lead by North Vietnam.

Finally, on the ground at Phu Bai, after my unusual flight, I headed out to find the Third Marine Division headquarters and my new job.

PHU BAI

The Third Marine Division Headquarters had sprouted up around this small Vietnamese village and was a large military facility providing logistical and artillery fire support to most of the units located in the northern military sector of South Vietnam. Phu Bai was just a few miles from Hue, the old Imperial City of Vietnam, bustling with activity as troops and supplies were moved unceasingly through this base.

Aircraft were constantly taking off and landing as they flew combat missions in support of engaged infantry units deployed over a wide area within the *Division Tactical Area Of Responsibility,* (TAOR). This is a defined area of terrain for which responsibility is specifically assigned to the commander as a measure for control of his forces and coordination of support. Amidst all this activity, the artillery was engaged in fire missions around the clock. Frequently the base would also experience enemy activity in the form of rocket and mortar attacks as well as periodic probes by enemy ground troops and *sappers* (enemy-carrying explosive devices). An infantry Battalion, the 2nd Battalion 4th Marines, was currently providing security and defense for the base.

After reporting to the Division Headquarters and receiving my unit assignment, I immediately met with the Commanding Officer of the Battalion. He was a crusty combat veteran of a couple of wars and had gained the nick name "Black Jack." I would only spend three weeks in the Battalion and so, didn't get to know him as well as I would have liked. His reputation was that of a hard-nosed leader, one of those breed of officers who obtained his commission on the battlefield rather than through academic pursuits. Many such men lacked a college education, usually the prerequisite for an officer commission. They had to have worked twice as hard as their peers to have broken through the enlisted ranks. They were often what you might call, street-smart, and possessed great natural ability and intuition. Those I encountered or had the good fortune to serve under, I always found to be dedicated and highly decorated combat veterans who knew their jobs well and performed them in a most effective manner. It was a pleasure to have known them and learned from them.

Upon meeting with Black Jack, I was told there was no specific job opening available at that time and until a position came open, I was to conduct inspections, or rather, an Operational Effectiveness Review, of the Combined Action Groups (CAG) which were under his command.

These small units were comprised of Marines and South Vietnamese army troops numbering about twelve to twenty men in size. Each CAG unit, of which there were about a dozen, were located in small villages around Phu Bai. Their mission was to protect the village against Viet Cong infiltrators and to assist in the general *pacification* programs initiated after the war started.

Pacification included everything: medical aid to the village people, assistance in rebuilding destroyed homes, protection against enemy demands for food, and deterrence of Viet Cong forces taking conscripts. The theme was to preserve and maintain peasant loyalty on the side of the South Vietnamese Government. Many of these programs were successful, especially the medical aid provided for the young and old - the ones that usually need it most. Villages had little resources for the treatment of diseases and even routine health problems.

I spent two weeks visiting all these units, inspecting, interviewing, and evaluating their operations and activities. My inspection team consisted of me, a jeep driver, and one *shotgun*, (an armed trooper). He was our lone security element as we drove the back roads to visit small villages. We were a prime target for ambush and hitting a recently laid mine on the road was a constant threat. Consequently, we always made our road trips during daylight hours to minimize the possibility of surprise attacks. But I must admit, we were more than a little concerned as we made our way through the remote areas. Fortunately, our visits went without incident. It was interesting, though, that on three separate occasions the Viet Cong attacked the CAG units the night after our daytime visit! I don't know if this was a coincidence, but it raised some question as to whether we prompted those attacks by our inspections.

At the conclusion of the operational review, I spent a couple of days compiling my report and submitted it to the Battalion Commander. He read it immediately as I sat in his tent, answering questions on the spot. Unfortunately, it contained some unfavorable information that didn't make my debriefing a pleasurable experience.

For example, in a couple of cases I had to report that the units did not have adequate artillery support plans in place in the event of attack. The Viet Cong could have overrun some of these units easily if the enemy pressed an attack.

In another example, I recall two cases where Marines were paying rent out of their own pocket for houses in villages which they maintained as their living quarters. This may have been a unilateral decision on their part so they could have better living conditions, but I found this unacceptable. If they were to live in designated villages and be part of that community, they needed to have safe and adequate facilities to support them in their pacification and security efforts. Logistical support I found to be inadequate also. In some cases they had to purchase their own foodstuffs from the local villagers, again out of their own pocket.

Some of these units were apparently not being supplied on a regular basis - a major problem if you run out of the *Three B's*: Beans, Bandages, and Bullets. The *Three B's* is a euphemism frequently used to designate the primary logistical supply components.

Also questionable, was the support and effort given them by the South Vietnamese force. Some Vietnamese soldiers fought with pride and were aggressive, others were on the take, interested only in their personal welfare, and had a way of disappearing whenever hostile action occurred. In some cases the South Vietnamese soldier was actually more disposed toward the enemy, serving at cross-purposes with their own army forces.

This was the way the game was played in that war. Many times you didn't really know who was friend and who was foe, unlike previous wars where Americans could clearly demarcate the hinter-lands as friendly held or enemy terrain. Some peasants would toil the fields by day and conduct raids and ambushes against the U.S. occupying forces at night in black pajamas (uniforms worn primarily by the Viet Cong) and then be back tilling fields the next day, living their lives as peaceful, friendly peasants. This scenario created a lot of confusion in the minds of troops and accounted for a lot of the prevailing attitudes of distrust and hostility toward the Vietnamese people.

None the less, I had completed my lengthy written report complimenting the efforts of the Marines and their personal dedication, briefed the Commanding Officer, answered his penetrating questions and was told that these matters would be looked into. Whatever happened as a result of my operational review, I don't know. Such is the way things happen in the fluid environment of war.

However, these units were successful in their pacification efforts, but the war eventually out ran their usefulness.

Probably, everybody involved with the program moved on to other jobs, or the units were assigned to other tactical areas of responsibility. This occurred frequently as emphasis was placed on more critical issues.

I also moved on. Within days of completing my assignment I had orders to report to the 3d Battalion, 4th Marines, based out of Dong Ha, located North of Phu Bai, and the forward headquarters of the 3d Division.

My transfer occurred as a result of an accidental meeting with Colonel A. D. Cereghino, the Commanding Officer of the 4th Marine Regiment. The Colonel had been my boss at Camp Smith, Hawaii, and had told me prior to his transfer to Vietnam, which preceded my orders by about four months, that when I arrived in Vietnam I was to look him up and he'd have a job for me. I took his recommendation with a "grain of salt," but little did I realize the significant role he would play in what became my eventual destination in South Vietnam.

When I met him in Phu Bai, he was en route to a staff meeting and we exchanged warm greetings during which he inquired as to my job. He was the big boss of the 4th Marine Regiment, consisting of three Infantry Battalions and supporting arms, all located in the northern area of South Vietnam. So, I didn't hesitate to tell him I didn't have a real job. I wanted to command a rifle company and asked if he could help me. I didn't remind him of his promise but he quickly concurred that I should be in a rifle company and that he would look into it. To wit, I received orders within days and was on my way, again moving further north to a new job in a new Battalion. If I had not encountered Colonel Cereghino I have no idea what fate would have bestowed on me. When I had worked for the Colonel in Hawaii, I had apparently satisfied him with my performance as his Operations Officer because he was certainly fulfilling his promise and I counted myself extremely fortunate with my new assignment.

The Third Battalion, commanded by Lt. Colonel William Masterpool, was an excellent Combat Unit that had recently been engaged in a bloody battle on *Mutter Ridge* where they had been successful against a Northern Vietnam Army Regiment. The battle occurred north of Cam Lo, in the mountains of Nui Cay Tre. The name of the battle however, had been changed to *Mutter Ridge* after the radio call sign of Masterpool's 3d Battalion. The Marines had suffered moderately in this hard fought struggle, loosing 20 men but accounting for over 100 North Vietnamese Army (NVA) dead. Two Marines from his Battalion would later receive Congressional Medals of Honor for their heroic efforts in that battle. The assignment to the 3d Battalion was the stepping stone to command of a rifle company - my earnest wish and objective when I requested transfer from Hawaii to Vietnam.

A few weeks hence, after fulfilling the responsibilities of another job in the Battalion, I would be made a Company Commander, a position that would require all the skills I learned the proceeding seven years as a Marine Officer.

With my new orders in hand, I packed my gear and caught a uneventful flight to Dong Ha. It was now December 1966, the war was becoming more intense each day and the U.S. manpower strength committed to the war, was growing daily.

DONG HA

Arriving in Dong Ha, I made my way to the headquarters of the 3d Battalion, located in a series of tropical wooden huts built by military construction crews, arranged in line with sandbags stacked around them. These makeshift buildings were used mostly for administrative and logistical support purposes and served as the rear headquarters for the deployed units in this northern section.

The village and base were ten miles south of the *Demilitarized Zone* - (DMZ), located within artillery range of the NVA gunners. The enemy guns were probably just North of the DMZ in North Vietnam or, concealed in the DMZ. Upon reporting, I was told that the combat elements of the 3d Battalion were about seven miles West in an area named for a small village, called Cam Lo. I completed my administrative processing and issue of combat gear and was to be driven to the combat base the next morning.

Dong Ha was located at the Junction of Highways One and Nine and about 10 miles by the Cua Viet River to the South China Sea. The air strip, highway, and the developing port facilities at the Cua Viet base on the South China Sea, were utilized for re-supply of the forward headquarters of the 3d Marine Division and all combat units deployed in the Northern sector.

Highway One ran North and South through South Vietnam, directly into North Vietnam by way of the DMZ, while highway Nine ran almost due west from Dong Ha to Khe Sanh and eventually into Laos. Some feared the NVA would mount an armored attack southward down Highway One, push through the Northern Provinces, and attack all major bases and cities. I believe, this eventually happen in the early 1970's.

Dong Ha was part of the area called *Leatherneck Square.* Each corner of the square was anchored by a combat base: Cam Lo west of Dong Ha, Con Thien, the high ground, North of Cam Lo, and the fire base Gio Linh, due North of Dong Ha. These bases, so positioned, provided artillery fire support and troops for all the combat operations within the region.

In addition, naval ships patrolling off the adjacent coast in the South China Sea could also perform fire missions in support of these bases and their infantry missions. Even with this firepower and the capability of mutual support, the bases were still susceptible to long range NVA field gun attacks from north of the DMZ.

On three different occasions while in Dong Ha, I experienced enemy artillery shelling. The last time was in the summer of 1967 after landing in a chopper on the airstrip. We had just disembarked from a chopper and were walking across the airstrip when the first rounds fell. The chopper was blown apart and we were running for our lives, diving into the nearest bunker along the edge of the strip with incoming rounds pounding all around us.

It was a well built bunker, amply covered with sandbags. I can still recall sitting below ground in the darkened cavern as the impacting rounds shook the ground unmercifully. The only light inside the bunker filtered through the single opening that served as a doorway and only point of egress. The room was a tomb. We crouched waiting, watching, as little strips of dirt trickled down from the roof through the stacked sand bags as each round shook the ground. Minutes seemed like hours. Finally, the attack ceased. We scrambled through the tiny orifice as one body desperately seeking the light, freedom, and relief from the maddening anxiety of the shelling. It occurred to me, then, that at some point during the attack I lost my soft-cover hat. I found it on the ground not far from the nearly demolished chopper. Upon inspecting it I found a large jagged rip along the top, obviously caused by exploding shrapnel. I assume an errant fragment pierced it as it lay on the ground. At least I hope I didn't have it on my head when it was struck as we scrambled for cover. That would have been too close for comfort.

In every serious situation there is always some humor, and when we cowered in the bunker with the enemy artillery falling all around us, one of the men informed the group that he had been hit by a small piece of shrapnel. He said he was hit in the back of the head, when the shelling began, while taking a leak off to the side of the bunker. With mocking horror he exclaimed how awfully glad he was he had not been peeing the other way, lest his wife would be furious if he returned home with his pecker blown off. We had a good laugh and a momentary relief from the anxiety of the shelling.

On another visit in May, 1967, prior to a search and destroy operation that was to be conducted in the DMZ, our Battalion, which had just returned from Rest and Relaxation in Okinawa, was bivouacked in Dong Ha. On the night before our Heli-lift, about midnight, the base came under heavy rocket attack and our Battalion seemed to be located in the principal impact zone. We lost several Marines killed and wounded even though we had foxholes to help protect us from attack. Unfortunately, some of the casualties occurred as a result of direct hits on the foxholes; which left a grim reminder to all who witnessed the carnage.

I can only guess that this was not a premeditated attack, but one of opportunistic shelling by the NVA spotters and gunners upon seeing the massing of troops at the Dong Ha base. They naturally seized the moment to inflict as much damage as possible in anticipation of an attack on their position. I remember, during the attack, pressing myself down into the bottom of a fox hole which was about four feet deep. I was aware of my radio operator, Lance Corporal Evans, lying across one of my legs, which was shaking terribly. I looked over at him and asked if he was trembling, or was it me. We agreed we couldn't tell the difference and decided it was both of us.

Dong Ha, the Southeast corner of *Leatherneck Square* left me with many memories, mostly unpleasant and frightening. It was a base I would visit many times over the next several months, but for now, early December 1966, it was the entry way to my next job. I left early the next morning to join the forward combat elements of the 3d Battalion 4th Marines at Cam Lo.

CAM LO

The jeep ride along Highway Nine was slow and uneventful. However, one always scanned the road surface to detect any fresh disturbance of the surface that might hint at a landmine.

The terrain between Dong Ha and Cam Lo was fairly level and cultivated with populated areas along the river. North of Cam Lo, the terrain consisted of rolling hills covered with shrub growth and coarse elephant grass. West of the combat base the low ground rose to a series of ridges and steep hills at an elevation of 550 meters and looked down over the base. (At a later time at this location, while my company was manning an outpost, we received heavy mortar fire from the enemy located in these menacing hills.)

Heavy vegetation and rough terrain made ground movement north from the base difficult. Conversely, it provided the enemy good concealment for their deployment. Cam Lo was only 8 miles from the southern boundary of the DMZ and some of the heaviest fighting of the war occurred a few miles north of Cam Lo and 2 miles south of the DMZ, in the Song Ngan Valley.

Upon arriving at the Cam Lo Combat Base, I located the Commanding Officer, Lt. Colonel William Masterpool. His command tent was perched on the top of a small hill protected by extended ridges. I made my way up to the nose of the incline leading to his quarters. He was sitting inside reviewing some maps. I announced myself, handing him my orders and personnel file. He was a warm, friendly, and hospitable person, the type you could not help but like immediately. He sat in his field chair and inquired about my background as he read through my file. He noticed that I had received a letter of Commendation from General Krulak, Commanding General of Fleet Marine Forces Pacific, for the Jungle Warfare training program implemented at Camp Smith. He then, immediately launched into a discussion about counter-guerilla tactics. He wanted to know what we had done, about the training in general, the tactics taught, and what results were achieved. In many respects, I think he wanted to know what I knew, if anything practical, about this warfare. We even talked about the type of personal gear that should be carried on long patrols or sweep operations. He went so far as to show me his multi-pocket vest. It resembled a trout fishing vest containing all kinds of items: flashlights, matches, string, knife, medicine kit and many other miscellaneous items.

He also showed me the Third Battalion, Fourth Marines' "Thunder Mug" - a ceramic toilet with attached seat that was used as a type of punch bowl whenever a social event was held by the Battalion. It had been dedicated at a *Mess Night*, a kind of dinner-and-dining party for officers, held on the Marine Corps birthday, November 10, 1966. That was when the Battalion was located at Camp Carroll.

Masterpool had a wonderful reputation as a combat leader, and his Battalion had shortly before distinguished themselves in an overwhelming victory over the NVA. He was a *mustang* - an enlisted Marine who had obtained an officer's commission. He was intuitive, gracious and gregarious with a personality that flowed with charisma. He was the type of leader men would happily follow. I liked him immediately and my respect and admiration for him grew over the next few months. "We hit it off well," as you might say. Our paths would cross again later, when we were both stationed in Phu Bai, at Third Division Headquarters. Materpool's personality was infectious and he made a personal impact on me, as had the Regimental Commander Colonel Cereghino.

I liked these men, got along with them, and did everything I could to fulfill their demands while working for them. They were bright, resourceful officers, professional in all regards and I considered my time under their tutelage highlights in my career and passage through the Marine Corps.

After Masterpool and I concluded our conversation and he had briefed me on the Battalion and our current situation, he informed me that I was to be the S-4, Logistics Officer of the Battalion. All the Rifle Company Commander positions were filled, but he promised I would get the next one that came available. I was disappointed to say the least. I had come so far and truly believed the timing was right and that I was ready to take on the responsibility. But it was not to be - at least, not this day.

I had never been a Logistics officer before and knew little about the responsibilities of the position. But the Marine Corps believed in on-the-job training and with time and a good staff, a Marine Officer should be able to properly handle any job they were assigned.

Prior to leaving his command tent, another surprise befell me. A big lumbering Major entered the tent just as I was preparing to depart. I was presented to the Battalion Executive Officer, Harry Field.

Major Field had been the Company Commander of Charley Company at Camp Lejeune and was the Captain who had chewed me out so unmercifully because of my bad attitude and expectation of special treatment, when I played football while in his unit. The Marines were a relatively small force, and if you remained in the Corps long enough your paths with fellow officers would cross many times at different duty stations.

Captain Field had made a big impression on me three years before, consequently, I had made some attitudinal changes and we got along fine after that. I held him in high regard and was happy to see him and to have an ally of sorts in this new situation. He had recently been wounded in the battle on *Mutter Ridge* and had a few metal fragments in his back from an enemy mortar. The wounds were minor and the tiny pieces of shrapnel were working their way out of the skin. I'm sure they were uncomfortable but Harry never complained. He was not athletic, awkward in many ways, but determined, with a forceful personality and booming voice to match.

I assumed my new responsibilities and immediately went to work trying to figure out what I should be doing. I quickly learned how to acquire, for our active rifle companies, the logistical supplies we needed, the *Three B's*, beans, bandages, and bullets. I found myself immersed in paper work, filling out requisitions, forms, meeting the needs of the Battalion, and so on. I made frequent trips to our rear headquarters at Dong Ha to check on the flow and storage of supplies. It took me about two weeks to get the handle on the job, and when I did, Masterpool had another task for me. He asked me to develop a plan that would help protect the bridge that crossed the Cam Lo River from Highway Nine, a short distance from our base camp. The bridge was guarded around the clock as it was on the main supply route from Dong Ha to the Cam Lo base and points further north to Con Thien. If destroyed, the units North of the river could be in jeopardy of being re-supplied on a regular routine.

The troops stationed at the bridge provided adequate security from enemy ground attacks but Masterpool was concerned that *sappers*, enemy demolition troops, might float an explosive charge down the river and detonate it under the bridge. Or, perhaps, they might attempt to swim to the bridge under the cover of darkness, and place explosives on the bridge pilings.

It was a thought provoking exercise and the solution was not simple. We didn't have the proper physical resources available to solve the problem. But after studying the terrain, width, depth of the river, currents, and our troop disposition, I presented a plan to Masterpool, which he liked and told me to implement.

We would place several large cargo type nets connected across the river, ends anchoring on each side and attached along the bottom with 55-gallon drums filled with rocks and concrete. These would hold the net in place on the floor of the river. The river was neither terribly deep nor particularly swift. The net would be located about fifty yards upstream and serve as an obstacle to floating objects or water borne enemy troops in reaching the bridge. We did not have any concern downstream from the bridge, concluding that any threat would come from the west with the water flow out of the mountains. Both the bridge and obstacle would be guarded and observed on a twenty four-hour basis. The problem was to find large cargo nets, sufficient rope, and drums to put the plan into action.

I began searching for the necessary supplies. Masterpool didn't care where I obtained my materials and wouldn't ask me any questions. The nets and rope would have to come from the Navy. We started a diligent search or, "midnight requisition" that is, acquisition without approval, or better yet, confiscation under the cover of darkness. I knew it would not be easy, but I was prepared to do whatever it took to finish this project.

But events overtook the project, and I never got to finish the job. The Cam Lo Bridge remained an important feature of the re-supply routes, and I believe a similar plan was put into effect by another unit at a later date.

We moved on. We were to conduct a sweep from Cam Lo to Con Thien, occupy the base, and conduct combat operations in the area north to the DMZ.

This was to be my first combat operation. I was excited, scared, and unsure about my abilities to perform in combat. However, I would be indoctrinated quickly.

CON THIEN

This base was part of *Leatherneck Square*, located on the north west corner and was reachable only by helicopter or a shabby, dirt road which ran North from the Cam Lo base.

Con Thien was a 158-meter hill over looking the DMZ which lay 2 miles to the North. It was the only high ground around in an otherwise flat region. It offered the best observation in the area and was a critical terrain feature for both the Marines and the NVA. Throughout the war, the base and the adjacent terrain would be the sight of numerous battles and heavy casualties on both sides.

This operation would be the first of three times I would visit the general area. This was not uncommon for units operating in this area, as they were routinely rotated in and out of the base, due to the heavy fighting and constant shelling from the enemy.

Battles in the area were never conclusive. We located enemy, engaged them in battle, finally they would retreat and we would chase them up to the DMZ, where they would then retreat to North Vietnam. Our units returned to base, and later, while on patrol or a sweep, we would engage the enemy, often the same enemy all over again. Win, lose, or draw, the battles seesawed back and forth, just like that, for years in this northern sector.

No one really owned the terrain. Both the NVA and the Marines moved through it regularly, engaging each other, and moving on. All this was followed up with frequent artillery and rocket shelling from the NVA, their rounds dropping on our set-piece bases (fixed in position). The Marines shelled at will throughout the zone with harassment and interdiction fire, whenever and wherever enemy troops were spotted. Unfortunately, our firepower produced uncertain or undefined results much of the time.

The longer the battles raged back and forth inconclusively, the more resources we committed and, the more the enemy threw into the fray. The situation would continue to worsen as it escalated in the years ahead, even with the construction of the so-called, *McNamara Wall* - a highly publicized solution in the newspapers of the time, but with little or no recognizable results on the battlefield. The *McNamara Wall* was an invisible boundary about fifteen miles long, paralleling the DMZ on the southern side. It was composed of electrical sensors planted in the ground to detect enemy troop movement through the zone. It was supported by a series of combat bases that could provide artillery and troop support to meet the threat of the NVA movement through the DMZ. This "electronic wall" was installed after I left this area, but again, I believe history reflects that the results were given mixed reviews.

Our Battalion moved out by foot one early morning in mid December, 1966. We headed North and experienced no contact with the enemy all day. It was a five-mile march through the rolling terrain from Cam Lo, to the high ground at Con Thien. The Battalion deployed its units into a tactical formation and we moved out smartly toward our objective, reaching it by late afternoon.

We had been on the march for only a couple of hours, moving slowly, using caution at every possible ambush location, checking potential enemy positions at critical locations - I mean, we were primed! In addition, we had a section of three *Otters* attached to our Battalion. *Otters* were armor plated, tracked, mechanized vehicles. They were armed with fifty caliber machine guns mounted on the top of the vehicle. They trailed our command section in single file. I was walking just ahead of them near the rear of our Headquarters column. Had we come under attack from enemy small arms fire, they would have provided both fire power and vital protection with their metal hulls for the command group.

We halted briefly at one suspicious point, while our security elements scanned the area looking for enemy emplacements. As we waited for an "all clear" signal, I moved from my position in front of the lead *Otter* vehicle to check on another matter. Within a few seconds I heard a loud explosion immediately to my rear! Thinking we had come under attack, I hit the ground like a brick, as did the entire group of men around me. However, as we presently discovered, it was not enemy fire but *friendly* fire - our own.

The gunner in the lead *Otter* had accidentally fired one round from his fifty caliber machine gun. The impact of the shell tore a huge hole in the ground just a few feet in front of the vehicle, right where I had been standing just seconds before. After checking out the situation, I was both frightened and relieved. The gunner made a mistake and was genuinely stricken by his action and thought of what might have happened. Thank goodness I was the busy body type, otherwise my war and maybe my life would have ended unceremoniously by "friendly fire.".

I had a friend and fellow classmate from Basic School who unfortunately lost his life when an artillery round from "friendly fire" fell "short" on his position when this same Battalion was engaged in the battle on "Mutter Ridge." My friend, Captain J. J. Carroll, was both an outstanding officer and individual. Colonel Masterpool, during our initial meeting talked with me about Captain Carroll, who was the Company Commander of Kilo Company at the time of the incident, and he told how the mortally wounded Marine had died in his arms. J. J. , as he was called, was a handsome, hard charging, professional Marine Officer, well liked, and always with a great smile on his face. He was posthumously awarded the Navy Cross. Camp Carroll, in this northern area, was named in his honor (the camp where the "Thunder Mug" was initiated.)

We moved into the Con Thien base a little later, relieving the Battalion located there and began to occupy their positions and conducting all the myriad tasks that are necessary to establish a sound defensive perimeter. There was an artillery battery in place to support the base and to conduct fire missions for the maneuvering units operating in the tactical zone. It was not a large combat outpost and was usually occupied by only one Battalion and a gun battery. It had a helicopter landing zone inside the perimeter.

It looked in disarray to me with empty shell boxes and casings lying all over the place, I suppose, from the constant fire missions that were being conducted by the battery. (Incidentally, wooden shell boxes, filled with dirt, were highly revered by the troops as material for fortified bunkers. They provided protection from enemy fire and their shape and strength facilitated the preparation of the bunkers. The base was surrounded with foxholes, with triple concertina wire placed in front of the positions, along with anti-personal claymore mines that could be detonated by our troops from their foxholes. These were deterrents to enemy attacks and were normally located in likely avenues of ground approach. When detonated, they could blast an area several yards wide.

My baptism of enemy fire took place around midnight of the first day by way of a typical wake-up call and welcome from the NVA to the new boys on the block. I'm confident that the NVA gunners and spotters observed our movement into the base during the day, knowing we were a new unit, and had not totally organized our emplacements. Seizing the moment, they peppered our position liberally with their guns, probably from just across the DMZ in North Vietnam.

We were on the high ground, such as it was, surrounded by relatively flat terrain. We could observe the ground around our position, but then so could the enemy watch our every move.

I'm reminded of the nature of the situation then, at Con Thien, by a "Murphy's Law" type of phrase, that originated in the war: "Remember, when the enemy is in range, so are you..." A very endearing and appropriate observation.

Fear and confusion occupied my top priorities when those first artillery rounds slammed into our position. You wake-up to the noise, and hopefully, you do wake-up. You're not certain what's happening; the explosions are deafening; people are running and moaning if they'd been hit; your brain is scrambled from the confusion; you're not sure what to do next. Finally, your training takes over; you automatically grab for the ground; and begin a crab like dash to the nearest hole you can find. Then you sit, crouched in the hole, waiting for what seems like an eternity as the concussions rock and shake the very earth that encases you. Fear and terror streak through your mind, and you ask yourself, "What in the hell am I doing here? I could be home and not in this hellhole risking life and limb. What about my family, are they going to live the rest of their lives without a husband, a father, and a son? Why did I choose this as a lifestyle?"

These are reoccurring themes which will reenter your mind each time you come in harm's way. I guess this thought process is common among most people, who go through these frightening experiences. You do finally adapt, somewhat, to the explosive outbursts. Over time, you learn to live with them, to accept them, and to do your job in spite of them. You've been trained to do it and inside you know you must.

But you're still scared; I made no pretense otherwise. Once your nerves have settled down and you've found all your body parts in place, you contain the adrenaline that flooded your body during the hostilities. I made it through that initial test, but there were more to come, and unfortunately they seemed to get worse.

After that first night, we pulled ourselves together - at least I did and got on with the business at hand. Supplies were coming to us by heli-lift daily from Dong Ha. My job was to see that our own needs were met logistically on time, and the fighting units got what they needed when and where they needed it. Kick ass; take names; and don't leave any need unfulfilled. Do whatever it takes to get it done. That was my mission, and I did it while I learned my job.

After a couple of days we had a surprise visit from the Commanding General of the III Marine Amphibious Forces, Lou Walt (MAF headquarters was based in Da Nang). The General was Commander of all Marine troops in South Vietnam. He was on an inspection tour of the bases and was to be briefed as to each unit's status during his visit. I can recall, standing on the edge of the landing zone, inside our perimeter, speaking with the General and he asked me if we had everything we needed.

I immediately responded "Yes Sir."

He did not recognize me from my three-day stint as his Aid-de-camp in Hawaii where he had his third star pinned on, and I didn't dare remind him. That would have been out of order, at least I thought so. Another piece of vital information I did not disclose was that our unit did not have enough combat equipment available in our supply to outfit new troops when they reported in for duty. We would not, and could not, put troops in a combat zone unless they were fully outfitted with flack jackets, helmets, rifles and other significant equipment. Because of these shortages, and our inability to locate the proper equipment, we were required to detain our much-needed replacement troops in the rear area for several days, until they were outfitted. This situation was ridiculous, but I can only assume that many units were experiencing the same re-supply problems at that time in the war.

I didn't say anything to General Walt, that was the CO's job and I didn't want to appear a "Horse's Ass" with my astonishing demonstration that I knew all the problems, but didn't have any answers. Life and the war would go on, without my revelations and lecture on supply problems to the Commanding General.

We spent several more days at Con Thein - our units searching for the enemy, conducting ambush operations and shelling everything that moved around the base night and day. I don't recall any significant battle during our stay. We were soon relieved by another Battalion and moved our headquarters back to Dong Ha, except for one Rifle Company, and assumed security for that base.

In Dong Ha we were moved into the tropical wooden huts that were surrounded by sandbags for protection against enemy shelling. A bar was available for an occasional libation in the evenings. Compared to living in the field it was first class, but it wouldn't last long, at least for me.

We had been at Dong Ha, it seems for just a few days, when I received an urgent call from the (XO), the Executive Officer, Major Field, to come to the Commanding Officer's *Hootch*, another wooden hut. I hurried from my office where I was probably counting gear and bitching about shortages caused by inadequate re-supply and thievery. It was amazing how combat gear could disappear from secured storage. Later, I was to find on a visit, that the local Vietnamese black market in Saigon, seemed to have anything and everything you needed for sale and on displayed in various street markets.

I knocked on the screen door and received the traditional response "enter" and I walked in, saluted, and found my two leaders having a drink and in a deep discussion on some subject matter. I was soon to discover that the subject was Me. I was told to have a seat and Major Field quickly got to the issue. He informed me that one of the companies, Mike, was in bad shape: declining leadership, low morale, and terrible performance. He told me to catch a jeep that afternoon and get out to their location at Cam Lo ASAP. This was the company that had not return to Dong Ha from Con Thien with the rest of the Battalion. They had been assigned to maintain a base at Cam Lo for security and to conduct patrol operations. Apparently, this was not being done adequately, and both the CO and XO were furious with the current leadership.

Major Field asked me if I had any questions, and I responded, "No. " I don't think he was interested in questions at that time, because he was really pissed at the Mike Company Commander for whatever reason.

He said, "Good. Catch a jeep and leave here within the hour". Finally he said, "Get the fucking mess squared away." We think you can do the job, and we're counting on you." It was over that quick and I started getting my gear together to depart, as ordered.

When things happen in war, they happen fast. I had not expected this opportunity so quickly, or under these circumstances. I didn't know nor could fully appreciate the problems with Mike Company and didn't care. This was what I wanted, what I had worked toward, and now was presented the chance to make or meet my destiny as a Marine Rifle Company Commander in Combat.

CAM LO REVISITED

The drive to Cam Lo was only about thirty minutes by jeep, on mostly hard surface road through the rural agricultural area. We drove across the guarded bridge onto a rough dirt trail that led to the company's position. Mike Company now occupied a part of the base where the 3d Battalion had been located prior to our deployment to Con Thien. Cam Lo was the southwestern corner of Leatherneck Square, an important adjacent to the overall security of this area. Additional bases were being developed further west, Camp Carroll and the infamous Khe Sahn, which was to receive a great deal of publicity in the early 70's when under heavy attack by the NVA.

Upon arriving at the base, I had a friendly discussion with the outgoing Company Commander. He was helpful, provided orientation and status of the company. I didn't know why he was being relieved, didn't really care. He was tired. I was ready. He'd been through major battles, and was ready for an easier lifestyle. We shook hands as he stepped into the jeep that brought me to the base, and headed back to Dong Ha. I never saw him again. He seemed like an o. k. person to me - probably had some tough breaks and was too weary to overcome them.

In my mind's eye, even today, I can picture the company position. The command post, 81mm Mortar section, and other supporting units were located in a deflated bowl. The perimeter was surrounded on three sides by small hills with the forth side consisting of gently rising ground. A Northern knoll contained our 60mm mortars and had good observation over the general area and northward to the mountains.

Concertina wire had been placed in front of the foxholes. The Company had scaled down their position to fit their defensive requirement for what was earlier, a Battalion sized position.

It was now nearly 4:30 PM, still on my day of arrival and it was getting late. I had only a little daylight time available to physically walk the perimeter and be introduced to the Platoon Commanders and Senior Non Commissioned officers. I made the tour, offered a few suggestions, ate my c-ration dinner, had some briefings from the Lieutenants and my Gunny Sergeant. About 2200 hours, I laid down on my army cot located in a tent adjacent to the dug in command and communications center - for, what I thought, was to be a nice, well earned sleep.

The company position was well established - to well established unfortunately, having been in the same place for several weeks. I didn't know how aggressive they had been patrolling or ambushing the area because they had not engaged any enemy for sometime. But in no time flat, I learned the NVA had found us! Their wake-up call and "welcome" to the new Commanding Officer of Mike Company came soon enough.

At 0230 hours all hell broke loose. The sky lit up like Times Square on New Years Eve; the gunny was screaming, "Skipper, Skipper, Incoming"; I shot from the cot in a roll and hit the deck with the impact of a bag of wet sand. Gunny was clinging to the floor as I tried desperately to pull on my jungle boots. What a night to pick. One of the few times I slept without my boots on! I vowed it would be the last.

Mortar fragments slammed into the back of my head causing a sensation similar to the sting of a yellow jacket. I pressed my body even flatter against the makeshift wooden floor, still wrestling with my damn boots. Double rows of sand bags circled our tent standing about 3 1/2 feet high. I could feel the vibrations as shrapnel crashed deep into the bags. The enemy 82mm rounds kept peppering the company position. I knew I had to get to the command bunker and coordinate the counter mortar fire and defense against a possible ground attack. I scrambled from the deck, crab crawling the long, long 15 yards of ground that separated my tent and the command center.

As I rushed from the tent, the exploding mortar rounds continued to rain down on our position. I was scared, really scared as I skirted across the barren ground. But I forced myself to reach the safety of the tiny opening in the ground that lead into the protected bunker.

I made it through the tiny orifice and immediately began receiving compass azimuths. These came over the company command radio net from points within our position to the muzzle flashes of the enemy mortars.

The 82mm mortar was the principal high angle fire weapon of the enemy with a range of about 4,000 meters. When a round exits the tube, a profound flash is emitted as a result of the burning propellant increments affixed to the fin assembly that propels the round to it's target. The flash is vomited from the tube, vertically into the air, and if the tube is not concealed in a defile, it is not difficult to spot these flashes on a dark night. As soon as the azimuths are determined and distance from out position estimated, they are plotted on a map and artillery counter fire missions immediately requested through the Battalion fire support center, at headquarters. Of course, while all this is underway, a lot of other things are happening.

One such action took place almost immediately when the first rounds began to inundate our position. It involved two Marines manning our 60mm mortar. On the previous evening after assuming command of Mike Company, during the initial tour of the combat base, I had given instructions to the 60mm mortar section, that if we were ever hit, I wanted counter mortar fire to commence immediately toward the muzzle flashes using the free tube method. This is done without use of the tripod. One man holds the mortar tube, sighting over the top of the barrel towards the target, while the other man loads the tube with ammo. This method eliminates several seconds off the time normal aiming manipulation takes. I learned this technique at the British Army Jungle Warfare School in Malaysia.

The company mortars were located on the military crest of a small hill inside our position, and when the first enemy rounds hit, our mortar crew immediately began to return fire using the free tube method sighting on the distant muzzle flashes. We did not, and could not know at this time, but their quick response probably saved our unit from taking significant casualties.

As the enemy rounds continued slamming into our position, these stalwarts remained at their position continuously firing their mortar amidst flying fragments. One of them was later to receive both the Purple Heart and the Navy commendation medal for meritorious duty during this critical period.

During the confusion we somehow managed to get a fix, or approximate location, on the enemy mortars and relayed the fire mission over the Battalion Tactical Net. It was only minutes before we received an "On the Way" from the artillery gun position. However, much to our surprise, the first six rounds did not drop on the enemy position but fell well short puncturing our own perimeter. The concussions were so close to my CP that I thought the enemy had stepped up the attack. Realizing what was happening lead to an instant scream into the radio to cease fire. We were to find out later some stupid son-of-a-bitch transposed numbers in the coordinates we transmitted, causing a 3,000 meter error. Luckily, no one was hurt as a result of this error. It's one thing to be killed by the enemy in battle, but to "buy it" from "friendly's" makes it a futile ball game, indeed.

While we feverishly reworked the coordinates with the fire support center to bring our big guns on the enemy positions, our mortars continued to fill the sky with our own counter mortar fire.

After a few moments the artillery again signaled "On the Way", and our spotters directed the guns until no more enemy muzzle flashes were seen in the darkness.

The muffled explosions from the mortars had finally stopped as we prayed and cursed at the same time. Finally after a few minutes of deliberation, we sounded an "all clear" and began to clamber from our holes. Once on top of the ground, under a moon filled sky, I requested a status report from all of my Platoon Leaders, with some apprehension. This is one of the terrible periods that every commander must face; the stark realization that some of his comrades may be dead or severely wounded.

We stood wet with nervous sweat, waiting with bated breath. It was 0300 in the morning. The reports rolled in: 1st platoon, one casualty; 2nd platoon, 1 wounded in action (wia); 3rd platoon, no casualties; Weapons platoon, 2 wia; Tank section, no casualties; 81mm Section, one casualty; Twin 40 Anti Aircraft Section, no casualties; Headquarters Section, no casualties. Reports complete: five Marines wounded during the attack.

An immediate follow-up report from the company Corpsman indicated that none of the casualties required immediate evacuation. All wounds were minor in nature.

A great relief surged through me. We had survived, this time. Charlie, as we called the enemy, had thrown everything they had, with little results. It's kind of funny, but we considered this a major victory for us.

After some insignificant chatter allowed our nerves to settle, we climbed back into our bedrolls. I fell into a restless slumber. This time, my boots remained on my feet and would, at night, for quite a while.

In a battle zone, morning comes extremely early. At the first sign of light even the weariest begin to move about. They prop up their aching bodies from sleeping on the ground, pour a little water into a dirty C-ration can, mix-in some powdered coffee and cream and try to warm it with a heat tab or small fire. You try to get this hobo coffee down the gullet because it warms the body and provides some strength to get you going.

It's amazing how good it tastes. You try to remember how percolated coffee tastes, but you can't. It's been too long. This stuff is great; you force yourself to think. At least you're alive and in one piece, and therein lies the challenge, to stay in that condition for as long as possible. You open a can of rations. The choices are innumerable, that is, you have twelve different possibilities and none to great. Among them are beans and franks, ham fried, turkey loaf, and ham and limas. Perhaps you've saved some canned peaches, apricots or pears, and along with one of these, you might even enjoy some pound cake, date pudding, or fruit cake. You might even heat some white bread by punching holes in it and pouring water over it. You stick it in the fire till it gains the crispiness of toast, then eat it with a spread of peanut butter and canned jam. Although, none of these are the fancy of an Epicurean, I can assure you they somehow satisfy your needs and pack enough healthy nourishment to keep you going. In the box of C-rations (RATS) you are also provided with a plastic spoon and a compact utility pack, which contains such useful items as toilet paper, matches, instant coffee, sugar, salt, two pieces of chewing gum, and a small package of 4 cigarettes.

Each Marine in the field was normally issued three boxes of these "delicacies" each day. It was surprising how one did acquire an adequate supply of nourishment from this array of foodstuffs. That is, most did. Some chow-hounds ate everything they could get their hands on and would never be satisfied.

After breakfast, you relieve yourself into a hole and cover your evidence with several shovel loads of dirt. After all, one must practice the proper sanitary procedures to have an orderly camp. If you've occupied a camp long enough you might even have the luxury of a "head" made out of wooden ammo boxes and mounted over a half size 55-gallon drum. These are burned out every day with kerosene to help keep things clean, and military.

You can brush your teeth by chewing on a green twig if you don't have a toothbrush. If water is in surplus, you might even shave. But you remember not to use your hard hat, or helmet, to boil water in. Direct heat on the steel will weaken it and the old hunk of metal might just save your life someday... but, it does make an excellent wash bowl. When you finish your shave, you empty the water and put your helmet liner back in, fold the camouflage cover back in place, and look military again. But don't use after-shave lotion because the enemy might smell it, if later in the day or night you're in an ambush position. After these ablutions are complete, you organize for the day: clean weapons, dig foxholes deeper, hold police call of the camp - get it as clean as possible. After all, maybe one of the Big Brass will show up to see how your morale and defenses are.

The men look tired and young. As time goes on they will age before your very eyes. They will grow into battle-hardened old men. After they return home, their youth will somehow return, but in war, they look and act much, much, older.

On a day like this following an attack, there is always more to be done; conduct a *recon* of your camp, survey the damage, evacuate the wounded to the rear for medical attention. When the helicopter, or chopper lands, you place the wounded on it for evacuation. This process is properly called MEDEVAC, for, "medical evacuation". In the military all descriptions are in mnemonics because time doesn't permit long-winded discussions. Time is precious, and your responsibilities are increasingly infinite.

We got a platoon of 43 men ready to move out at 0800, to patrol the area where the enemy mortar positions of the previous night were suspected to be. They moved out in single file; always single file with 10 to 15 yards between each man. Vegetation in the area was too thick for men to move in a dispersed formation. The prescribed distance between men had to be maintained to keep casualties to a minimum in the event of surprise enemy fire. The casualty radius of a grenade is 12 meters, a mortar 25 meters and an artillery round about 50 meters. Even a single bullet from a high powered weapon can penetrate several men if they were aligned just right.

We surveyed the camp and noted the damage. We found two hundred and forty seven holes in the ground. This means our company received 247 rounds of enemy mortar fire. We conducted a crater analysis to determine the direction of fire. Six big craters were located about 50 yards from various foxholes. These were from the "friendly" in-coming the night before. It could have snuffed out a bunch of lives! We cursed this stupidity all over again.

At 1000 hours I received a message that the Assistant Division Commander was going to visit the camp to view the results of the previous night's actions. Another opportunity to excel, I cursed to myself. Moments later a chopper circled our position and my forward air controller (FAC) established radio contact and threw a yellow smoke grenade to signal where the landing zone (LZ) was. As the chopper settled roughly to the ground, the General jumped out. I saluted him smartly with one hand and with the other tried to contain my body and clothes under the hurricane blow from the chopper blades whirling overhead disengaging everything within a 25 meter radius.

The General returned my greeting as we shook hands and strolled away quickly to review the damage once again.

On occasion I might sound discourteous to rank but I do not mean to give that impression. I never wavered from the rule to always respect rank and position even if I didn't respect the man or agreed with actions my seniors took.

After a lengthy discourse on the attack, I presented to the General in detail, my evaluation, subsequent action and future plans. The General congratulated the unit on it's fine fighting spirit, dedication and other amenities; told us to keep up the good work, jumped into the chopper, and was gone. The short duration of his visit suited me just fine because I needed take a piss almost since the time he arrived and my bladder had been about to burst. Unfortunately, my military training did not cover the proper way to excuse yourself from a Marine General, while in conference, when nature called. Sacrifice can be endured in many ways.

About 1600, the platoon returned from the sweep with negative results. I was disappointed. The no-contact report from the Platoon Leader, Lieutenant Jim Conklin, indicated no enemy activity anywhere within their assigned patrol area. I dismissed the Platoon Leader, broke out my map case and began studying the terrain once again to determine the position of the enemy location. After further study we determined another possibility. I called the Platoon Commander on the ground line telephone and told him that he would be going out again the next day. I chose the same patrol because of their intimate knowledge of the terrain. The Platoon Commander "thanked" me and also cursed me under his breath. But that's o.k. because that's nature, and more importantly, you need to know how they felt about you. It keeps you on your toes, and helps to create better understanding when things really get tough.

After I briefed all my unit leaders, each retired to his section of defense to ensure that final precautions were taken before nightfall. Fortunately, the second night was peaceful except for the cold caused by the northeast monsoon, which starts in December and lasts until late February. I half enjoyed the decent nights sleep - only minor interruptions occurred when reports were sent in by ambush squads and our outposts.

The next morning at 0800 hours, the 3rd platoon again departed with a mission to search out a different area and locate the enemy position.

The routine the second day approximated the first. There is always more to do than time allowed. But it keeps every one busy and time passes more quickly.

Then, at 1300 we received a radio message that the platoon had found the enemy position! - unoccupied, but with a supply of mortar rounds and other accoutrements. Elated, we ordered them to finish their search and to get back to camp ASAP. Around 1700 hours the platoon dragged into camp tired, dirty, and wet, but pleased with their results. The platoon leader broke out his cache. The contents included 16 82mm mortar rounds, several bags of propellant charge, carrying poles for hauling the rounds on the shoulder, some miscellaneous equipment, a rifle, ammo and food stuffs.

Our evaluation was that the little yellow bastards got out fast after they hit us. Matter of fact, they didn't finish their mission as they had ammo left over. My belief was that the rapid reaction of the 60mm mortar crew, on the night of the attack, caused them to cut their attack short, thereby saving some lives. This was confirmed when the platoon sergeant reported that a number of mortar craters were located close to the enemy mortar positions. This meant that our counter mortar fire did indeed scare them off.

After the debriefing was completed, a full report was sent to Battalion in the form of a Situation Report (Sit Rept). The captured equipment was sent on by vehicle the next day and the company spent another peaceful night. The next day brought new challenges with an order to move out in the attack.

A message that morning from Battalion Headquarters at Dong Ha directed me to report back ASAP to receive an operation order. I readied myself quickly, called my driver and two Marines to ride shotgun We jumped into my company mighty might jeep, and headed for the Battalion Command Post.

On arrival I went straight to the S-3 combat operations center to receive instructions. In the usual fashion, orders were brief, and to the point. My mission was to abandon my present position and move with my company, reinforced with tanks and self propelled 40mm anti aircraft vehicles, to establish a blocking position some 5000 meters north below the DMZ. The rest of the Battalion was to commence a sweep occupying a zone of action 3000 meters wide parallel to my position. It sounded simple and easy to execute. Then the parameters were thrown in. I had to close out my base by daylight tomorrow. This meant undoing everything that had been done in a two month period, remove all booby traps and destroy everything that the enemy could use against us if it got into their hands. I had to leave a platoon at the base for one day to assist in the cleanup and move out at daylight with the rest of my company and supporting units. I looked at my watch; it was almost noon and only 6 hours before darkness. There was no way. I cursed to myself and them, I cursed everybody in sight. I guess my driver thought I had flipped my lid.

I wanted a beer badly, but I didn't have time and I guess that perplexed me even more. As soon as I could divest myself of the rest of the bullshit, we hit the road again, and upon arrival at the camp, began shouting instructions to every swinging dick I could find.

We prepared most of the night and somehow, someway at daylight the next morning, we were moving toward our objective. We moved in a tactical column with tanks and 40mm self-propelled anti aircraft mechanized vehicles sweeping our flanks. The terrain was flat and rolling with heavy vegetation. I located a mine-clearing unit with my lead platoon to assist in the location of mines. Our movement was very slow at best, because the mechanized vehicles were inhibited by the rough terrain and areas that provided potential ambush points.

At 1000 I began receiving hell over the Battalion tactical radio net from the old man because we weren't moving fast enough. I assured him that we would make our destination on time, and thought to myself that if they'll leave me alone long enough I'll get this mess organized. Later, several of our tanks became bogged down in some very wet rice paddies and after about two hours of screwing around with them, I was ready to abandon the lumbering sons of bitches. Finally, we got them out and before long moved into our blocking positions. This was situated about 400 meters due south from a small, recently abandoned village. Only an expansive field with towering grass separated us from the village that was circled with trees and centered around a large Catholic Church. The church had a tall steeple and proved to be a good point for orientation. I placed one platoon on a small hill overlooking the ville (as we called the village) with one section of tanks - that is, two tanks. The other section I moved into a position immediately south of the village. I had a good observation point and could easily command the action from my location. Our other platoon, that finished the clean-up at the Cam Lo base, joined us in the late afternoon and I moved them west some 300 meters to occupy another small hill that had a good approach from the north.

Once into position we immediately began digging in and preparing fields of fire for our automatic weapons. After this was under way, I called my first platoon leader, Dick Scolio, and told him to take a reinforced squad, 18 men in all, and head into the ville for reconnaissance to determine if we were alone, or with company.

This was the Platoon Leader's first combat action and he would damn well remember it. Within 30 minutes, he had his squad moving towards the village and we had our heavy weapons covering his approach. The first 200 meters went without incident but then all hell broke loose. A tremendous explosion rocked the ground, followed by 3 or 4 more. Automatic weapons opened up from enemy positions all around the squad, pinning them down in the open field. I stood nearly paralyzed watching the debacle, trying to contact the Lieutenant, but none materialized. I was later to find out his radio operator had frozen and they couldn't get him to move. I could neither determine what they had run up against, nor could we provide weapons support because the squad was in our line of fire. Against my better judgement, I readied another platoon but before I could dispatch them for assistance, the Lieutenant was on the radio. I ordered him to disengage and they didn't waste time getting their asses out of that mess. Within five minutes we opened up with our tanks and 40mms, tearing the hell out of the area. I then called in artillery and when the shelling was lifted we had a couple of Huey helicopter gun ships, pepper the area with machine gun fire and rockets. As soon as the Lieutenant returned, he gave me a brief of what had happened. He had sustained two casualties, and he had received a small flesh wound in the face from a piece of flying shrapnel. He was scared and shaking. I had to get him squared away quickly or he might never be able to lead his men under fire.

I ordered him to take the rest of his platoon, and go back, into the village, as soon as the supporting arms lifted their fire, and clear the resistance. He looked at me in disbelief, then he turned and yelled for his squad leaders to give them instructions. Within minutes he had his platoon moving and we laid in another concentration of artillery fire to cover his advance. The platoon moved hastily across the grassy area and into the tree line. They received only scattered shots and then nothing. The enemy was dead or had withdrawn. After about 30 minutes, he gave me an "all clear" over the company radio net and I told him to hold what he had.

Meanwhile, we had called for a MEDEVAC chopper to carry the two wounded Marines back to the rear for medical treatment. Before the choppers arrived, the company Corpsmen reported that the wounds were not serious. Relieved, I went over to see them and found them in good spirits, and questioning me extensively about the results of the action. I told them they would be all right, and that we would miss them. Before I could say more both of them shouted, "Don't you worry skipper, we'll be back just as fast as we can".

Then the chopper was there and we loaded them aboard. I saluted them as the bird lifted off and we returned to the business at hand.

It was starting to get dark. I knew well that the enemy had a fix on our position, and I didn't relish the idea of being mortared that night. I requested and received an OK from Battalion Headquarters to move the company into the ville under the cover of darkness.

My theory was to do the unexpected as it was normally illogical to move once you are dug into a position. This was an unorthodox tactic I picked up at the Jungle Warfare School. With this rationale, I issued orders to relocate into the ville, I thought that this would be the last thing the enemy would expect and we moved hastily to join the platoon already in position. The maneuver went well and we were in a good tight company perimeter defense as total darkness set in. We used the old church as our central point and I moved my command post into the abandoned building. The night was uneventful, but daylight brought new instructions from Battalion as they were beginning to move toward our position. My orders were to hold, but send fan patrols out to reconnoiter the area in all directions. We patrolled the area all day without incident and spent another night in the ville. The next morning the Battalion joined up with our forces; we turned the position over and moved out to patrol further north toward Con Thien. We patrolled for several days through numerous villages and dense terrain with only limited contact. After about one week our intelligence told us that the enemy had probably moved out because they didn't have the strength to meet us on our terms, or, were only probing our positions to determine capabilities and troop strength.

We continued to patrol vigorously, splitting platoons off from the main force to patrol areas singularly, while the remainder of the company moved at some distance to see if we could trap the enemy into a contact. Nothing seemed to work. At night, we moved into different villages along our patrol routes and established defensive positions. Our reasoning was that some of the enemy males had probably been recruited from these same villages, consequently, as they were still inhabited by women, children and old men it was unlikely that the enemy would mortar us because some of their own family members might end up casualties.

We also figured we might catch some VC attempting to return to their village to visit the family, and it was unlikely that they would suspect a Marine rifle company waiting for them. We did detain several young male suspects and returned them to the rear for interrogation, but we seldom learned the results of these interrogations.

On one occasion, we moved into a small village prior to darkness and began consolidating our defenses. Intelligence reports indicated that this ville was sympathetic to the VC cause. In addition, many males had been recruited to fight with the VC and I had hopes of capturing some who might return during the night.

As we moved in with our tanks, we tore up quite a few beetle nut and banana trees. Some of the Marines chopped down trees to use for cover, over their fighting holes, and also to clear the area for fields of fire.

The next morning, several Vietnamese women were brought to me complaining about the damage. I was surprised and shocked because as I looked around I could detect nothing that appeared out of line, however, I'm afraid my perspective was from the vantage point of a combat leader not a property owner. I tried to realign my thinking and look at the so-called devastation from their point of view.

We had destroyed plants and trees that supplied them foodstuffs. One woman actually carried a section of bananas over from a tree that had been torn down by one of our vehicles and matched it to the stem that it had been growing on. The bananas had been cut by some well meaning Marine, who only wanted some fresh fruit. We had returned the bunch to her and she wanted to have them returned to the rightful owner. By matching the severed bananas to the proper limb she was able to prove the rightful owner, which, interestingly enough was not her. Ostensibly, they belonged to a neighbor, and she then took them to her. We had also destroyed several beetle nut plants when our tanks had unintentionally run over them. The local villagers were terribly upset, as these plants supplied them with a type of chewable nut that was used much like our own chewing tobacco. Supposedly, it protected their gums, although, I believe it was also a type of aphrodisiac. The beetle nut plant, when chewed, turned their gums and lips reddish and their teeth black. During my time in some of these rural villages, I saw many beautiful women, but if they used beetle nut, and if they happened to smile, all of their beauty dissipated quickly. Their mouth was not a pretty sight.

Some Marines, like many other men after a lengthy time in the field or in a remote location, without female companionship, can easily develop a strong desire for sexual gratification. I could never totally understand how these men would take any available opportunity to "buy it" from these rural Vietnamese women. I was concerned that they might "hook up" with a Viet Cong woman soldier unknowingly, and experience a terrible result, death, infection, or ever painful dismemberment, as a kind of retribution for being the enemy. My feelings didn't align with my men, and they would avail themselves of any and every opportunity they could, even on a search and destroy mission in enemy territory.

Once, in a different village, we experienced a minor problem when a young woman, about age 25, came running and screaming from her thatch hut, over what I thought initially was perhaps a rape situation. She was in an uncontrollable state of mind, and her ranting and raving was not doing our cause any good in that village. I didn't know what the real problem was, or what to do with all the frightened and disturbed village people assembled around me and my command group.

Finally, my Vietnamese interpreter, talking with her and some of the elders, determined that she had not been accosted, as I suspected, but only propositioned by one of our Marines when he entered her thatched home finding her asleep on a straw mat. Relieved, although the screaming and hollering continued, we finally concluded that all she wanted was an apology.

My next challenge was to locate the Marine in question, and without her help as we didn't need the extra commotion. While she looked over and through our troops for the offender, the village population was getting more upset. I wanted to diffuse the situation without further incident and as quickly as possible. After some interrogation, the guilty young Marine stepped forward, admitted to his trespass, and after some "encouragement" on my part, apologized to the young lady, graciously, and in front of the entire population, including his fellow troopers.

He was probably scared to death and I'm certain, concerned as to what would happen to him later. Nothing did. His embarrassment was lesson enough for him and we let the matter drop except for a "morals" lecture that was conducted at a later time for all the troops.

To help install ourselves in the good graces of the local population we offered some C-Rations for their trouble and a few *piasters*, local money, to help "buy" their friendship. I didn't want them coming after us, or sending any friends, to mortar our position for our transgressions.

No harm resulted from the incident, and we wanted these people to believe we were their friends, to assist our side and not the North Vietnamese or Viet Cong in the war. No matter, I don't think we won the "hearts and minds" of the peasants that day, and these incidents, although minor, I'm confident were typical throughout the war.

Unfortunately, some terrible events did occur, resulting in death and total destruction of entire villages during the Vietnam conflict. The My La incident was the worst that I heard about - caused by a fury out of control among some U. S. soldiers and their irresponsible leaders. This highly published incident had repercussions then and after the war. It continued to greatly impact the lives of the members of the platoon involved and some high ranking officers in the U. S. Army. Troops, excited and scared by the shooting from the enemy, seeing their buddies wounded or killed could become over aggressive when under attack from a village location. The attacks, in many cases, were instigated by an occupying enemy and not necessarily the intent of the local inhabitants. The result, unfortunately, was that such a village was condemned in the minds of the U. S. attacking force as being Viet Cong, or NVA. Once it was overrun and the enemy departed, the natural follow-up action was to "level" it beyond recognition. Logic did not always prevail, nor did cool heads in the heat of battle.

Our company burned huts in some villages after we had come under attack by the enemy, but this was not standard procedure, and did not occur after we were able to evaluate the action more rationally. In situations like these it was easy to conclude that every Vietnamese was the enemy, unless proven exclusively that they weren't. This was a state of mind that was incorrect, but it can be understood, because it was not easy to determine the good guys from the bad guys. There was no clear-cut separation of enemy vs. friendly held terrain, and in many cases everything outside a tactical perimeter was appropriately termed "no man's land." Guilty unless proven innocent seemed to be the best approach to most situations.

Is it any wonder that we never fully gained the support and approval of the South Vietnamese peasants. That is, "Won their Hearts and Minds" - a cliché that was used frequently by military personnel in our pacification efforts. We couldn't tell whose side they were on, didn't trust them, nor understand their mores. We accidentally destroyed their property, burned their homes, solicited their women, and generally treated them as third class citizens - I suppose because of their lack of education, rural backgrounds and lifestyles.

This is not a moralistic lecture on the U. S. soldier. We just didn't fully know enough about them or how to handle their situation. We were helpful in many ways, such as providing medical aid, but unintentionally we probably fell short in our accomplishments with many villages of the countryside when the final tally was taken.

We continued our search and destroy operation for a few days more without any major contact. The enemy had departed the area, but in the future would return again and again. We received orders to relocate back to Dong Ha, along with the rest of the Battalion, with the mission for base defense.

We had seen limited action, engaged in a few skirmishes with the enemy, and the results had been mixed. It had been my first command of a rifle company in combat, and I had done a satisfactory job, I hoped.

But, I must admit at the time of our initial enemy contact, when my First platoon members were pinned down on the first day of the operation, I had to run the gauntlet of fear in my mind. Could I make a decision or was I too traumatized and afraid to take control and do what was necessary? I guess it was possible that I could have gone either way. Somehow my sense of responsibility and concern for the men reached a higher plateau in my subconscious, and gaining my senses I took action and command of the situation. Do most so-called leaders react in a similar way, or experience the same insecurities, when placed under that kind of stress? I don't know, but I do know, at that time, I was at a critical juncture. I had to overcome my demons and potential indecisiveness or shrink from my command and the battlefield. Thank God, I passed that test, finally, if only so I could live with myself for the rest of my life. Otherwise, after all the time in the Corps, extensive training and leadership training, it would have had an emotional, long term crippling effect on me. But, there would be many more opportunities ahead for me to test my mettle and conquer my fears.

Receiving our new instructions, we hiked back to the Cam Lo area where we were picked up by trucks and driven to Dong Ha. Our stay there was to be short lived as we were immediately assigned another mission. We were to depart by boat the next day to take over the security of a small re-supply base at the head of the Cua Viet River and South China Sea. We would basically be on our own and would be responsible for planning and conducting all our operations. It was an interesting assignment. We would be ten miles from any other unit and have a huge *tactical area of responsibility* (TAOR) in which to operate. Our assigned area extended along the coastline of the South China Sea from the DMZ south, for about fifteen miles and inland about three. I didn't know at the time, but, I was given the most flexibility and freedom of command, that any Company Commander could ever hope to have in his career.

I assembled our troops for a little pep talk the next morning, prior to our departure, in a broad grassy site near the airstrip. This was the first time since assuming command nearly ten days past, that I had the opportunity to introduce myself and to talk to them as a group.

This became a motivational talk. I guess I got excited and began espousing how we were going to kick the enemy's ass and beat him into the ground. I assured them that we were a great unit, that we were going to win our war, take care of each other, and go home in one piece. Carried away with the exuberance of my own verbosity, I told them, only the failure of consciousness or the loss of will to go on would keep us from our destiny, and I would supply the ingredient to ensure that the loss of will did not occur. I really over did it, I'm sure, but I felt emotional. The good thing about it was, they believed me. They had never been talked to like that before, and I apparently touched a cord inside them. We began to jell at that moment as a real team. Later, I was to learn from several of the men, that our little talk was a turning point for the company as they began to believe in themselves and their abilities to overcome any obstacle. In short, they told me they knew they could win - and would.

Afterwards, we hauled our gear over to the river, boarded the Navy landing craft and headed down the river to our new destiny. It would be there, at the Cua Viet, that we would discover a different way to fight the enemy in that devilish war.

CUA VIET RIVER BASE

It was about a two-hour boat ride down river from Dong Ha to the Cua Viet base. As we slowly motored through the meandering water route, I half expected some kind of hostile action, at least a couple of indiscriminate rifle shots in our direction, but it was not to happen that day.

The Navy dropped us at the loading area, which was only a small beach of sandy soil with no docking facilities, of any kind, in place at that time. And that was it. Now the base and surrounding area belonged to us. We stood hesitantly, viewing this odd looking base which was surrounded by water on two sides - natural barriers to enemy ground attacks, a swamp on one flank, and the terrain composed of sand dunes. A sparse stand of pine trees running through the area was the only ground cover.

The previous companies assigned to this port facility had worked on the defensive positions and they were in relative good condition. Since the base was on sandy soil, it was quite easy to dig fortifications and utilize sandbags to reinforce the bunkers. The base provided protection for this major re-supply port. Supplies would be off loaded at sea, just off the coast, and the navy landing craft would ferry it either to our base or up river to Dong Ha. It was a slow, time consuming, inefficient method. The RMK Construction Company, a civilian company, had men and equipment located at the base and were dredging the river mouth to enlarge it so ships could offload directly on land at the base. This would greatly facilitate resupply.

Over 360,000 gallons of aviation fuel were stored in flexible tanks, located in a centralized area within the base, on top of the ground with sand piled up around the sides. We worried and wondered what would happen if one of the fuel storage containers were hit by enemy shelling. Thank goodness we never found out. We assumed, if the tanks were to explode, that very little would have been left of the base. It would have made one hell of a fire. To provide adequate protection, one reinforced rifle company was assigned for security. In addition, an amphibious tractor company (AMTRACS), with about twenty amphibious troop-carrying vehicles and five LVTH'S (landing vehicle tracked howitzer) with mounted 105 mm howitzer, were provided for direct support to our company. Each AMTRAC vehicle had a 30-caliber machine gun mounted in a small gun turret on the top of the hull and could carry unlimited amounts of ammo. This fire power and transportation capability gave us great striking power with ease of movement and flexibility in our operations.

In normal ship to shore amphibious landing operations, the AMTRAC is used to transport troops. The vehicle weighs about 26 tons and it's steel hull provides some protection against small arms fire. In the water, most of the hull is submerged below the water line, providing a low profile. It can carry about twenty four combat laden troops at a speed of about thirty miles per hour on the ground and six knots in the water.

The AMTRAC was critical to our mission to protect this facility for several reasons. First, they provided added muscle for the defense of the base. Second, they could assist in transporting supplies from the off shore re-supply ships to base. Third, as we had a large area of responsibility, they could transport us throughout this zone quickly, allowing us to conduct search and destroy operations in remote regions within our TAOR. Equally important, we would be able to return to the base by nightfall to provide security for the base during the crucial night time hours. We normally left one platoon at the base during the day for security and to recover from the previous night ambush duty. Usually, we had two to four squad sized ambush positions established for early warning of potential attacks and to trap any moving enemy near the base.

Without the transportable capability and the requirement to man the base at night, we would have been limited to operating only a couple of thousand yards from the base, leaving much of the area un-patrolled and exposed. The enemy would have had unlimited access and free reign to roam the area and mortar or rocket the base at will.

The AMTRAC Company, with the self propelled howitzers, also provided us with mobile and fixed artillery - unique for a rifle company. We used these capabilities in several ways.

At night, designated target areas were assigned to them for fire missions. These included likely avenues of enemy approach into our position, potential assembly areas, and trail routes. These harassing and interdiction (H&I) fire missions were usually selected as a result of what we learned from our daily sweep operations and intelligence gathered from any enemy contact.

I cannot unequivocally state the effectiveness of the fire missions, but we were never shelled. On a number of occasions after encountering the enemy during our operations, we followed up with fire missions that night. When we returned the next day to the area, we would occasionally find fresh graves.

Periodically, we would utilized a couple of the mobile howitzers in our search and destroy operations for direct fire missions on targets of opportunity or to provide preparation (Prep) fire, prior to our sweep of an objective. We worked well together and developed a cooperative spirit in completing our mission of base defense and elimination of the enemy within this TAOR.

The civilians employed by the RMK Construction Company, went about their daily work and didn't seem to pay much attention to the activities around them. They were friendly enough, and assumed the Marines would provide them with adequate protection and security.

The mouth of the river, adjacent to our base, was only 100 yards wide and did not offer a great deal of maneuvering capability for the navy ships. Immediately across from our base, which was located at the mouth of the river and the sea, was an old oriental tug boat that had been trapped at low tide and settled on the adjacent shoreline. Below the focsle, the forward part of the ship's hull, was a huge black hole caused by an explosion. It stared across the river providing a constant reminder of what the enemy had done to the ship, probably after it had beached, and could do to ours, given the chance.

Approximately one mile southeast from our base, was a small village and a contingent of Vietnamese soldiers, who were to provide boat patrols in the river and small adjoining streams. The senior officer of this rag-tag outfit was somewhat lackadaisical with his responsibilities, but wanted us to provide him with artillery and mortar support in the event of attack. In essence, we were supposed to work together and coordinate our combat activities, while providing mutual security for each other.

As was common with many of the Vietnamese officers, they seemed to expect more than they were willing to give. Case in point, I asked him to provide a boat to patrol the river in the immediate vicinity of our base since it bordered on the Cua Viet. As it was only 100 yards to the adjacent shore, an aggressive, wily enemy might swim the river on a dark night, plant explosive charges, and blow-up some of our facilities.

My concern was real. Since his unit conducted river operations it was not out of the ordinary to request this kind of security measure.

He refused, stating that it wasn't his responsibility, and he didn't really have the desire to expose his men in that type of operation. My immediate, hot- headed response was that it would be a cold day in hell before he received any support from us, if he were attacked. I was ready to let him burn in his own self-created mess. However, sometimes issues take an interesting twist and resolve themselves. That very night, after our negative exchange, his base received some enemy activity. When a few mortar rounds fell within a few hundred meters of his position, we did not return counter mortar fire. Frankly, we didn't think the attack was a threat and the shelling was over quickly. He was on the radio pleading for support, but we didn't respond. We would have done whatever was necessary, if the threat were real. It was not, and he didn't realize it. After he again expressed his concern over our lack of support the next morning, I reiterated my position to him. Without boat security in the river next to our base, he wouldn't get shit from us. The solution to the problem was simple.

That night there was a great deal of activity on the river. We laughed commenting that there was so many boats floating around out there that they were bumping into one another. Henceforth, we had adequate security on the river at night, which made us very comfortable. We reassured the Vietnamese Captain that our artillery support would be available if he needed it. We became "buddies" again, but we had to scare the hell out of him to get his attention.

Our medical personnel did an excellent job providing aid to several small villages near the base. Whenever possible, they would conduct sick call, a kind of in-the-field medical first aid clinic for all Vietnamese civilians that would come for help.

We put the word out to the "locals" through our interpreter and normally had a good turnout, especially from young children and elderly people. Our troops would give them food and in most cases were extremely gentle and friendly to them. This was the contribution that most military units made to the people, who lived close to their base and was appreciated and much needed by the rural Vietnamese. Fortunately, this was something we could do that was positive to prolong life, rather than most of the military activities, which out of necessity, shortened life. We felt good about helping and did all we could whenever possible.

One of the great benefits we had at this base was our own mess hall. We had cooks who prepared two meals each day, which meant we only had to eat C-Rations for lunch while on patrol, or search and destroy missions. We normally left at first light each morning making sure we filled our stomachs well before we left, with pancakes or whatever our mess hall served up at the time. It was always hot, good and satisfying, and a lot better than ham and limas, chopped eggs, or some other "delicacy" from the C-ration box.

One of the tricks you learned early on was to carry a large metal tablespoon with you at all times. I carried my spoon in my breast pocket for so long it turned green. Whenever hot food was available, it was wise to be equipped and ready to take advantage of the situation. You grabbed your spoon and ate, sometimes right out of the pot. When hot, everything was better and tastier than rations, even powdered eggs. A small bottle of Tobasco sauce came in handy. Only a few drops were required to either smother the original flavor or provide an unique or more pungent kick to most food. The small size bottle made it easy to carry around and have always available.

We began to settle into our routine, making some general improvements to our base perimeter, putting out more claymore mines, and studying our maps to develop a thorough understanding of the terrain and general lay of the land. I was able to conduct some reconnaissance by helicopter, which was helpful early on and expedited our knowledge of the TAOR.

The area extended along the South China Sea and was therefore, mostly composed of sandy, beach like soil with scattered pine trees throughout much of the region. The only open area, was the central part of the sandy plains and it too was lined on both sides with a growth of trees. There were about twenty or so small villages located throughout the area, among the trees off the coastline. Several of the villages, north toward the DMZ, had been vacated and only the skeletal remains of the huts remained. Children lived in many of the villages and they were always friendly to the Marines as we traveled through them. Probably, most of these villages provided resources of one kind or another to the Viet Cong, but we could never determine if any VC manpower came from this area. Over time, we located numerous enemy hiding in tunnels in the villages. We thought they had to be foreign to the area, otherwise, they could have blended with the regular inhabitants during the daylight hours in their normal activities.

Naval ships could be seen frequently from our coast. They were positioned there to provide fire support to the Marine bases and to conduct fire missions into the DMZ, North Vietnam, or in support of ground operations. On one hazy afternoon, while at our base, we could see a Navy Destroyer, no more than a mile or so off shore, sitting still in the water. It was engaged in a fire mission sending its big payload north somewhere. As we watched, the enemy returned fire and rounds began splashing around the ship, each impact getting closer to its intended target. Black smoke began pouring from it's large smokestack as it started maneuvering in the water to get the hell out of range. Fortunately, no rounds hit the ship, and it moved seaward. Watching the action, and the tremendous amount of smoke produced to get underway, we laughed in a convoluted way speculating how they were probably using everything on board for fuel, including the furniture from the normally, nicely furnished officer mess hall, to move that metal monster out of harm's way. These ships were called on frequently for their massive firepower and were very important to the Marine's mission in the region.

We began with our own operational plan and would submit situations reports (SITREPS) daily to Battalion. We received little advice and recommendation and were basically left to our own devices, including tactical initiatives. This flexibility enabled us, over time, to react quickly to suspected enemy movements and was a key ingredient, along with our knowledge of the terrain, to our ultimate success.

Our initial plans were to take us south of the river, because there were more villages with people, and we believed the likelihood of contact was better. Motivated, we were ready for action and we wanted to test our mettle. As the new boys on the block, the enemy probably was also wondering how we would play their game. We surprised them, we played it our way.

CUA VIET SOUTH

The Cua Viet Coastal terrain and the large tactical area of responsibility provided new challenges to our normal methods of engagement. We were accustomed to operating in a hilly country with dense elephant grass.

Our current terrain was basically flat with soft, sandy soil, covered with an ample supply of trees and small brush vegetation. Observation was easier. You could see great distances, but you could also be seen. Concealment for the enemy, as we came to learn, was not provided on top of the ground but under it. Digging was not difficult and the enemy could quickly and easily disappear when we approached, by constructing makeshift spider holes - a small hole in the ground covered with grass or other debris. The VC, who were the principal insurgents in this area, knew the terrain and had an unholy alliance with the local villagers. They could obtain food stuffs from them and occupy hiding places in underground holes located within the village proper. I never fully believed that these rural people truly cared about the VC. They were forced to submit to their requests or suffer the consequences. The Viet Cong were not as disciplined or tenacious as the NVA, who we were to engage in the northern sector of the Cua Viet. But, they were demanding of the local population and could be ruthless in dealing with then.

We would depart our base camp each morning riding on the AMTRACS, normally traveling along the water's edge or a few feet into the water. It was nearly impossible for the enemy to lay mines or booby traps along this route, and we never experienced a problem.

As we rumbled down the coast to our pre-selected sweep area, it was always interesting to see the large number of poisonous sea snakes, basking in the sun, just beyond the treads of our vehicles. These snakes, with rings of black, red, and yellow, encircling their bodies, could do massive damage if they were to bite you, but riding on top of the AMTRAC'S about 8 feet above them we felt secure. We never attempted to disembark from the vehicle in or around these critters, believing that they were entitled to their resting place, and we were happy to leave it to them, unaccompanied. Once our column of vehicles came to the appropriate map coordinates, or pre-arranged sweep position, they would do a flanking movement, move across the dunes through the tree line and further inland as quickly as possible. Reaching our destination, we would dismount, move into formation, usually on line with the command group in the center, with a couple of squads in the rear for security.

The AMTRACS, after we deployed, would move hastily to another location on a flank, or several hundred yards to our front and establish blocking positions. They would trap or contain any fleeing enemy we might flush during our sweep through the area. I didn't worry about the vehicles, as they were usually in a group of ten. All had three men crews and 30 caliber mounted machine guns. They could put out a lot of firepower if engaged, and their armor would deflect small arms fire. Also, they were durable enough to smother small exploding booby traps with no damage to their mechanized tracks. If they hit a large land mine, it could disable the vehicle or destroy it totally. However, we did not encounter any during our deployment at the Cua Viet.

Our initial tactics involved continued movement within our *zone of action*, striking different random areas each day. These fast moving, *search and destroy* operations, showed no pattern of deployment or obvious objective. We zigzagged and crisscrossed our way throughout the area. Our seemingly haphazard movements might have appeared a bit like the keystone cops, but we kept the enemy guessing. With our mobility we were able to execute this plan and obtain a thorough base of knowledge of the terrain, villages, and people's activities.

Our problem was, we were not encountering the enemy, except on a minimal scale. Obviously, the use of the tractors, while facilitating our movement, alerted the VC with their loud engines, well before our deployment into an area. The VC would have ample time to hide before we arrived. We had the element of speed, but not surprise.

Their hiding spots were ground holes or tunnels, inside or in close proximity to villages. This ensured their safety, because they did not believe we would search the village ground thoroughly, but would instead spend our efforts looking through the homes or huts of the people. They also liked locating inside a village proper, because they reasoned it was most unlikely we would shell those locations. In essence, a village, was a safe haven for the VC. We knew from evidence, discovered through our sweeps of the villages and surrounding areas, there *were* Viet Cong operating in the zone. We just couldn't find them. They would not engage us, and we were certain they were trying to covet or convert the people in the area to their cause, so they would turn against their own local government and take up arms against the newly arrived U. S. troops.

It was a discouraging situation, and we needed a new plan or technique to locate this elusive enemy. There is a biblical expression that runs, "seek and ye shall find", and that's exactly what we attempted. We couldn't find them on the surface, so we concluded they had to be below it. How to get to them, posed a different challenge, but "necessity breeds invention.".

We needed a kind of "Divining Rod" a method used, almost intuitively, to locate water or minerals underground. The solution to our dilemma began to unfold. Almost accidentally, while on a routine search mission early one morning, a couple of our troops were using long wooden sticks with sharpened points to probe into some of the sandy soil, almost as an extension of their arms. Previously, some had used their bayonets held in their hand or attached to the end of their rifles. The problem with that method was the probe was too short to penetrate very deeply into the soil or any other substance, such as the side or roof of a thatch hut, where weapons or other items could easily be hidden.

For some reason, perhaps on intuition, one of our Marines, plunged his long sharpened stick into a brushy area and on through the soil, striking something solid a few inches below the ground's surface. Curiously, he probed with his stick several more times and at each instance brought a resounding thud as he penetrated the soil. Inquisitively, he began spreading the loosely aligned sand until he located a small wooden plank that appeared to be a cover to an opening of something buried below the ground. Calling for assistance, he was joined by two other Marines. They began systematically, to search for booby traps. Finding none they slowly removed the wooden door and found a small opening to a cache of ammunition and weapons. This was a revelation for our group. Happily, we had finally located definite indications of the enemy's presence. Gathering the captured supplies, we reported "our find" by radio to Battalion Headquarters. Pleased with our efforts of finally establishing some evidence of enemy presence, we returned to our base for the night responsibilities.

The next day we again launched our normal search and destroy operation. Having learned from the results of the previous day, we had more of our troops carry a long stick with a pointed end to use in their search of the area. Over the next few days we extended our success from the initial effort as our men found more concealed caches and enemy hiding places. Another revelation presented itself when we found the method effective in locating *punji* pits and booby traps. Our learning curve went straight up as a result of these encounters. We had found no enemy, but we were getting close. We knew it, and they probably did too.

We had a problem which we discussed nightly after each day's experimentation. The sticks kept breaking, bending, and were usually not stout enough to be used more than a few times, requiring our troops to replace them often. We decided we needed a more permanent solution, and metal was the only answer. We needed a thin rod about three or four feet long, sharpened to a point on one end. It also had to be strong and durable so it could be used with more force when pushed into the sandy soil. The big question, where would we get the material to make our newly "thought up" weapon out in the field? I was going to send some of our resourceful men to the rear area in Dong Ha, to look for the appropriate solution. This team was made up of our top scroungers and we knew that we would have to "midnight requisition" what we needed. We were still planing the "excursion" when our artillery forward observer, First Lieutenant Gus Donnelly, from Asheville, N. C., proffered an idea that turned out to be the solution to our problem. It was so obvious we were stunned with its simplicity.

We had our own artillery, located at the base in the form of LVTH6's, which were the AMTRACS with mounted 105 howitzers. They were continually firing missions on our behalf and had accumulated a large number of empty wooden crates that housed the ammunition for their guns. There were three rounds in each crate. As luck would have it, to separate the rounds and hold them in place, were two steel rods over three feet long and about one-third inch in diameter! The rods were easy to remove once the ammo was taken from the wooden containers. The answer to our problem in more ways than one, was within our own confines, controlled by us, offered in unlimited supply.

Furthermore, the RMK construction company had tools, lathes, and other machines that could sharpen the steel rod to a point, and they were happy to oblige our request. Especially, since our success in the field, would be important to their job livelihood and personal security.

Grasping the bonanza in our own backyard, we went to work and within a few days we equipped every Marine in the company with the probing tool. To extend its depth penetrating capability, we also affixed bamboo or wooden handles to the hand held end of the rod, which added another six to twelve inches to its overall length.

After this project was completed we needed a name for our new weapon and creatively, but simply, decided on "The Mike Spike", for Mike Company.

It was to be our "Divining Rod", our edge, and the enemy would learn shortly to fear its use in the hands of our troops. Over time the Mike Spike would become a symbol for our company. It was to be the common denominator among our troops that signified success and combat professionalism. It helped develop unit pride and a strong sense of brotherhood among the men. It was not a toy, or a cheap flimflam device. It was a weapon, an instrument of combat, and the results spoke loudly to all who read about it or witnessed its deadly usefulness.

Later, the success with the Mike Spike necessitated that we develop an emblem to wear on our uniforms. When two of our company members went to Okinawa for R&R, (rest and relaxation), we gave them money and a diagram of our symbolic use of the spike in hopes they might find some one to produce patches that could be attached to our jungle utilities. Several days later they returned with the patches. They had a yellow background with Snoopy the dog dressed in combat gear with a rifle in one hand and a spike in the other. At the top of the patch embroidered in maroon was Mike-3/4 and at the bottom "Snoopy Poopers".

Everybody loved them. We pinned them on our uniform pocket, but were advised not to sew them on as it was not military. The Mike Spike and "Snoopy Poopers" were our trademarks. The men took great pride in being part of this elite group and enjoyed the recognition they experienced as a "Snoopy Pooper".

Nearly twenty-five years later I was to attend a reunion held for all members of the Third Battalion Fourth Marines, in Washington, D. C. and ran into some of the men that served in Mike Company at the Cua Viet. Several of them had their patches with them, and one Marine, (there is no such thing as *former* Marines) had his pinned to his shirt. I took a picture and only wished that I could locate my patch. Some things from Yesterday go on Forever.

After the success in developing "The Mike Spike" with the RMK Construction Company, I had one other request while we were on a roll with them. I wanted them to make us a small steel base plate for our 60 mm mortar that could easily be carried on our operations. I had insisted, when I assumed command of the company at Cam Lo, that we use the free tube method when firing our mortars, especially in emergency situations. We eliminated the use of the bipod, and consequently, also its sighting mechanism which required precious minutes for adjustments when sighting on the enemy target. The new base plate was less than half the size and weight of the original and could easily be strapped to a pack for carriage. It worked perfectly in the field.

I reasoned that since the mortar was such a great weapon with its significant explosive power, we needed to be able to put it to use quickly and effectively regardless of where the enemy was located. In my mind, it was an offensive weapon and I intended to employ it in that manner and would frequently locate it with my foremost squads while on the move. This technique allowed our units to put maximum firepower quickly on the enemy and gain fire superiority. In place of the weight eliminated by not carrying the bipod, the mortar section carried extra mortar ammunition. In addition, each man in the company carried one round in his pack.

We did not take mortars on every sweep, especially if we were only out for a day, but for extended operations they were always with us and ready for immediate action.

All the adjustments I had in mind were made, arms and equipment techniques were ready, weapons refined, employment decided, formations established, Mike Spikes issued, and we aggressively stepped up our *Search And Destroy* operations to find and eliminate the enemy.

Each night we studied our maps attempting to out-think the enemy in their movements. Since we had no limits placed on us by Battalion, we were free to roam the countryside as long as we remained inside our elongated TAOR. Our only requirement was to report in daily with our plan and to radio situation reports when we encountered the enemy, uncovered booby traps, or located caches of enemy supplies.

We mounted our vehicles each morning and went in search of contact, varying our attack plans regularly. Our pattern of attack was without routine. The unexpected, the unorthodox, the unsystematic were the tenets we practiced. Our knowledge of the land worked in our favor and I believe we eventually knew the terrain as well as the enemy. We would strike south, then north, north again and then south on successive days constantly creating different routines and locations of deployment.

The method worked. We started to catch the enemy off guard, what they expected didn't materialize. We thought like, and emulated guerrillas in our tactical methodology. The men relished the unconventional approach and were excited with each new day and crazy plan. Even the AMTRAC Marines began to feel the same energy and enthusiasm for our results. It was one-upmanship, and we always came out on top. At one point, over a thirty-day period, we had enemy contact twenty six times, mostly by catching the enemy off-guard in their hiding places. They could not mount an attack, and between our daytime operations and aggressive use of ambush and nightly shelling, we severely limited their ability to maneuver successfully in our TAOR.

Using the Mike Spike, we also located and uncovered large numbers of booby traps. Some of our men, however, were wounded as a result of these concealed devices. One case was most unusual. We were on a mission a couple of thousand yards south of the base, moving though a heavily wooded area along a well-defined trail. Our troops spread out on line, and a couple of fire teams, with four men each patrolling our flanks for security and reconnaissance. We halted our advance at one point along the side of a trail where one of my platoon sergeants came upon a signpost written in Vietnamese. This was obviously a frequently used trail between villages and the Sergeant, a hard-nosed, hard charging career Marine, who had seen his share of combat, moved to check out the sign. Unable to read it, he pulled it out of the ground to take back to our Vietnamese interpreter, who was with me in the command group fifty yards to the rear. As he pulled it from the ground a small explosion occurred from a booby trap device attached to the sign. He was hit in the forearm with shrapnel. As his wounds were not serious, he shrugged it off and carried the sign back to us. The interpreter read the sign and almost went into hysterical laughter. I asked him what it said and he responded "Danger - Mines." So much for our understanding of the Vietnamese language.

We called a MEDVAC chopper and had the Sergeant return to Dong Ha for medical treatment, but by the time we arrived back to the base, later that day, he was there to great us. He told me he was fine and didn't want to miss the next day's action. I told him he should have stayed in the rear for at least a good night's sleep and a beer, but "no," he responded. He would rather be with his troops, as they were counting on him to lead them. This was a case of real leadership and courage.

On another occasion we did have a couple of men scratched when they stepped into a *punji* pit, but each time the injury was minor. In one case a Marine slipped into a pit and the bamboo spike punctured his boot, missing the flesh totally. The booby trap devices were horrible and could result in death or permanent injury, but with the use of our Mike Spike we located over 700 booby traps using our probing techniques.

During another sweep operation we were rapidly moving through the outskirts of a small village, when I heard shooting from one of our flanking security squads, about 200 yards away. Unable to reach the squad leader on the radio, I moved forward with some men to check out the situation. As we came up behind the squad we found them deployed in a semi circle, in a sparsely wooded field. They were facing toward a large mound of dirt and debris that appeared to be a kind of old makeshift outdoor cellar, twenty five yards to their front. The local village probably used it to store foodstuff. Now, however, the Viet Cong occupied it, and they were firing at our troops with their automatic rifles. The squad had them surrounded and there was no escape route possible, unless they could shoot there way though our force. The VC had been caught in the open by our flanking security and had run into the cellar and was now using it as a bunker - but trapped.

Upon arrival, I saw three Marines standing on top of the bunker, shooting into it and grappling with the rifle barrel of a VC that was protruding through an opening on the top of the mound of dirt. The Marines, average age about 20, were firing their rifles furiously into the opening. The VC on the receiving line, were equally busy with their weapons. Within minutes, all grew deathly still as the firing ceased. The three Marines standing on the bunker had done their job, killing the enemy in the close, point-blank, hand to hand firefight.

I moved forward to the battle sight and the squad leader stepped off the bunker to meet me, while his other two men searched the make-shift bunker. I asked him what had happened. He told me they had physically chased the three enemy into the ground cover and two men from his squad had engaged in the hand to hand fire fight. One Marine had been shot in the foot, luckily only a crease along his heel, and the other, while holding on to the rifle barrel of the VC, had a slight scratch on his forehead from a passing bullet. Both were extremely lucky to be alive. One quarter inch more and they could have been severely wounded or killed. He then told me, he personally assaulted the bunker to help them out. I questioned him why, as the enemy were surrounded with no retreat possible, had he risked his life instead of pulling the other two back to his position? He responded quickly, "Hell Captain, I had to do it, my men were in trouble and I needed to look after them." That was that, no more explanation required on my part. All of them were later recommended for Bronze Stars for Heroism in action. Such was the stuff of our American youth.

We cleaned up, buried the VC in the abandoned cellar and continued with our mission. Results reported to Battalion were, three enemy KIA (killed in action) and 3 automatic weapons and miscellaneous equipment captured.

TET, the Vietnamese holiday celebrating the New Year, was observed for three days beginning at the first new moon after January 20 each year. During this time in 1967, it was normal for all troops to disengage from the fighting to honor the special holiday. Supposedly, it was to be honored by all sides, North and South Vietnamese, as well as all U. S. Troops. However, there had been times in the past, when the enemy used this three-day hiatus from the fighting to improve their position of attack or to occupy positions more favorable to their battle plan.

Our concern at the Cua Viet base was that unless we were active during this period, we could put our base in jeopardy of a potential mortar or rocket attack. This would have been disastrous, especially if the fuel storage tanks were hit. Normally, the U. S. forces, in keeping with the intent to honor TET, pursued only defensive operations during this time.

One year later, the TET offensive mounted by the NVA, demonstrated clearly that the enemy would use every advantage they could to better their cause. Several cities were hit in South Vietnam, including Hue, the old imperial capitol of Vietnam, in the I Corps area, and it was devastated by the fierce fighting during this so called Vietnamese special holiday period.

We planned daily defensive patrols in company size strength within several thousand yards of our base to ensure no enemy activity was occurring or preparations being made to attack. We were not conducting offensive operations and thereby maintaining the spirit of our orders to stand down, only protecting "our interests." At least that's the way I defended our operation when I was criticized by some "higher ups", after we had engaged a small enemy force on the second day of the TET celebration, 2000 yards from our base position.

On that occasion, we were patrolling nearly due south from our base when we altered our sweep direction, moving into an adjacent occupied village that looked suspicious. We searched the huts and the surrounding terrain as part of our normal process. Of course, everyday we were in the field someone found a booby trap device with our "Mike Spike". These were always destroyed and reports made to Battalion. This day was no different, and as usual, we located several explosive devices, disarmed them and moved on. So far, we had not found any evidence of enemy troop movement in the area.

It was lunchtime and as a matter of practice we always ate our meals on the move. Normally, we carried a couple of C-ration cans in a military issue sock tied to our cartridge belt or shoulder suspender straps. It was easy to pull out a can, open it with the small can opener and indulge in a meal without being distracted from the day's activity or halting the march. I never liked to stop our momentum when on an operation, except at night, when we were not as much of a target. (Typically, when evening approached on an extended operation and it was time to stop, we would first move into a defensive position and always assume we were being watched. We would establish a perimeter as if settling for the night, and then, just as dusk faded to dark, we would abruptly move a couple of hundred yards to another location. By keeping the enemy guessing, they couldn't get a fix to mortar your position.)

I was standing on a tall sand dune with my radio operator on the edge of the village we had just searched, and had given the order to our sweeping troops to pivot left and head off in a different direction. From my elevated position I was able to observe the entire movement of the line. No more than twenty yards from where I was standing, one of our men was strolling along a village path using his Mike Spike, almost unconsciously, to probe the ground as he proceeded to his new troop position. For some unknown reason, his actions caught my eye. I watched him thrust his spike into a pile of human excrement positioned in the middle of the trail in front of him. It was not uncommon to find evidence of the local inhabitants waste matter spread through the village, especially in the cultivated fields. But crap in the middle of the trail, that was out of the ordinary and perhaps is why the Marine plunged his spike into the mess, or he was just being crude. I don't know the reason.

As his probe sank through the waste and pierced several inches of sand we heard a loud "clunk". He obviously struck something solid buried below the surface of the ground. Again, he thrust his probe into the muck and another "clunk" resounded. I was watching from my perch on the dune and could see and hear everything clearly. I yelled at him to get a couple of men and check it out. Meanwhile the rest of the company was completing their turning movement. An entire platoon of 35 men were now passing in close proximity to the evolving show.

As three men began carefully cleaning the sand and other debris from the suspicious sounding area, they discovered a small wooden trap door large enough for a human to enter. It was obviously an entry way into an underground passage of some kind. One Marine slowly and cautiously, began to lift the door from its resting-place, while the other two checked for booby traps. I stood there watching, eating my lunch, beans and franks (probably the best meal of all the c-ration packages.)

As the entry door was raised to a height of about one-foot off the ground, we heard the unmistakable "ping" sound of a hand grenade being armed. When the safety pin is pulled on the grenade, the spoon or handle is released under tension and springs free creating the sound, igniting the fuse that causes it to explode in a matter of seconds. Hearing the "ping" sound, I yelled to get the hell out of there, not that they needed any encouragement. The Marine dropped the door, as the VC hiding in the hole tossed his grenade toward the opening. The falling door and the rising grenade met in flight and the grenade fell back into the hole, exploding. Seconds later another explosion occurred from a grenade in the hand of another Viet Cong.

At that juncture, after watching the play unfold, and the muffled explosions coming from the concealed hole, I knew that the hiding place of the enemy had now become their tomb. Nothing could survive the consequences of the grenade explosions in those tight quarters.

The Marines, after a few seconds waiting for the dust to clear and ensuring themselves that no one else, or other grenades were ready to detonate, began to check out the devastated hole in the ground. As they looked over the human debris, because that was all that was left, they found three dead bodies, and a bunch of equipment and weapons. We reasoned that the VC were probably moving into position to attack or mortar our base and were probably part of a larger group also in hiding.

As they hauled the dead, mutilated bodies from their grave, I was still eating my lunch as I had been doing throughout the action. After witnessing that carnage, it was a long time before I could eat beans and weenies again.

We put the bodies back in the hole, their tomb, and covered it with the sandy soil. We questioned some of the villagers but could obtain no information about other VC. It was obvious though, that they had received "help" in concealing their hole and must have believed that with the human excrement on the top of the entrance no one would ever find their location.

They were wrong, thanks to the Mike Spike, quick reaction from the troops and presence of mind. We sent a message to Battalion: three enemy KIA, three weapons and miscellaneous captured equipment.

We were not attacked after that incident, but without our "defensive" patrolling throughout the TET holiday, it was highly likely we would have experienced some offensive action from the enemy. We headed back to camp, pleased with our results and relieved that none or our men had been injured during our discovery of the enemy location.

A few days later, we were engaged in a mission at the southern most boundary of our TAOR when we ran into a reinforced squad of Viet Cong hiding in a group of mutually supporting spider trap positions. We had taken fire and had captured and killed a couple of Viet Cong and were searching diligently for more. At that time we received a radio message that the Third Division Commander would be landing by chopper to observe our progress and prepare to receive him by securing a Landing Zone (LZ) site. Just what we needed, observers in the middle of a fire fight.

Two helicopters settled down in the middle of our deployed company as sporadic shooting was occurring, and we were trying earnestly to maintain the momentum of our attack.

Major General Wood B. Kyle stepped from his Command Helicopter; I went to his side to brief him on our contact and progress. He was surrounded by aids, and I cautiously advised everyone to stay in the rear of our troop disposition, as we were in the midst of a dug-in enemy force.

General Kyle wanted to move forward and observe more closely our attack and we walked along the top of an elevated rice dike to a position providing a good view of the company in action. Most of this area consisted of rice paddies; each field was partitioned with dikes to help control the flow of water. These mounds were of sufficient size for the VC to locate hiding holes inside the embankment with entry points from either the top or sides. Actually they were the only place free of water that provided any opportunity around a rice field for concealment and protection from the water. The VC probably concluded that these were the last places any "sane" person would search for them.

As General Kyle and I walked toward our company front, I began briefing him on our results of the day and answering his questions concerning our activities over the past several weeks.

Suddenly, about 20 yards to our front on the dike we were walking, a startling commotion occurred and I respectfully asked the General that we stop where we were, until I could determine what was happening. One of our Marines was probing the top of the dike, plunging his spike several times into the sandy soil. Each time it sank deeply revealing a cavity below the surface. As he probed for the extent of the subterranean chamber, he would lunge forward with a hearty shove, the probe would nearly disappeared into the ground, he'd yank it out and plunge again a foot or so along. He had followed this rhythm a few times when suddenly, trying to retrieve the spike after another lusty plunge, the spike wouldn't budge. It just stayed stuck like the mythical Excaliber

Sword. He attempted to pull it out and it wouldn't move. He attempted to free it several more times and still it remained uncommonly fixed in the ground. Finally, calling some more men forward, he exerted one more powerful pull on the handle of the spike and the ground heaved upward bursting forth a VC rising vertically from his hiding place in the dike, holding the pointed end of the spike in a vise-grip with his hands. He immediately surrendered to some very surprised Marines.

I grabbed the General and forcefully pushed him back from the scene. He didn't seem concerned with my protective demeanor for his safety, and gladly relocated to a more secure area. Leaving him in the safety of one of my men and his staff, I went forward to check on the situation. The VC soldier was shivering, scared nearly out of his wits, and displayed no aggressiveness whatsoever. He was still holding on to the spike, hands and arms extended in the air with the spike vertically suspended in his outreached hands.

It seemed that as the Marine trooper was probing the dike, on one particular thrust with the probe, he ran the spike into the ground, penetrating the hole and hiding place, and actually scrapped the skin from the VC's back with the pointed edge of the steel probe. After several more attempts with the spike plunging deep into the hole, the VC must have concluded that it was safer to surrender than be impaled by a crazy American with a menacing piece of sharpened steel, flashing through the ground all around him. We gathered his weapon and took him to our rear for evacuation to Division Headquarters for interrogation.

Actually, we much preferred to take prisoners and always made every effort to salvage the enemy's life. It was much better than fighting to their death, or our men's possible injury or death. Taking prisoners was more humane. They were removed from battle and with proper interrogation; we could learn about their unit's identification and probable future plans. Several VC and NVA soldiers captured by the U. S. Forces, were eventually converted to our side and assigned combat units to assist in fighting their former comrades.

We had one such soldier assigned to our unit. They were called "Kit Carson Scouts" and were helpful in explaining the tactics and battle behavior of their former comrades in arms.

General Kyle was very impressed with our efforts, praised the troops, and then decided he should move on to a safer haven. It was not a good thing to have a high-ranking officer with you when engaged with the enemy with "shit hitting the fan".

General Kyle was a good General Officer and did seem to take a strong interest in the men of his command. He later sent a message to the entire 3d Division, praising our combat effectiveness and results. The troops very much appreciated the recognition for their stellar efforts. For me personally, that message was the summarization of all the commitment and effort that I had given to the Corps and perhaps the capstone of my eight years.

A few weeks later, Colonel A. D. Cereghino, Chief of Staff of the Third Marine Division, published a bulletin on the "lesson's learned" as a result of our sweep techniques. This document was also sent to the attention of all units in the Division. We were proud of our results and the recognition our company received. We were finally beginning to, detrimentally, impact the Viet Cong forces operating within our TAOR.

With each success our unit gained more confidence and enthusiasm as we stepped up our search and destroy missions. Even though our results were gaining momentum, it was critical that we not lose our edge or become over confident. Safety of the troops and constant attention to their livelihood was paramount in our minds. We wanted all of our men to go home alive and in one piece. That was the mandate we had placed on ourselves. Consequently, I challenged the Officers and staff NCO's to do everything possible for their welfare. Sometimes, this attention could get out of hand because they tried extra hard to take care of their troops.

An interesting situation occurred when our entire company was spread out over an open field during a long day's mission. It was very hot and we had been on the move most of the day and had stopped for a short break to reorganize our line of movement. A raucous suddenly occurred behind me and glancing around, I was surprised to see the Company Executive Officer, Lieutenant Bill Curt, hitting a Marine on the back with his Mike Spike. Lieutenant Curt was a former enlisted man, with nearly twenty years of service. Now he was a superior Marine Officer in every conceivable manner, and totally beyond reproach. Consequently his behavior caught me off guard, and I quickly sent another officer to his side to bring him to me. Many of the men in the field witnessed the scene and were surprised, to say the least.

When I finally retrieved Curt to my side, out of sight of the rest of the company, I ask him what he was doing beating up on that man. For some weeks we had been preaching to our men not to drink any water from the rice field or from any other local source as it was certain to cause diarrhea or possible dysentery, thereby, creating a potential casualty. If absolutely necessary, local water can be made safe to drink with two purifying tablets that cleanses bacteria from the fluid, and even that method was not fool proof.

It seems Bill, when checking on the troops, had happened on the Marine drinking untreated water directly from a small pond. He obviously lost his composure. He began striking the young enlisted across the back with his spike, hitting the man's pack. He didn't hurt him because of the padding from the pack, but he sure as hell surprised him with his "expletive" screaming along with the almost abusive activity. Bill had bellowed, "We told you not to drink the fucking water. What in the hell is wrong with you?" Everybody heard it, and everybody saw it. I had to contain the emotion quickly and did so, but after the fact. Bill was trying his damnedest to keep our men alive and well. He went a bit overboard that day. But interestingly, we never saw anyone attempt to drink from any foreign source other than what was provided by our logistics, nor did we ever lose a man to dysentery. I guess Bill's tirade, got everybody's attention, and made them realize we were going to take care of them or make them take care of themselves whether they liked it or not "even if we had to beat hell out of them."

As a matter of fact, we were so under manpower strength that the loss of just a few Marines could have a deleterious effect on us and jeopardize the safety of the entire company. Another reason to do everything possible to keep our men healthy. The event passed and was soon forgotten. I reasoned that the incident served as a lesson for all and I would do anything to keep our men alive and well as I had promised the first time I talked to them as a group on the airstrip in Dong Ha, before we came to the Qua Viet River base.

Each day in the field brought new revelations to us from our methods and the behavior of the enemy. Sometimes we needed to question our own actions, as I did on a particular sweep operation one late afternoon in February.

We had stopped for a rest break after a long and fruitless day. No contact and no evidence of enemy movement had been discovered by our troops throughout the operation. I recall that I seemed to have a difficult time staying in a single location for any lengthy period of time, and liked to roam amongst the men or around the general area, when our company periodically halted.

For some unknown reason, we had stopped at the edge of a hedgerow of trees, and I decided to take a short walk into the tree line, no more than thirty yards from where the company was resting. Intuition is an unusual characteristic and there were many times it worked for us as we made a choice of one direction over another, which eventually led us to an enemy location, or a hidden cache of supplies. My intuition told me to look around in this small tree stand, as it seemed like an ideal location for a hidden storage area. As I walked through the woods, looking at the ground for some unusual sign, or evidence of disturbed ground cover, I halted at one spot that differed from the surrounding area, and began to examine the earth with my K-bar (long handle knife). I began sticking it into the ground, sweeping away debris, when I discovered a small makeshift wooden door buried a few inches below the ground surface. I thought this must be a buried cache of enemy supplies and using my fingers and knife looked for possible booby trap wires attached to the small covering. Finding none, I began to gently lift the lid of the opening, and as I did, an NVA soldier popped up out of the hole, almost in my face as I crouched down looking into the darkened space. He immediately extended his arms over his head to signify his surrender.

I was scared beyond description. I didn't expect anyone to be in the hole, and my knife was the only weapon in my possession. I had left my pistol and gun belt back at the rest stop. I don't know why I didn't plunge my knife into the NVA soldier from fear and excitement.

I immediately yelled for help, and one of my Platoon Sergeants, walking in the wooded area only a few yards away, came running to my assistance. Finally, gaining our composure, mostly my composure, we subdued the man - although, there was no resistance from him. With his hands tied behind his back we took him forcefully over to our company's location to the surprise of everyone else.

This was a stupid stunt on my part. He could have easily killed me with the U.S. carbine he had in the hole. Why he didn't, I don't really know, except, perhaps he was more afraid than I was. This was not bravery. It was a piss poor judgment on my part and my actions could have easily put the entire company into a very serious and critical situation. Not only could I have been killed blundering around on my own, I could have initiated an attack on the company while it rested in an unguarded moment, if other enemy were in the area.

We spent some time interrogating our prisoner, trying to learn where his comrades had gone, their unit designation, the location of any stored arms and supplies and the reason he was apparently left behind. With the help of our interpreter, we learned that he had gotten sick and had been left to recover from his illness. He didn't seem to know much, but after a lengthy period of coercing, he took us to a small, buried supply dump containing some small arms, ammo, and other supplies. We decided to send him to the rear the next day for more interrogation.

We then boarded our AMTRACS and headed back to base. We moved out in a ten-vehicle column spaced about 20 meters apart, with the troops sitting on the top. After only a few minutes of travel along the edge of a tree line paralleling a 300-yard wide-open area, we took a few rounds of automatic rifle fire. None of the enemy fire hit any troops or the vehicles.

I ordered the vehicles to stop in place. It was getting late, and we didn't have time to investigate. We needed to get back to our base and man our night time defensive positions. Also, I didn't relish the idea of crossing the extensive open area on

AMTRACS in the fading light. We would have presented an excellent target for an enemy antitank weapon in that exposed position.

I ordered the ten AMTRACS with their 30 caliber machine guns, to open fire on the suspect tree line. Each gun fired about 2,000 rounds, a total of 20,000 rounds of automatic fire over a couple of minutes. Every standing tree for about 200 yards opposite our position, was cut down by the massive gunfire. No enemy fire was returned. We devastated the area. If any enemy were hiding in that clump of trees, none would remained alive after that deluge of firepower.

I ordered the vehicles to resume their course of movement, while muttering to the men on our vehicle, "That'll teach 'em, not to fuck with the Snoopy Poopers". Everybody laughed and we relished the moment, as we hurriedly returned to our base.

Upon our arrival at a camp, we deposited the captured prisoner in our "home made" prison compound. As I indicated earlier, we preferred to take prisoners whenever possible and with the use of the Mike Spike, probing hidden places, we had captured over 20 enemy over a two month period. It was impossible to have them transported immediately to the rear, so we built our own compound where we locked them in, under guard, usually only overnight. The next day we would send them up river to Division for further disposition. Now, when I think about it, we probably operated the Marine Corps only rifle company prisoner compound in the War Zone. It was small, well constructed with barbed wire walls and top. It served a good purpose and got a lot of use.

That night, I had time for a little self introspection and thought about the day's activities, especially the captured NVA. I pondered my personal stupidity in wandering around unaccompanied in enemy occupied territory. I hoped I had learned my lesson and I knew I was fortunate to be alive.

Probably, if the NVA had been healthy, he would have shot me with his U. S. carbine (ironic) and attempted to escape. After all, he couldn't have known how many Marines were in the general vicinity of his hiding place. I did keep his carbine as a war trophy, and today I have the weapon in my den. It serves as a constant reminder of that ridiculous folly.

I was not then, nor am I now, a brave person, but something inside of me caused me to take risks that were not necessary. Was I trying to prove something to myself, or just wanting to do the best job I could at the time? I don't know, but I was a slow learner. I would pull another similar stupid stunt a few weeks later, in the northern sector of our TAOR.

In the heat of combat, funny things happen to people as their emotions overwhelm them, causing them to do things almost compulsively, including putting their life at risk. Afterwards, they wonder why or what compelled the irrational act on their part. Perhaps it was concern for another fighting man's safety, patriotic response to the mission, massive responsibilities, or just a driven impulse caused by the excitement of the moment. Whatever my reasons or compulsions, they were reckless in nature, and it was wrong for me to undertake a risk that was not necessary at the time, especially since I was the Commander in Charge of a large group of men, who depended on me to make good decisions. Fortunately, neither situation resulted in harm to me, or the company, but the end did not justify the means. I had to learn to control myself or suffer severe and serious consequences.

Within a couple of days I would have the opportunity to test my rational thinking when we were again involved in another search and destroy operation at the southern most tip of our TAOR. We had departed our AMTRACS on the sandy beach outside of a tree line and immediately located a couple of "just vacated" bunkers. Obviously, the enemy heard the motors of our approaching vehicles and quickly departed their protective holes. We found some gear they had abandoned in their hasty retreat, including a commercial radio which we used back at our base for a few weeks. Incidentally, we did check it out before using it to make certain it wasn't a booby trap. We didn't trust anything or anybody, including a Catholic priest who brought some sweet cake and a bottle of vino for us at our Cua Viet Base. We were overly cautious, but that was the way to stay alive. We didn't drink the wine or eat the cake, probably missing a good treat.

As we moved inland a hundred yards, our men located a spider hole containing a VC and he was quickly eliminated when he fired at our troops. We continued to search the terrain, which transformed into a series of rice paddies surrounded by large, six feet high dikes.

One of our men using his spike had located a possible hiding place in one of the dikes. We moved to check it out more closely. The VC hiding inside pushed a concussion grenade through an air vent on one side of the dike, just as I was ascending the incline of the dike's rise. The grenade exploded. The concussion knocking me off the incline into a small puddle of water. As I landed on my back the VC leaped from the hole, literally jumped over me, and took off running toward a tree line.

I pulled my pistol to shoot him, but as I did a dozen or so men also pointed their weapons at him. They were spread out in a semi-circle in the direction he was running. I reasoned very quickly that there was a good possibility errant shots might hit our own men. I quickly dropped the weapon to my side and screamed "don't shoot"! The VC was running at full speed with his weapon in hand, and was now outside our troop position and a safe target, about to disappear into the forested area. I shouted, "Shoot him." One of the Marines on the flank got him in his gun sight and fired one round, hitting him in the back of his knee. He went down like a rock and it was over.

The nearest squad carried him back to our command group. He was in terrible shape. The rifle round had splintered his lower leg at the knee and he was in shock. We administered morphine and called for a chopper to MEDEVAC him to a hospital for treatment.

I don't know if he lived, but we did all we could for the poor man, even though he attempted to kill us with his grenade. This was the savage part of war no one liked but it was necessary to you harden your own feelings. As warriors, it was our job and acceptance was mandatory. Always in our mind was the mandate, get them before they get you. It was the law of survival in it's most obscene and crudest interpretation.

The concussion grenade used by the VC, caused more of a shattering and stunning effect from it's explosion, than the release of shrapnel. The concussion effect knocked me from the dike but inflicted no damage from shrapnel, however, one of our men was hit in the foot, suffering a minor wound. Several of our men were in proximity of the explosion, and if the grenade had been of the fragmentation type, all would have been injured. Such an explosion releases a large quantity of metal chunks up to a casualty inflicting radius of about 10 meters. Again, I had escaped serious injury or death, but this time I was doing my job rationally, not necessarily in a risk taking way. Nevertheless, I happen to be where the action occurred, which was my normal standard of operation, because it was the best way to influence the action.

We were taught early in our training, that a Commander influences the out come of battle in one of two ways - through the use of heavy arms, such as artillery, or by his personal presence on the battlefield. To be an effective leader, I learned, whether in combat or in business, you must be willing to sacrifice and demonstrate your leadership capabilities by doing the same thing you ask your people to do, and by being with them at critical times. This was my personal approach then and has been over the past thirty odd years.

I read somewhere that men continuously take the measure of those over them, and I am certain that my actions, were under constant evaluation by our company personnel. I tried to be a good example to those young men and it was important to me that I did the best I could.

We had our own direct support artillery in the AMTRAC Company and a section of 81mm mortars, which were used nightly to provide harassment and interdiction fire on likely areas of enemy movement. On one particular night, our mortars were firing on pre-arranged coordinates at designated times, a couple of thousand yards from our position, we noticed after each round exploded, secondary explosions followed a few seconds later in proximity to ours.

Initially, we thought that we had hit an ammo cache, or enemy troops carrying demolitions. We increased the rate of our mortar fire, scattering it around, and still each time our round exploded, an unknown secondary explosion occurred. This was unusual, and we were perplexed as to the reason.

Finally, we heard a voice on our radio asking if we were under attack. No, we responded, but who was calling us? It turned out that a Navy patrol boat armed with an 81mm mortar was patrolling in the South China Sea a thousand yards off shore, adjacent to our position. Each time they saw an explosion they fired their mortar at our exploding round.

We reassured them that we were not under attack, and would they please stop shooting into our TAOR until we requested their assistance. It was Murphy's Law, in all its glory. "If anything can go wrong it will, and at the most inopportune time."

CUA VIET NORTH

The search and destroy operations in the northern sector of our TAOR took on a different dimension from the southern area. We would engage a more resolute and tenacious enemy in the form of the North Vietnamese Regular Army Forces. The Southern boundary of the DMZ was only eight miles from the Cua Viet River base and the NVA could easily penetrate the DMZ and emerge in our area of responsibility almost at will. The terrain in the DMZ was heavily vegetated offering good routes of egress north and south. The remaining terrain was similar to the southern sector with a heavy stand of trees along the coast and an open sand dune area flowing inland for several hundred yards. Sporadic patches of trees and dense vegetation were interspersed among the sand dunes. The land was basically flat, normally providing good long-range observation and ease of travel by AMTRACS.

Because of the close proximity of the DMZ, we believed that any rocket or mortar attacks on our base would eventually come from the North. The NVA could easily mount such an attack and then scurry back through the demilitarized zone to a safe haven. It was an accident looking for a place to happen, and we knew that only our aggressive patrolling and ambush activity could prevent the accident and potential destruction of our base. We essentially utilized the same method of operation in this sector that had been successful in the southern area. However, we developed one more tool for our bag of tricks.

We developed a "J" hook, which was nothing more than a steel hook shaped like a "J", with a twenty yard line of heavy string or rope attached. We needed this device to pull tops or doors off of the caches and hiding places, and to detonate booby traps we could not easily disarm. When we came upon a suspicious looking hole or item, buried in the ground, we affixed the hook to the cover or debris. We would then back away to a safe distance letting the line out. With all the troops laying down on the ground, weapons ready, we give the line a hard jerk. If enemy troops were located in the hole we were ready and prepared to take them on, at something greater than point blank range. If an explosion occurred from a booby trap, the troops were far enough away to minimizing the likelihood of injury from the explosion.

We lost a lot of "J" hooks when they blew up as a result of an exploding device, but saved our men from certain injury. The hooks were expendable and easily replaced. We had the RMK construction group make us an ample supply.

With the continuing success from our operations, the RMK work crews grew more secure in their work, and were happy to provide us with any crazy thing we needed as long as their safety was perpetuated, and their work uninterrupted. Actually, they were very helpful to us, and really became apart of our team from a support function.

We augmented our fire power capability in the northern sector by including two or three of the AMTRACS with their 105 Howitzer on our search and destroy missions. Since we were patrolling very close to the DMZ, we were more concerned about running into larger ground forces, or artillery shelling coming from either the DMZ or North Vietnam. The vehicles gave us a direct artillery fire support capability in the event of ground attack, as well as the ability to return counter battery fire, if we were shelled by the enemy.

We continued to use the "Mike Spikes" on our operations. They were as effective as ever in the soft sandy soil. Each morning when we departed our base, the AMTRACS would first launch into the river carrying our troops aloft on their hulls. Then, after "swimming the river" on our vehicles, we would immediately drive to our designated points and commence our mission for the day. The tractors were placed in blocking positions with their firepower directed to cover our approach. At times, we would position them in front of the troops to lead us across ground suspected of harboring booby traps. As in the southern area, they were indispensable to our operations. Without the transportation and direct support the tractors provided, we could not have roamed our TAOR thoroughly, nor could we have moved into areas so quickly that the enemy did not have adequate time to escape or conceal themselves properly.

When ambush parties were sent north to their designated sites, they crossed the river under darkness in small paddle boats. AMTRACS were noisy and the roar of their engines would obviously eliminate the element of surprise. While the enemy wouldn't see our men, they sure as hell would hear them coming and have an opportunity to preempt with an ambush of their own.

Nightly ambush parties were a fact of life for us, and some nights we would send as many as four groups out to establish ambush positions. These squad sized groups usually consisted of 12 to 18 men. They would move out under the cover of darkness to occupy pre-designated locations, primarily on trails, or areas of likely foot movement, in hopes of trapping the peripatetic enemy. Because of our sensitivity of the NVA having good access through the DMZ, we established more nightly ambush locations in the northern section than we did south of the Qua Viet River.

We had been at the river location for about two months when we dispatched a reinforced squad, about seventeen men, across the river to man an ambush site about three thousand yards north of our base. We believed the timing was right for an attack on our base because of the success we had experienced. The port facilities for off loading supplies was functioning and there was a build-up of supplies at the base.

Our team moved out as usual under the cover of darkness. Each ambush party would check in periodically by radio to let us know of their progress. (Throughout the night they provided status and up-dates.. Most of these messages were by code or some pre-arranged sound, directed over the radio. This method was used to keep noise to a minimum while in the ambush, so as not to give away their position in case the enemy was monitoring our radio net or were in proximity. It was impossible to take to many precautions, even wearing after shave lotion was taboo, as the enemy could detect the smell, if they happened to be close to a position. The fragrance would carry for several yards and was foreign to all other jungle odors. It was better to stink just like the battleground.)

Our ambush party was close to their site, as evident by a recent radio check, when all hell broke out. It was 2130 hours; the ambush party had been on the move for about two hours and was about two thousand yards from our base when we heard the rifle fire and grenade explosives. The sound cut through the cool night air like a knife and we knew immediately that our team was in trouble. They were not in their position so we concluded they had been ambushed by the NVA while en route. We kept trying to make radio contact but couldn't get a response. The firing went on for several minutes as we tried to get a fix on their exact position. We could only guess at there situation. Finally, the shooting stopped. A voice came over the tactical radio net. "We've been hit hard and taken casualties, we need help!" We had already mobilized a platoon and several AMTRACS were ready to transport them to the contact point so they could extract the ambushed party.

We plotted artillery fire around the reinforcements to cover their routes of advance and withdrawal. Artillery barrages were also plotted around our ambush team to help protect them in case of a counter attack from the enemy. We also plotted artillery shelling north of the team's location in the direction the NVA would probably retreat after the fire fight.

Meanwhile, our reinforcements had crossed the river on their AMTRACS, and were moving to locate our ambushed team. We did not know the extent of damage. They would be excited, we knew. There communications were limited , we later found out, because the radio operator had been wounded. As they recovered from the attack they would be in a state of disarray while attempting to determine their situation. It would be important that they quickly consolidate their position in the event of another assault.

It took nearly two hours for our reinforcements to reach their position, get them aboard the vehicles, and bring them back to base. We were now able to get accurate reports on the action. They were not good. We had lost some men, and some were wounded. We prepared to receive them. All our Corpsmen came together in readiness to assist the wounded. MEDEVAC choppers in Dong Ha were put on alert to carry our wounded to the rear when they arrived. We waited for, what seemed like an eternity as the AMTRACS carrying our men, made their way back to the base.

They finally arrived and we assisted the men to the ready tent where our Navy Corpsmen began emergency treatment on the wounded. The MEDEVAC choppers were called again and were shortly at our position to evacuate the wounded and the dead. The squad leader who headed the ambush team had been killed in the attack and his radio operator wounded as we had already concluded. The squad leader, a corporal, was well liked and a personable young man, about twenty three years old and an outstanding Marine and person. It was terrible to see young men killed in their prime in this terrible war. Their lives snuffed out before they could begin to enjoy and experience the wonderful meaning of family creation and the ultimate fulfillment of dreams. This was a painful experience. They were the first men in our company killed since I had joined, and the realization of this horrible tragedy knocked down some of the hardened barriers that had been internalized to block out feelings and emotions.

After the groups were settled down emotionally, and the casualties were evacuated to the rear, we began to debrief the remaining ambush team members to obtain a clear picture of the action.

After they had crossed the river by boat, they began their patrol in single file, apparently with the squad leader and radio operator near the head of the column. They had been moving quietly under the darken sky in the tree line that ran parallel to the coastline. It was very dark with no natural glow from the moon, and the route was difficult to follow because of the tree canopy and heavy vegetation. As they moved toward their ambush site they heard a noise to their front a few yards away. Realizing that it was probably enemy troops, they formed the entire unit on line, abreast of one another with about 3-5 yards between men, and began an assault. The NVA having arrived at the same conclusion also formed into a skirmish line formation. When contact was finally ascertained a simultaneous attack ensued with no more than twenty yards between the two patrols. Neither group realizing how close they were to the other because of the subdued light and heavy bush. Both sides fired their weapons at a rapid rate at practically point blank range. Our squad leader fell mortally wounded with the first volley of fire from the enemy. One other Marine was killed and two more wounded including the radio operator. The firefight was over in minutes and the enemy withdrew leaving three dead NVA.

Our team didn't know how many enemy they encountered, but believed the unit was of similar size, 15-20 men. When our reinforcements arrived, they looked over the area and from bloodstains could conclude that some of the enemy had been dragged away with the retreating force. While no mortar tubes were found, several rounds were located, and considering the size of the group, it was clear that this enemy patrol was en route to mortar our position. Such an attack would have clearly resulted in the loss of many lives and potential destruction of our base, especially if any rounds hit the gasoline storage tanks or other ammo stored at the dock for transport to Dong Ha. Our thinking and timing about a potential attack was on target and those men did not die in vane. Their heroic action saved many lives.

Doc, the Corpsman assigned to the ambush team (all Corpsmen are called Doc) had done an excellent job caring for the wounded and through his diligent efforts helped preserve the lives of the wounded. While I spoke with him, I reached down and picked up his helmet. Much to my amazement and his shock and surprise, there was a bullet hole in the front, about three inches below the top of the helmet. Turning the helmet around, I found another hole in the rear where the round had exited. The bullet had penetrated the steel pot, ricocheted around the ballistic helmet liner then blasted out the rear. Doc recalled a sudden shock to his head but had not realized the nature of the impact. He was quite shaken and nervous to think how narrowly he had escaped instant death. I suggested he send the helmet to the rear for storage to take home with him later as a reminder of what could have been. It would make a great story someday for his children.

We fed the men and then dismissed them for some shut eye - if they could. The incident, as terrible as it was, could have been a lot worse for many of us had it not been for these gallant men.

The contact did confirm our suspicions about the enemy activity and their probable intentions in the northern sector. We knew we had to step up our operations in that zone, and quickly, or suffer consequences that would endanger all the forces and activities at the Cua Viet River base. The overwhelming success in the southern end of our TAOR had bought us some time, consequently, we believed we could concentrate more of our time and effort in the northern sector without jeopardizing our strong foothold in the south.

We launched our search and destroy missions north with a vengeance, and unknown to us at the time, we would quickly encounter the NVA and find out just how tough and resilient they were. We had decided to move our forces north to the southern boundary of the DMZ, to catch the enemy as they crossed through the Zone into our TAOR to establish base camps, or to entrap them returning north for re-supply.

On one of the early operations we made contact with a small party of NVA dug in around a sand dune, almost four thousand yards from our base. We had been patrolling most of the day when we noticed signs of enemy activity in the form of a fire pot and freshly dug fighting holes arranged in a circular pattern amongst sand dunes and thick ground vegetation. While investigating the area, we were taken under fire from three NVA, whose concealed hole, had been partially broached by one of our troops with his *Mike Spike*. One man was hit by rifle fire in the arm suffering only a slight, non-debilitating wound. A couple of rifle squads quickly surrounded the position. The remaining units posted security outposts and continued to conduct a search of the area. And then we waited.

I moved up close to the enemy position for a better look at what we were facing. We had to determine if we really had them surrounded, or if we were in the middle of a larger dug-in force ready to spring an ambush on us. After our outlying units reported no enemy activity in the general area we began our attempts to flush the NVA from their fortified position. We wanted them prisoner and hoped, once they determined that they were surrounded by a superior number of troops, they would surrender to us without a fight. We wanted them for intelligence, hoping we could gain valuable information on the enemy forces operating inside out Northern TAOR.

We had our Vietnamese interpreter call out to them, telling them they were surrounded and if they surrendered, no harm would come to them. We waited but no response came. They had no intentions of surrendering and were ready to fight to the death. They quickly demonstrated their tenacious combative attitude during our initial attempts to force them from their position.

We began with tear gas, in conjunction with yellow smoke grenades, by tossing them onto the top of their position thinking that this might change the enemy's attitude. (Using the two types of grenades together helps to contain and localize the gas in a specific location.) Just as the gas was dispensing from the exploding grenade, the wind changed to our direction and we ended up getting a high dose of the stuff in our faces and up our nostrils. We did not have gas masks, and the out come was not favorable to us. As we were coughing and sneezing, the NVA, who were also suffering the effects, jumped desperately from the bunker firing automatic weapons and tossing grenades.

I was close enough to the position to see their faces through the yellow smoke washing over them. It was one of the most surreal sights I have ever witnessed. The swirling smoke around their position accented their brownish yellow complexion, and their faces possessed a demonic look. Their eyes glowing in hate and anger convinced us they were going to fight to the death, ours or theirs.

As quickly as they appeared from the bunker, momentarily catching our troops off guard as we confronted our self-induced gas, they disappeared back into their hole. We suffered another wounded Marine, and decided that it was foolish after that display of their determination to fight, to continue coaxing them from their bunker.

We had to kill them or risk more harm to our troops. An assault on the position would risk further casualties. Instead, we decided that fragmentation hand grenades would do the job. We could easily lob the grenades the twenty-five yards from our position on top and inside the bunker. We were in for a shock.

Over the next few minutes, we threw over twenty grenades at them and not one exploded. Each time we tossed our grenades, the NVA would pop-up from their position with bursts of automatic rifle fire in all directions, toss our grenades back at us and duck back into the bunker. With all the confusion, gas in the air, grenades bouncing around, and enemy aggressiveness, I kept our men pinned to the ground so they would not be hit by the erratic rifle fire from the NVA.

We were going no place fast with this resolute and aggressive enemy force. We gathered more hand grenades from the other troops, and decided to eliminate this irritant once and for all. This time we tossed both gas and fragmentation grenades at the enemy position, but no smoke, we wanted to see clearly. As the grenades exploded, the NVA come out of the hole - for the last time. We caught them in a hail of cross- fire and it was all over, finally.

We had three NVA dead, automatic weapons taken from them, and only two minor casualties on our side. We called in the MEDEVAC choppers, sent our injured to the rear, buried the NVA, and continued on with our search of the area. We believed this three-man group was probably part of a larger force located somewhere in the area. We spent considerable time trying to find indications of their presence but there were none to be found that day. But a few days later, however, we would find the rest of the enemy, a much larger contingent.

For the moment, as we headed back to our base, my immediate concern was the problem we had experienced with our fragmentation grenades. Over twenty we threw at the enemy were inept. Grenades were an important weapon, both offensively and defensively. They were particularly effective when attacking fortified positions because of their explosive power and capability to destroy or blow-up rudimentary barriers. As a defensive weapon, they provided both shock power and a casualty-inflicting radius of shrapnel up to ten to twelve yards. Obviously, this made them a potent influence when used against massed troops at close range.

We primarily depended on our grenades and Claymore anti-personnel mines, as major deterrents to a ground attacking force at the Cua Viet. Now, based on the recent experiences of the day, it was painfully evident we could not depend on our current supply of grenades.

The M-26 fragmentation grenades, which were smaller in size than a baseball, weighed about a pound They contained serrated bands of steel, and when exploded, filled the air in all directions, with tiny flesh tearing steel fragments. There was a rubber washer that separated the main body of the grenade from the triggering device and was supposed to keep moisture away from the powder train responsible for detonation after ignition. Apparently, the heavy rains and wet conditions from the prevailing monsoon season were pervasive and detrimental to the rubber washer. It had hardened loosing some of it's flexibility, and no longer provided a tight fit on the grenade body. This condition allowed a substantial amount of moisture to seep in and destroy the powder charge.

In short order, I was on the radio to our rear supply area, informing them in no uncertain terms of our problem, and immediate requirement for more grenades. We had to have them at our base position before nightfall. I was not adamant with my request, I was over demanding to a fault. Shit happens, and it always happens when you're not prepared, or haven't done your homework. I kept thinking it would be ridiculous if we were hit by the NVA that very night and we didn't have sufficient supplies of ammo or grenades to meet the threat. It would be worse if we had not done everything we could to solve the problem, before we had a problem.

When we arrived back at base, there were twenty-five new cases of M-26 fragmentation grenades waiting on us, , about 600 grenades. The old boxes containing the dudes had been picked up and taken to the rear for disposition. I guess the squeaky wheel gets the oil, and I had been squeaking real loud that day.

We didn't get attacked that night at the Cua Viet or any other night for that matter, but our men were prepared and always had what they required when it was needed. As their leaders we owed that to them.

I have spoken about intuition a number of times, and to this day I don't know what causes it or where it comes from. Is it the combination of experience, training, and knowledge, or is it an inner voice that whispers to you, at critical times, with sound reasoning and advice? A kind of spiritual reckoning to guide you when you most need it. Wherever it comes from, it came to me a few days later as we were again in the northern sector looking for more NVA perpetrators. We were operating in the same general area where we had experienced our most recent combat.

We had been on patrol all day finding no evidence of the enemy. I was about to call it a day as it was late afternoon and we had to head back to the base to prepare our usual nighttime defenses. Our AMTRACS were in a blocking position to our rear. For some unknown reason, as we moved, pivoting from a westerly advance to a southern direction, which was where our vehicles were deployed, I stopped the march and called my Platoon Commanders together. I told them to turn north for a few hundred yards, and to search in that direction. Why did I suggest that course? I remember looking at a bush on the trail as we passed, and something didn't look normal, at least in my mind. But why north? Why not east, or south? I didn't know, but I felt compelled.

The first and second platoons moved out in the lead, on line, with the command group in the center, and a squad for rear security. After making our turn north and moving about two hundred yards, a commotion occurred in the rear of our formation. About twenty yards behind the command group, one of the Marines had probed a small rise in the ground when a concussion grenade came at him from an enemy hiding in a hole. It momentarily stunned him. An NVA soldier with an AK-47 dressed only in short pants and "T" shirt, jumped from the hole and took off running south. His route was to take him across three hundred yards of open sandy area, and he was determined to reach the distant tree line, alive. It would provide protection and the ability for him to disappear in the heavy vegetation.

When he took off running three of our men took off after him. I was close to the action and found myself drawn into the foot race almost without realizing what was happening. The only thought in my mind was to catch that little SOB, before he escaped, so we could interrogate him and learn something about the enemy's plans.

Driven by some internal force, we gave chase and it was the second time that I had given into my emotions without giving serious thought to the risk I was assuming. Again, it was stupidity on my part. Be that as it may, we ran through the open area, dislodging our heavy gear as we ran. Our men halting periodically to take aim with their rifles at the fleet-footed, unencumbered, dodging NVA soldier. After a couple of minutes he disappeared into tree line, and I knew we had no chance to catch him. Screaming at our chase party, I got them under control, including myself, and we headed back to join the rest of our troops. The ground we had just crossed was scattered with discarded gear; packs, helmets, canteens, ammo belts, and panchos were lying all around. We retrieved them as we walked back, somewhat embarrassed about our actions, because we didn't catch him and the realization how we had blatantly exposed ourselves. If any enemy had been located in the tree line they would have had a field day shooting us in the open area.

I've often asked myself how anyone with leadership responsibilities could do such a stupid thing. I still don't have an answer. We were caught up in the excitement of the moment and the possibility of capturing an enemy soldier. It was a blunder on my part, and we were fortunate that we didn't get ambushed during the chase. Returning to the rest of the company which had halted in place, awaiting our return, we decided to push on and check out the remainder of the area.

Almost immediately we made contact. A squad of NVA was in a series of fighting holes, more or less on line, perpendicular to our approach. They too, were ready to fight.

Our lead platoon took them under fire. Several enemy soldiers came out of their holes throwing grenades and firing their weapons attempting to escape the attack. They were killed instantly. While we engaged these, others further along succeeded in fleeing their holes and escaping into their rear. The battle lasted only a few minutes. We took no casualties and managed to kill eight NVA. We estimated that five to seven fled the battle scene during the action. We were unable to give chase at this time due to the late hour, and inability to ascertain the actual directions they scattered toward. We thought it best to wrap up the day, collect the enemy weapons, bury the dead, and get back to our base before nightfall. We would come back again tomorrow and start looking for them.

I walked up to my Second Platoon Commander as we were concluding the consolidation of the battle site. The Lieutenant was standing over an NVA he had just shot and killed with his pistol as the enemy jumped out of his hole in front of him. He was still shaken from the incident when, glancing down, I noticed an unexploded grenade laying on the ground a few feet from where he was. As I attempted to help him regain his composure, complimenting him for his personal bravery and his platoon's aggressiveness in action, I pointed to the inert grenade lying at his feet. That was too much for him, his knees nearly buckled and I had to help stabilize him. That must have been the grenade the dead NVA tossed as he scrambled from his hole. Fortunately, it didn't explode.

Within a few minutes he was back in form, and I got him moving on his responsibilities so he wouldn't have time to think about what could have been. He was now under control and began to move about with his men getting them organized and prepared to move out.

It was wise not to let men dwell, mentally, so soon after the action, especially, if they had experienced a close call with enemy contact. Their concern could traumatize them and they might become overwhelmed with the emotion, unable to perform their duties or even take care of themselves. It was better to keep them moving and active. They would have plenty of time later to think and talk about their experiences with their buddies. Time would have passed and they would be more sanguine and calm, able to digest and rationalize the action better. I always hoped that the approach and attitude would work for me. So, I too, kept my mind occupied with things to be done.

As we departed the area, riding on the AMTRACS, the sky was beginning to darken as we hastened to return to our base. We needed to be there before nightfall to prepare our security. We also didn't like traveling under reduced visibility because it made us more susceptible to enemy ambush.

We routinely traveled the water line along the coast, because we had three open visible sides and only our inland flank with the tree line to worry about. If attacked in that type of situation, our immediate action response drill, was to pivot our vehicles toward the attacking force, putting them on line from out of the single file column. We would then open fire with our vehicle mounted machine guns and assault the attackers. It was a simple plan giving us potential fire superiority and momentum in the attack. Except for the one time when we were shot at in the southern region and responded by leveling the tree line with our guns, the enemy never fired on our column in that position. I guess they rationalized that it would be suicidal to take us on with our firepower unless they possessed heavy anti-tank weapons along with overwhelming troop support.

On arrival at the base, I called the artillery liaison officer to plan our nightly artillery shelling. We decided to hit the area where we had just engaged the enemy at frequent intervals throughout the night. We knew the NVA were still in the general area, and they would be moving around that night, returning to the battle site to retrieve their dead from the graves we dug and rebury them. This was standard practice, it seemed, associated with their religious beliefs that the soul would wander this earth unless properly buried. Intermittent artillery shelling might catch them in the open if they came back into that location.

After the fire plan was put in place, I took the opportunity to reflect on the day's activities. What had started out as a slow day of monotonous patrolling in our northern zone, concluded with a foolish wild chase of an NVA across an open sand dune area, followed by a deadly battle with the enemy in a dug-in fortified position. Though eight NVA soldiers had been killed, and several unfortunately escaped, we were lucky not to have taken casualties.

The result from my sudden intuition to make a right turn with our sweep force at the end of a long day took only a few minutes to erupt and then conclude. Had we continued with our original mission we would have missed the enemy completely, perhaps engaging them at a later time and under more unfavorable conditions to us.

In retrospect, that situation could easily have resulted in an enemy ambush. We were clearly in the middle of the deployed enemy force with at least one NVA soldier to the rear of our company and several to the front. We never did determined if any were on our flanks due to the rapid engagement our lead platoon concluded on the dug in enemy squad. My suspicion was that we caught them unaware, and if there were others in the area, they slipped away quietly or decided not to engage us at that time. Our troop strength was probably superior, and they had not yet at consolidated their troops for a large battle.

It was a serious situation we had stumbled into on a whim, but prevailed. This was a critical engagement because the NVA were clearly building up forces in our northern sector. We were fortunate to discover the smaller sized contingents and eliminate or scatter them, before they could mass enough troops for a possible major attack on our base, or ambush our company.

The Cua Viet River base, as I have emphasized, was an important re-supply point for all units in the northern I Corps area. The enemy knew this and if it could be neutralized, it would eliminate some of the threat to their forces by slowing down the flow of critical logistical supplies to the front line Marine units. Therefore, each terminal contact with the enemy, enhanced our control and surveillance throughout the area and stymied the consolidation of their troops. We fractured their battle plans and coordination efforts, and kept them from achieving momentum and control of this theater of operations. Constant pressure, aggressive search and destroy missions, knowledge of the terrain, and unorthodox methods, provided us with an advantage that we never relinquished to the enemy, during our deployment at the river base.

Several months later, after we departed the Cua Viet and I was reassigned other duties, I would again visit the Base as an advisor sent by the 3rd Marine Division Commander. I would learn that much we had gained had been lost and the area was then, more or less, being dominated by the North Vietnamese. Gains made on the battleground were never permanent. When the terrain was vacated or we ceased to control it with aggressive action, the NVA and VC would immediately reoccupy it with new troops. As one writer noted, in his book published several years ago, Ho Chi Minh would send more soldiers down the trails from North Vietnam, to match our troop commitment and occupy any areas that we left unattended. That was the terrible part of this yo-yo war, and one of the reasons it went on for so many years. The NVA were unrelenting in their aggression and willingness to continue the battle by replacing troops in a constant flow to face their enemy. When we lost momentum or relieved the pressure, they would immediately capitalize on the situation. They perceived this as weakness on our part and would increase their warring activity. In essence, they would always seize the moment. It worked for them and prolonged the war, which was a major part of their strategy, and it worked.

We intended to keep up the pressure in our area, and so the next morning, after shelling the previous day's battle site, we returned in force, in hopes of locating them once again. We were not surprised that the graves in which we had buried their dead had been dug up and the bodies moved, maybe even carried back to North Vietnam, as we found no new graves during our search.

After the battle when we had departed, the NVA had come back during the night, and while under artillery shelling, gathered their comrades' remains, relocating them to another area in keeping with their religious rites. One had to admire this tenacity and resolute devotion to duty, and their religious belief system.

We were also resolute in our desire to win our war and within a couple of days, launched a search and destroy mission to the southern edge of the DMZ. We assumed that our prey had moved back in that direction to regroup. We had never conducted an operation in this area, so the timing might carry the element of surprise and benefit our efforts.

This area was more heavily vegetated than any we had operated in throughout our TAOR. The Ben Hai River, the actual border between North and South Vietnam, was about three thousand yards further north, and emptied into the South China Sea. Another smaller river, a couple of thousand yards inland from the coast, connected with the Ben Hai, flowing south to join the Cua Viet west of our base. The confluence of water in the region helped promote the thick growth of trees and underbrush.

Several times while working in this area, we were unable to determine our exact location due to the heavy underbrush and the inability to guide off major terrain features. We had our artillery forward observer call for illumination rounds to be fired and exploded in the air at designated coordinates. Using our compasses and maps, and sighting on the air explosions, we could determine our location within a hundred yards. If we were attacked and needed artillery fire called on the enemy, we had to be absolutely certain of our coordinates, otherwise they could miss the enemy altogether, or worse, drop artillery shells on us. Much of the time we carried our maps and compass in our hands, tracking our progress as we moved over the ground. I told my forward observer that if he ever had a question on our location, he was to let me know. We would halt our march immediately and recalculate our position.

We had fire power available to us in many forms; our own mortars, Marine artillery Naval Gunfire, helicopter gun ships, and aerial bombardment from both Marine and Navy planes. I wanted to be prepared and ready to use these resources quickly when we needed them.

As we patrolled through this densely vegetated area we located a number of trails that seemed to crisscross leading off into several different directions. It was obviously an area befitting concealment of troops and the establishment of enemy base camps. As we moved about in this almost jungle like thicket, one of our lead units was fired on by an NVA. They gave chase, killing him as he retreated from his position. Thinking we had encountered the security guard of a larger unit, we deployed our force and began to move through the area in anticipation of engaging remnants of the unit we had battled a few days earlier.

We found several blood trails and a small camp out post scattered with gear and a smoldering fire. Food was still simmering in a pot sitting on the edge of a fire pit. We had found a base camp, but the enemy had escaped just prior to our arrival, probably as a result of the outpost guard that had taken our unit under rifle fire.

This was obviously a heavily used area by the NVA, and we thought it probably served not only as a route of egress through the DMZ, but also as a major staging area and base camp location in support of their forays into our TAOR. This thicket of vegetation was of sufficient size to conceal a large number of troops. The formidable and eerie looking jungle had a density of trees and bush that made foot travel nearly impossible, restricting movement, primarily to the trail system. We searched the area for most of the day finding hiding holes and other evidence of their activity, but could not uncover any enemy troops.

In one hole we located a small tunnel with a 1941 bolt action German made rifle resting in an upright position at the bottom of the pit. The hole had obviously been occupied recently, and the trooper had quickly departed, leaving his weapon behind. I have that rifle in my den at home. It was then and still is a wonderful shooting weapon. Many times I have considered having it altered for big game hunting, but it represents too many memories of those days at the Cua Viet to alter it in any fashion.

Success is a wonderful thing but sometimes it can be a nuisance. A young captain, with no combat experience, had been dispatched to our base to observe our operations, and to report back to Division headquarters. He was a nice enough young man, probably about twenty seven, full of piss and vinegar, but a little too aggressive and somewhat of a loud mouth, a know it all, if you know what I mean. Nevertheless, we were hospitable, we had him join us on our operations over a two-week period and told him all we could about our methods. A couple of times he unnecessarily, and without forethought, created some dangerous situations by wandering off from the group and on another occasion nearly stepped on a booby trap. I found myself under a lot of strain watching after him and admonishing him for his battlefield behavior. I didn't want to see our guest go back to wherever he came from on a stretcher.

As we headed back through the woods from the action in the DMZ, our company was spread out over a wide, flat, grassy area, with most of the men in visual contact with their individual platoons. Our erratic guest was strolling in the rear of the command group when we heard a loud "ping" sound. It echoed through the open field, reminiscent of the sound from an armed grenade after being thrown, when the spoon or handle jettisoned in flight. Without hesitation, one hundred and forty five Marines hit the ground waiting for an explosion or possible attack. Nothing happened, no explosion. And as I glanced around, the only man standing was the young captain ten yards to my rear.

It seems he had been shuffling behind our command group, kicking items on the ground. Finding a desolate tin can, he gave it a good kick with the toe of his boot, creating the "ping" sound as it sailed through the air. At the time, we had engaged the enemy twenty six times, over the previous thirty-day period and our collective nerves were stretched to the breaking point and raw at the edges. As I looked up at the Captain from where I was lying on the ground, while he stood there rather sheepishly, I decided he had to go. He had learned enough and it was time for him to report back to his boss with his report. After some instruction on my part about his conduct and inability to appreciate the seriousness of his actions throughout the two-week period, I suggested strongly, that he catch the first re-supply boat back to Dong Ha as soon as we returned to our base. He was gone the next morning and I never saw him again. I hope he survived Vietnam, or better, if he ever had a command, I hope his men survived him. Some people are just slow learners and that trait can get people killed in combat.

There are always undesirables in every unit and we had one such person in Mike Company. Of all things, he was a Navy Corpsman, whose duties and responsibility were to treat the wounded and keep people alive if seriously injured. You expect them to be the most humane people on the battlefield. Most are just that, many times exhibiting great feats of bravery under enemy fire as they go about their duties. In my mind, this included administering first aid treatment to the wounded enemy when necessary.

However, this particular man had seen a lot of combat and to my knowledge had done his job satisfactory. But, he frequently displayed a personal hardness toward people and an edge that bordered on cruelty. On one occasion in the field as we were patrolling, he had found a snake and ran a stick down it's gullet. He held it up for all to see as he walked through his platoon members, proud of his achievement. This action seemed ridiculous to many of us and was not appropriate in our environment. On another occasion, after we had engaged the enemy on one of our operations and had shot an enemy soldier, he was asked to check him for possible signs of life. The soldier was dead and our Corpsman was found attempting to dig gold out of the man's teeth with his knife. When I was informed of this I was furious and called for him. I don't believe I ever chewed out any human being as badly as I did him. After my tirade, to which he had no response, or showed any concern, I told him to report to his unit in Dong Ha as soon as we could arrange transportation. He was gone that night, and I don't know what happened to him and I could care less. He was an insult to his profession and the Marines with whom he served. There is no place for people like that in the military, or any place else as far as I'm concerned.

Most of the Navy Corpsman I met in the service were outstanding and a credit to their profession. I could never provide enough accolades for their dedication and contribution to the Marines they supported.

Within a few days, we were ordered to board helicopters, and were dropped into another area near the Gio Linn firebase, which bordered on the Northwest side of our TAOR. We were to search for an NVA group that was operating in that area. They were harassing the base with mortar attacks and nightly probes of its defensive positions. We departed with two platoons and command group, leaving one at the Cua Viet base for defense. We spent the first day searching the area but could find nothing. We had not taken our *Mike Spikes* with us and the next morning requested that a chopper pick them up at our base and bring them to us. The terrain was sandy, similar to our own operational area and we thought we might have more luck with our probing device. This was probably the only time that a helicopter was ever used to haul metal spikes into a combat area so troops could dig around in the ground. We found this humorous, but our request for the chopper was handled promptly, denoting the reputation we have had earned with our spike.

After another day on the sweep we were still unable to locate any enemy activity. We were returned to our base, disappointed that we could not deliver on our orders to find the NVA. We gave it our best try and though the search was fruitless, our activities did apparently move the enemy out of that area because it was some weeks before the firebase was hit again.

A few days later we were notified that our company was to join another Battalion involved in a major operation northwest of Cam Lo. This was to be a defining point and time in my career and would result in my decision to ultimately leave the Corps. For Mike Company, the war would change dramatically from this point forward, and unknown to me at the time, my command was entering its concluding stage.

MARINE CORPS HISTORICAL TAPE INTERVIEW

ON CUA VIET SEARCH AND DESTROY OPERATIONS

[Content unedited]

INTERVIEWER:

This is a historical interview with Richard D. Jackson, Captain 080223, United States Marine Corps, Commanding Officer of M Company, Third Battalion, Fourth Marines, Third Marine Division. Name of the interviewer is Gilbert Oles, Sergeant 617947, United States Marine Corps. The interview is being conducted at M Company, Third Battalion, Fourth Marines command post at the Cua Viet River in South Vietnam. The date of the interview is 18, February 1967.

RICHARD JACKSON:

I am Captain Richard D. Jackson, 080223, Commanding Officer, M Company, Third Battalion, Fourth Marines, Third Marine Division. This narration is an account of the action that took place today and involved a village search and destroy mission that was conducted approximately 15,000 meters south of the mouth of the Cua Viet River along the coast of the South China Sea, coordinates vicinity 47 35 77. Initially, Mike company moved out this morning at 0800 with ten LVTs, and two How' Sixes. The tractors carried the company south to the search area where the troops debarked the vehicles. One group of vehicles, with the How sixes moved to the west side of the village and set-up in a blocking position, another group of tractors moved over on the coast and set-up another blocking position. The area that was to be swept today was approximately 4,000 meters in length. We only swept 1200 meters.

Initially, we jumped off at 0930 hours. After we had moved approximately 100 meters we began to encounter booby traps, and punji pits. Most of the booby traps that we encountered were rigged with Chicom grenades. A couple of the punji pits also had Chicom grenades rigged in conjunction with the booby traps. All of the grenades were recovered. All the booby traps were destroyed. After we had moved approximately 250 yards we located one spider hole containing two VC.

Our method of locating these holes is a little unique. Our movements are a little unique, probably differ somewhat in what many of the units use. We have taken the metal rods found in the 105 ammo boxes, tapered the ends, and screwed them into a little wooden handle, giving you a, more or less, a poker about four and half feet long. All of the troops conducting this sweep are equipped with one of these pokers. We merely go along, and each of the Marines carries the poker in his hand and jabs the ground as he goes along. We can conduct a thorough sweep -- search of all the rice paddy dikes and high ground. It's useless to search the paddies themselves because normally on the coast they're under water. We poke around in the dikes and any sand dunes that we encounter and so forth. It's not uncommon to follow behind a squad that's conducting a sweep and find numerous little holes all over the

place. We know if we find these that the
Marines are doing their job. The Marines
stick the poker into the ground as they
move along checking the areas trying to
check out all suspicious areas, and those,
sometimes, that are not too suspicious.
Once the poker is stuck into the ground it
will go in anywhere from one to four feet
in many cases. If it strikes something
hard we're not too alarmed, the poker's
withdrawn, inserted again into the ground,
and, on maybe the third or fourth occasion
if we continue to strike something hard
then we feel that we have encountered a
spider hole, or a tunnel, or a cave,
whatever you may desire to call it.
Sometimes we locate rocks beneath the
ground, sometimes roots, and so forth also,
which slows our progress down. However,
once that we feel that we have located a
spider hole, it's marked with the poker
still remaining in the hole. The small
unit leader then takes charge, we hold up
the advance of the remaining search squads,
which in today's case was a total of six
squads on line, and a fire team is then
brought up to take on the hole. Normally
if we have an interpreter with us we try to
talk them out of the hole.

This is not always a real good idea,
because a lot of times they come out
throwing grenades. After the squad -- or
fire team, I should say, is brought up into
position, a few more stabs are probably
made into the earth to determine the exact
location of the spider hole. Then small
amounts of dirt are scraped away by
shovels. We carry large shovels taken off
of the AMTRACS and we also carry our
entrenching tools, but the larger shovels
expedite our jobs quite a bit. A little
dirt is removed from the hole until we

246

locate the entrance door. Once we locate
this, if there's been no activity from the
hole, we may fire a few rounds down into
the hole through the door. If no other
activity is encountered we may then follow
this up with a grenade into the spider
hole. After this is completed, we then
open the hole and search it out.

Our techniques vary considerably in this
approach. Sometimes, we may use gas, CS
gas, in lieu of the grenade. It depends on
the type of resistance that we're meeting.
For instance, on the 17th of February we
encountered approximately four holes of
this nature. We tried to take prisoners
initially, but in each case the VC, or
actually, the hard core NVA would throw
grenades at us, would come up out of the
hole, throw a grenade and try to take off
running. We killed a total of eight on
this day, and one NVA raced away from our
position and after a chase of about 300
meters, he eventually got away from us. In
this particular operation we took one
causality.

I don't feel that it's worth while to risk
taking casualties among our friendly troops
in order to capture one VC, or one NVA. In
this particular case we were meeting heavy
resistance and so we changed our methods,
began firing into the holes, and dropping
grenades into the holes as soon as we
encountered them.

Now, on today's activities it was a little
different. These people, we feel, were
local VC, they did not put up the
resistance. A couple of them threw
grenades at us trying to get out of the
hole, but we had several who just out right
gave up. We ended up today killing five

and took six prisoners. We also picked up two VCS. [Vietcong Suspects]

In some occasions, we have encountered here recently, methods that the VC are using to counter our probing methods. We uncovered a couple of booby traps today that had little doors, just a door more or less, over a hole in the ground. When you pull up the door there was a Chicom grenade rigged as a booby trap. We have another device that we use to counter methods of this type and we also use it to uncover most holes that we find in the event that they may be booby trapped.

This little item that we have rigged up, we call a J-hook. It is nothing more than a piece of metal shaped in the form of a J and attached to a strong 20 yard length of nylon rope or strong cord. Once we've located the hole and perhaps fired a few rounds into it, the hook is then hooked into the opening, the door, the Marine gets at the other end of it and jerks the door off. This will preclude any casualties in the event that the door is booby trapped. We have not taken any casualties -- or we did not take any casualties today in our operation. Three of the holes that we located today had different types of entries than those that we have encountered before. They were all located in dikes along side rice paddies, but all three entries were made through water. That is to say, that they went down into the water in the rice paddy, and then up into the hole in the dike. This is the first time that we've encountered holes of this nature. It makes it extremely difficult to locate. It means that you not only have to probe the top of the dike, you also have to probe the side of the dike.

In one particular case today one Marine
sticking his probe down in the ground, he
tried to pull it back and one of the VC in
the hole held on to the probe, the man
could not pull it out of the ground.
Needless to say he was a little surprised.
In this particular case these two VC in the
hole gave up.

We also encountered one VC today who had
been wounded last night or yesterday
morning. His story was that he was wounded
early in the morning. We do not know if
this was a result of some H&I fires from
our position or other action from the ARVN
Forces, as they had an operation going on
yesterday. He gave up also when we
encountered him.

Most of the VC that we encountered today
were in pretty pathetic shape. They were
ill equipped, we only took three weapons
today, and these were all M1 carbines. We
found a few Chicom grenades in the holes,
very little food, no cigarettes, and very
little money. Compared to the NVA that we
located the day before yesterday, all the
NVA had automatic weapons in excellent
condition, ample supply of ammunition,
plenty of clothing, plenty of cigarettes,
and, generally, most of them looked pretty
healthy. However, those today were in
pretty bad shape. We do know that one of
the prisoners we took today was a Lance
Corporal in the NVA.

Within our particular unit today we had
several attachments, which I feel worth
mentioning. One, was a representative from
the CIT interpreters, who did a real fine
job. Once we take a prisoner, POW, we
immediately turn the people -- the prisoner

over to the CIT and the interpreter. Immediately these people go to work on the prisoner, try to get information from him. We may even be on the move and, they're still working on him.

Today's operation we were able to get three kills because the interpreter was able to get out of the man the location of another spider hole containing three VC. This particular method not only saves the Marines' lives, but it enhances our total operation.

Additionally, we had four engineers attached. The engineers make a big difference. We've encountered a great amount of ordinance, bombs, mortar rounds, and so forth. We use the engineers to detonate whenever we locate them. Additionally, the engineers are used to detonate booby traps that we find and we cannot disassemble.

The probing method that we utilize does not always uncover VC or NVA, but when we're not getting people, we're getting equipment, gear, food, supplies, etc.

Yesterday's operation, for instance, we uncovered approximately nine holes. All of these holes were destroyed. These are potential hiding places that the VC may go back to, but we have destroyed them and now they are of no use to the VC. In many of the holes we found rifles. Yesterday's operation, for instance, we found three rifles. We also found money, food, and clothes. These are holes that the VC live in during the day and at night, and perhaps they've gone out to take up another occupation and they leave their gear behind. We've uncovered it. We gathered up a great deal of gear and clothing yesterday. So, if we're not getting people then we're getting gear, supplies, and so forth. We're putting a hurting on the VC one way or another. Using this method we have encountered, or killed, or captured now in the past 21 days a total of 28 VC or NVA troops. These figures are a direct reflection of the method that we are using when we conduct our sweep operations.

From the action encountered on the 17th of February in which we killed eight NVA and buried them right in the holes in which they were hiding, on returning today we found that all the bodies have been dug up. Initially, we found two graves, and two of the bodies had been reburied in the graves in caskets, which is quite unusual. The other holes in which we had buried the bodies, the bodies are gone. We were unable to locate the graves. We felt that perhaps they may return to the area. Consequently, last night after we departed the ville, after the contact, approximately 45 minutes later we called in a fire mission, hoping that perhaps any remaining VC in the ville would, perhaps, be out looking around trying to figure out what had happened. Also, we called in H&I fire on the ville at 19:15 just as it was getting dark, and, again, at 0700 the following morning just as it was getting light, and hoping that we might catch any of the enemy moving about at this time.

As far as our operations up north and our TAOR was concerned, since we moved out to the mouth of the Cua Viet River we have stayed out of that area, completely out of the area, hoping that the VC might think that we had departed that area for good and would then jack up their operation somewhat.

We feel that this is exactly what they did. They, -- we were not in the area, there had been no one in the area for over one month. We waited, and waited, and waited, and we feel that they took the bait, moved into the area, and then we moved in and scoffed them up. So, I'm sure that we will probably hold off again for quite a while before we move back into that area.

Our anticipated operations in the future will probably take us back down south of our TAOR and even outside of it several thousand meters as there are quite a few hamlets [groups of small villages] in this particular area. All of these hamlets need to be searched out and we intend to conduct a very thorough sweep of this complete area.

We have some PRU units that have worked for us, (Provisional Reconnaissance Units composed of Vietnamese) on several occasions we've had these people out here in the area to go out and operate in the area trying to gain intelligence for us, so they we could come back and react on it. Our relationship with these people has been good. They have provided us both good and bad information. Just as anything else you may encounter there are good PRU's and there are bad. Some of them have done a tremendous job for us, others have -- the work has not been too exceptional.

We have a pending raid that we'd like to conduct on one particular hamlet. We have been setting up an operation there, we've made a couple kills there, we've uncovered quite a bit of gear, including fourteen mortar rounds and one Chinese carbine. This particular area is supposed to be a Charlie Papa (Command Post) for a VC platoon.

We have gotten a hold of one local Vietnamese fisherman, who lives in the ville, who has agreed to provide us information. We will pay him for this information. Every time we go in the ville, we sweep the ville, we check his house. If he has any information he will give it to us. One particular morning he met us on the beach at nine o'clock in the morning to give us information at that time. He wants to relocate his family.

He was at one time a Hamlet Chief. He's 48 years old, he has six children, and, as I said, he's trying -- he wants to relocate, I think, is going to provide us some valuable information as time goes on.

If we can determine a particular night that we think that the meeting will take place in this particular hamlet, we intend to conduct a predawn raid. We have learned that the VC conduct their patrol actions there around the ville when they're having meetings between eight o'clock at night, and four o'clock in the morning. We can move overland by foot from our position. We'll have to move a total of about four to five thousand meters into a position around the ville, and at first light we'll conduct a raid in that area. Once we can determine the exact location we'll be able to close swiftly, and I think get quite a few kills in this particular area. We're concentrating on this area and we're planning in the future to move down there and we hope bring back the groceries from this particular village.

The biggest problem that I feel that we have here in this area, and I assume that it's encountered by every Marine in Vietnam, is the ability to communicate with the Vietnamese. We have very few people in our company that can speak Vietnamese. We have these little fire team cards, the fire team leader cards. It has particular saying on those in Vietnamese and English. Our ability to communicate is almost zero. If we have interpreters with us we feel that we get information that leads us to locations where items may be buried, this has proven itself in the past and probably is our biggest draw back. We're beginning to understand the Vietnamese people a little bit better.

I think, in each particular area the people are a little different; here on the coast the villages are much cleaner than those that we have encountered in other locations, the people are much healthier, I guess the fact that they eat so much fish. - and they live principally through their fishing and their rice crops. They are much healthier, they look much better, they don't use as much beetle nut here as they use in certain areas.

However, our ability to communicate is big factor that's holding us back and it creates problems for us. Our hearts and minds program sufferers, We have PsyWar leaflets that we try to distribute whenever we can on our operations.

In many cases in using our LVTs we have to be extremely careful, we run down trees, run them across rice paddies and so forth, and, naturally, this is going to create ill will. We've got a problem here that boils

down to the old saying that you can't eat
your cake and have it too. We tried to get
the people on our side, but if you can't
communicate with them, if they don't know
what you're talking about, they can't help
you and you can't help them, and it make
for one great big problem and one problem
that we just haven't figured out how to
solve it at our level.

If we had interpreters on a permanent level
with us, at least two, we feel that it
would enhance our operations immeasurably.
Until we are able to get these people we're
going to be hurting. We don't understand
the Vietnamese. We don't know then, we
don't understand the way they live. We
don't know and can't understand the way
they think. Regardless of how hard we try
they're different than we are and we can
read all the books in the world, but you
just got to get down right on their level
and work with them 24 hours a day and live
with them practically, and operate with
them to really get the feel of these
people. It's extremely difficult and it's
a problem that's got to be breached and we
don't have the answer to it. But it is
holding us back somewhat.

INTERVIEWER:
This concludes the interview.

CAM LO WEST

All of us live in our own little world most of the time. This is particularly true in the combat zone where you live and operate in a remote area, nearly oblivious to everything that goes on outside your cloistered environment. There are no daily newspapers, radio broadcasts are infrequent, and reports on action in other areas are almost non-existent. When you do receive any shred of information, it's mostly outdated and insignificant. The intensity of hostilities in your own area, keeps you focused twenty-four hours a day, on your responsibilities and commitments to those things that will keep you and your men alive. Current events, outside your world, don't seem to amount to a hill of beans.

We were called to participate in an operation against a major thrust by a NVA regiment that had moved south of the DMZ into the Cam Lo area. We were unaware that this threat had occurred, although, it was about only 20 miles from our base. Other Marine units were also being mobilized to halt the enemy offensive.

One early morning we received a radio transmission telling us that Mike Company, less one Platoon to be left at the Cua Viet base, was to embark, ASAP, aboard Navy river-boats, which were to bring us to Dong Ha for further briefing. We were told we would have another platoon attached to our company and we would be involved in a tactical operation for several days. We were to bring all our equipment, weapons, and ammo. Knowing we would be going into mountainous terrain, we did not bring our *Mike Spike*.

With those orders, we gathered ourselves together, loaded on landing crafts and headed to Dong Ha, arriving in the afternoon. I went for my briefing to the forward Division Headquarters. We were to be heli-lifted the next morning, northwest of Cam Lo into the Dong Ha mountains, Hill 161, with the mission to envelope (attack from the flank or rear) an NVF force that had ambushed one of our Battalions and had it pinned down in the mountains. We were to land behind the NVA unit and maneuver to a position on the enemy flank. After relieving the pressure, we were then to link up with the Battalion and along with other units, continue the attack, driving the NVA back into the DMZ.

It was speculated that two regimental size units had moved into the mountains and were in the process of assaulting our bases and conducting ambushes and attacks on all our maneuvering ground forces.

Mike Company would be attached to three different Battalions over the next two weeks, operating mostly as a detached unit from the other forces.

We boarded the helicopters in the early morning, loaded with ammo, and were to be dropped off on the top of small mountain which was behind the NVA attackers. The assistant Division Commander, a Brigadier General, rode in my chopper with me and my two radio operators. The helicopter was piloted by a Colonel since the General was to be a passenger.

I didn't like this arrangement a damn bit. The General had no business being with an assault company and we had no idea what we might face when we landed. The chopper would go where the General wanted to go, not where I wanted to go, or needed to go. The General was known for sticking his nose into the operations of the combat units and his presence, in our chopper, on this day would cause serious problems for the company and me.

The birds launched from Dong Ha, and the landing began to evolve as planned. However, as my chopper began to circle to drop me and my radio operators off, the landing zone began to take incoming artillery and mortar fire. A terrific explosion occurred in the middle of the dispersed troops in the landing area below us. We were descending when the blast occurred and the Colonel hit the throttle for a hasty accent. I grabbed him by the shoulder from my rear seat, and told him I needed to get on the ground with my troops. He curtly informed me that he was getting out of there because of our passenger's safety and he would bring us back after he dropped him off in the rear. This situation wasn't good. My entire rifle company was in the landing zone on top of the hill, and they were taking incoming. A booby trap daisy chain explosion had been set off by some of my men when they stepped on a tripwire, causing a series of explosions in rapid order, seriously injuring eight men. I was in a helicopter with both radio operators, which meant there was no coordination of communications between my command group, the action on the ground, and the Battalion Headquarters. And worse, I was on my way out of the area, flying to the rear, in a helicopter with the inquisitive, peripatetic General. We were out of control and I couldn't do a damn thing about it.

We made it to the rear and dropped the General, with me bitching under my breath the whole way. The Colonel tried to find someone else to fly us back, something he didn't want to do, or perhaps didn't need to do - fly into a hot landing zone full of action. However, no other pilots were available and he had to do it. We made the round trip in about twenty minutes. He circled the landing site, dropped to about five feet from the ground, and told us to jump.

We leaped from the bird amidst the noise and confusion, crashing to the ground in a heap. I had to find out what was going on. My Gunnery Sergeant gave me a briefing on the situation and quickly we determined we needed to get the hell off that hill before we were annihilated by artillery fire. But first we had to get our wounded evacuated. The Medevac choppers had already been called. I got our radio communications organized and told the Platoon Leaders our plan was to move northwest down the hill into a draw, *On The Run*. Momentarily the choppers arrived and gathered up the injured Marines. I gave the order to move out as the skies darkened and shells again started hitting near our position. We were in an impact area, and we all knew it. We began evacuating the landing zone, running at full speed off the hill, in what I'm certain, seemed like a disorganized mob. Much later, we laughed about how we must have looked as we sprinted into the draw below the top of the landing zone, probably resembling a wild herd of rampaging animals. But, we made the right decision to get off that hill which had obviously been zeroed in by the NVA with their artillery.

Assembling at the base of the hill into an organized military unit once again, we gained our composure, formed a tactical column, and began moving towards the entrapped Battalion. The terrain was hilly and our direction of march was covered with elephant grass amongst heavy forestation. We had been on the move for about two hours when we came under small arms fire as we crossed over a densely vegetated ridge. We couldn't see anything, and couldn't determine where the weapons fire was coming from.

We were pinned down, but for some reason, it didn't really seem that the firepower was actually directed at our company. We were hugging the ground like we had a consuming love affair with it, as bullets flicked the leaves on the bushes inches above our heads. I got on the radio lying with my back on the ground and called the Platoon Commanders. I told them to hold their positions, keep their heads down and be prepared for anything. As I lay there talking over the radio, watching the bullets strike the bushes over my head, I knew if anyone got up on their hands and knees to crawl they would probably be hit by an errant round. Finally, Battalion called on the radio and told me that we had maneuvered into a position between an NVA unit and one of the rifle companies of the Battalion. The NVA were withdrawing, and the company had been ordered to cease-fire to allow us to move out of the predicament.

Apparently, we accomplished our initial mission, almost by mistake, as we had moved between the two units. The enemy was now breaking contact as a result of our arrival on the battle scene. Interestingly, we had not fired a shot, but we had plenty of rounds hitting near us in the crossfire from the NVA and our own troops. Fortunately, we had taken no casualties. We moved out of that area as soon as we received an "all clear" over our tactical radio net from Battalion. The firing finally ceased and the NVA disengaged moving northward, away from the battle. We were ordered to proceed in a southern direction and look for signs of other enemy base camps and troop movements. We started our march in the late afternoon, moving through thick vegetation, advancing only six hundred to eight hundred yards per hour. It was terribly slow movement as we worked our way through the elephant grass hills and streambed complex. After more than six hours of struggle through the mass of green vinery hell, we finally broke out on top a barren hilly area overlooking a wet, stream-infested low-lying area to our south.

It was now dark. We were on top of *the* critical terrain feature in the entire area. Surrounded by smaller hills on three sides, we could see in every direction. The ground provided excellent fields of fire for our weapons and troop emplacements. Fortunately, we had stumbled out of the bush, accidentally into an ideal location to establish our defensive perimeter for the night.

Then I received a call from the rear command center over the radio tactical net. It was some major who was attempting to express his superior tactical knowledge and impress me with his rank. We had just gotten all of our men into position; given them a chance to eat something for the first time that day and had put out security outposts and claymore mines around our defensive perimeter as darkness now surrounded us.

The Major told me we needed to move to another location, for what reason I couldn't ascertain. I guess we didn't fit the profile of the battlefield displacements in some way. He gave me new coordinates for the position. I checked them on my map and determined that he was recommending that we relocate from the high ground to a low swampy area some two thousand yards south from our current position. It was the worst possible location in the entire area. The whole idea was a disaster looking for a place to happen. From our perch on the high ground, I could see the location in the moonlit night. I told him that we were in the best defensive position around, and it was now dark and I didn't relish relocating to a much inferior, almost defenseless location in an open area surrounded by high ground. I thought that we would be setting ourselves up for an ambush to be moving at this late hour, and furthermore, his recommendation made no sense to me. After a bit of a heated discussion about the pros and cons of the move, he finally relented, and told me, as the officer on the ground, perhaps I had better perspective on the situation than he did from his rear command headquarters. I agreed with him, thanked him respectfully as much as I could for his keen insight, and signed off the radio with a very curt but military response, "Mike Six, out. "

It was time to get some shut- eye, so we would be ready for day two. The first day was a confusing mess; we had been run all over the place without firing a single shot at the enemy, we had taken casualties during the landing, been pinned down for nearly two hours by our own troops, chopped our way through the elephant grass climbing hill after hill all day trying to reach our objective. Then some "rear echelon" Major wanted us to risk it all by relocating to an inferior, almost defenseless position in the dark. Hopefully, day two would be better. It wasn't!

The next morning we were on the move early with new orders to move north, search the area for enemy activity and link up with the Battalion that had been engaged with the enemy for the past three days. Using our compass for direction in the thick vegetation, we moved out and spent most of the day looking for evidence of the enemy. We finally located their primary base camp which consisted of a series of mutually supporting bunkers, heavily fortified and dug in just below a ridge line in a heavy growth of trees. This was the base camp the Battalion had stumbled into days earlier and were ambushed. They had engaged the enemy in battle resulting in the deaths of the Commanding Officer, several headquarters personnel, and a large number of troops. The bunkers were now vacant, but we searched them out finding some ammo and a few small weapons.

The Battalion's front lines were only a short distance away from the vacated enemy base camp, and after our search, we proceeded to link up with them. I was stunned when we reached their position. It seemed in total disarray; men and equipment scattered all over the place, the remaining headquarters personnel and officers almost in a state of shock. I reasoned quickly it had been a helluva battle. As our column moved through their area, I looked over at what I thought was a group of Marines sleeping. Actually, it was a pile of bodies wrapped in ponchos awaiting transport to the rear. It was an awful sight, staggering every man who saw it. Due to the heavy fighting, no choppers had been able to fly into their position, up to that time, to evacuate the dead and wounded.

I was briefed by the acting Commanding Officer, the Executive officer, and told to set up our defense for the night. We spent the night without incident and the next morning a new Commanding Officer, Lt. Colonel Delong, joined the Battalion to assume command. I had known Delong in Hawaii at Camp Smith. He had an excellent reputation and was highly decorated in the Korean War. We had become friends at Smith and I really liked him and was glad that our company was to be attached to the Battalion under his command. Our friendship and mutual respect would save me some embarrassment in short order.

We spent a second night in a defensive posture while the command group and the rest of the Battalion was regrouping after their fierce encounter with the NVA. The next morning we began moving out to search for the enemy. As we were departing, a Marine combat photographer joined our unit and requested that he be allowed to accompany my lead squad so that he might get some action photos. I told him it wasn't a good idea and that he was putting himself in a very precarious situation. I laughingly told him I didn't even visit the head of the column unless it was critical. He pleaded, I relented, and he went forward to join the squad.

We moved and were fired on almost immediately, no more than two hundred yards from our perimeter. Rifle fire was intense at first, then silence. Within a couple of minutes the photographer came back to my position. Unfortunately, he was being carried in a poncho and had been shot in the chest by a sniper. He was alert. The wound was not critical. I looked at him as he gazed up at me in a kind of drunken stupor, and I said, "I told you not to go up there, but I hope you'll be al right." Our squad had returned fire and killed the two NVA, who had shot at them hitting the photographer.

As other units attempted to depart from their defensive positions, they also took small arms fire and some of the Marines began firing wildly. One of our men was shot and killed - we believed it came from an errant bullet fired by another Marine in an adjoining company, but this was never conclusively determined because rounds filled the air around us.

It became painfully obvious we were surrounded by a number of stay-behind NVA snipers who were taking shots at us as we attempted to leave our position. With this confusion, and inability to determine the extent of the enemy dispositions, Colonel Delong ordered us to hold fast and to move back and re-establish our previous positions. He was anticipating a possible attack and did not want to weaken our defensive posture if this was the case. Also, the indiscriminate shooting by the different units within our Battalion area, could only add to the confusion and result in more Marine casualties from possible friendly fire.

It was a chaotic situation, and we obviously needed more time to organize properly and determine the extent of the enemy dispositions. I ordered my lead squad to return to their original defensive position. I told them to place armed grenades under the bodies of the two dead NVA. I figured the enemy would return later to recover their dead and I wanted them to have a surprise welcome. We plotted mortar fire in and around their location, so, when we heard the grenades in the night, we would blast the hell out of the area, hopefully trapping them within our firestorm.

This accomplished, the squad moved back and we settled in for another night. Sometime later I met with Delong and when I told him of my plan to catch the NVA if they attempted to retrieve the bodies, he really let me have it verbally. He told me in no uncertain terms my actions were unacceptable, against the rules of war, and he could relieve me on the spot. He told me to send my men back to recover the grenades ASAP and that he would forget about the matter.

After the briefing, I called my Platoon Leader and told him to take two squads and retrieve the grenades. It was now dark, we knew we had enemy soldiers around our position and I didn't relish the thought of what could happen to my men, if they were to encounter them while they undid my previous order on the booby traps.

We had radio contact with the patrol and planned mortar fire around their route. They reached their destination without incident, gathered the grenades and made a hasty return back through our lines. I was one happy, much relieved person upon the successful fulfillment of that task. The next morning, when we again moved out, the bodies were gone, obviously carried off by the NVA, just as we expected.

As I reflected on my decision to booby trap the bodies, it was not the most humane thing to do. On the other hand, the enemy in other situations had done the same thing to our casualties. Also, the Battalion had taken a good pounding in the recent battle, loosing a number of men, and I rationalized that we should take every action possible to regain the advantage, protect our troops, and kill as many of the enemy as possible. I wanted to get even for what they had done and believed my decision justifiable. It was easy to excuse yourself from actions that you take when under stress of the battlefield. But the Battalion Commander was right, and I was wrong. That was my conclusion and I didn't try that trick again.

The next morning we attempted a second breakout from our position, and this time there were no enemy soldiers or shooting. We moved north in pursuit of the withdrawing enemy toward the DMZ and patrolled most of the day without incident. We did occasionally find blood trails and a few dead NVA. In some cases the bodies were located close to artillery shell craters, their death apparently caused by the exploding shrapnel.

The following day we were ordered to join another Battalion while Delong's battered group withdrew. Over the next few days we were used, more or less, in a reserve role, treated like stepchildren, unfortunately. Our new Battalion Commander gave me a lecture as soon as we joined up with his unit. We must be clean shaven he informed me, a role practiced by his men. I curtly informed him that we had been on patrol and in the field for several days, we didn't carry razors, and if we had any water we didn't splash it on our faces - we drank it. I told him we were a work group, not a show group. He didn't like my response worth a dam, and proceeded to lecture me on his view of personal hygiene techniques and method of command. He also made it clear that we were only going to be used in the event of an emergency and to get accustomed to his tactical style and leadership.

I didn't need his bullshit flare for the ridiculous, his egomania, or his obvious disdain for any unit that was not a permanent member of his so called "elite organization". He was full of himself, and it was clear that his number one priority was himself and his personal reputation. Obviously, he was in the fray to make a name for himself. His flippant remarks about the combat readiness of Mike Company, because we looked a little shabby, were really uncalled for. He didn't know us, what we had been through the past several days, or our capabilities. And it didn't matter to him. Even his own officers poked fun at his fastidiousness. But he was the Commander, and we were trained and obliged to follow his lead, regardless. We never shaved while attached to his Battalion, wouldn't have, if we had all the shaving gear in the world. Some things just don't matter when you're struggling for existence.

True to his promise to use our company in a lesser role, our first mission assigned by our new Commander, was to provide security for a troop-carrying helicopter that had crashed close to our position. We were to guard the chopper until it could be recovered and taken to the rear area for salvage. Frequently, when our aircraft went down, the enemy would make every effort to destroy it after recovering weapons, radio equipment and other usable items. The crew had already been evacuated, and we were told to stay in the area until the chopper was retrieved.

After receiving our instructions, we moved out, and sometime later located the downed bird. It had not been molested and we proceeded to establish security elements for protection. The chopper had crashed in an open field, located in a depression, surrounded by small hills with two well traveled trails crossing the area. Knowing we would probably be there for at least twenty-four hours, we decided to establish our defensive perimeter around the trail system at the foot of the hills close to the chopper. It was not an ideal location, but we had time to prepare and put out claymore mines and booby traps, as much for early warning, as for protection against potential enemy movement around our location.

Since the trails ran directly through the center of our defensive position, we placed automatic weapons on each trail where they intersected the entry into our perimeter. We thought any night "visitors" would probably be on the trail system since the surrounding terrain was woody with lots of thick underbrush. The position had obviously been occupied previously by someone, because there were a large number of foxholes located in the area. My radio operators and I found one previously dug foxhole; we cleaned it out, dug it a little deeper, and christened it our home.

In the middle of the night, all hell broke loose. Shooting occurred in two opposing directions. Immediately I thought a night attack had been launched on our position. I got on the radio and learned that the two outposts, on the trails, had simultaneous encounters underway - the rest of the defensive perimeter was quiet.

As usual, the shooting lasted only a few moments and then it grew quiet. On the radio, talking with one of the outposts located on the northern trail, I was told that a small group of NVA had come up the trail and were almost in our position when our men opened fire. They killed two and the others escaped in the darkness. I told the men to tie something around the bodies otherwise their comrades might come back and drag them off. The Corporal on the other end of the radio said he didn't think , it was necessary. I asked him why and he said, "Because I can hold onto them from my foxhole." The shooting had occurred at point blank range and the NVA had fallen to the ground adjacent to the Marine's position. I agreed with his analysis, and told them to stay very alert - not that they needed such sagacious advice from me at that time. They were very alert now, and would stay that way all night.

The contact made on the other trail, leading into our position, was covered by an M-60 machine gun and three men. Several NVA had approached our position on the trail, and instead of opening fire on them with the automatic weapon, one of the men drew his 45-caliber pistol and fired. Why he didn't shoot them with the machine gun I could never determine. As soon as he shot, the group scattered, one was killed and another somehow darted inside our position. He was running around within our perimeter firing his weapon creating a great deal of confusion. Our men began firing at him and very quickly we had a dangerous situation on our hands with rounds streaking across our position, both from the NVA and our own troops. I ordered a cease-fire as rapidly as I could to keep any of our men from being hit by "friendly fire."

It was then about midnight, pitch black dark, two NVA dead, laying adjacent to our men in their foxhole, one NVA dead on another trail leading into our position, and an enemy soldier inside our lines, firing randomly with his automatic rifle, trying to escape. In addition, we had a bunch of nervous Marines ready to shoot in any direction, at anything that moved. We were uncertain if this enemy activity was a prelude to a larger attack. This added further fuel to our nervous state. At this point, I decided we needed to turn "night into light". I called our rear artillery Fire Direction Center, and requested illumination over our position.

The illumination shell penetrated the darkness with a blazing flare that lasted for several minutes. The artificial light enabled us to view our position and the surroundings adequately to detect any movement.

The light kept our NVA perpetrator under wraps and may have inhibited further incursions by the enemy into our location. The shells exploded continuously over our position for nearly six hours. We were later informed that we used every round the battery had in supply at the artillery fire-base (around six hundred rounds.)

When daylight first broached the darkness, our NVA visitor surrendered, realizing his only other recourse was to fight his way out of our position - a choice he wasn't willing to make since the odds against him was about one hundred sixty to one.

He made a good choice, stayed alive, and we evacuated him to the rear for interrogation.

Everybody was dead tired from the night ordeal; no one had slept; nerves on edge; and we were fortunate to spend most of the day waiting for the downed chopper to be hoisted out and removed to its airbase. Later that afternoon, we were ordered to catch up with the Battalion in their search for the enemy. We reasoned that our previous night's contact occurred because we had occupied a primary trail system that had been used by the NVA as they moved north and south from the DMZ. Our encounters were probably stragglers, who had been separated during battle and were attempting to link up with their retreating units and we happened to be located on their main route.

Even though it had been a hectic night, we had been successful in eliminating three NVA, capturing one, protecting the helicopter and infuriating the fastidious ego centered Battalion leader, whose command had made no contact over the same twenty-four hour period. He immediately placed us in a reserve position, which meant that we were to bring up the rear as his other units continued the search and destroy operation.

We did have some limited contact over the next couple of days as we attempted to catch and trap the enemy, before they reached the safety of the DMZ. We wanted to be in the chase and believed we deserved more opportunity to do our thing, but it was not to be. We continued to receive his criticism for one thing or another and were kept in a supporting role until the last day.

We had been ordered to peel off from the Battalion and search out a series of hills and stream-beds. We spent the next two days crisscrossing hills and walking in water up to our knees, as we searched both the top and bottom of the hills.

This search technique is called cross grain patrolling and is physically demanding, as you are required to cross from valley to hilltop continuously. Much of this time was spent in the actual streams in hopes that we might locate base camps adjacent to the water supply.

Then we got our chance. A large NVA force was sighted north of our position, and we were the closest unit in proximity of their route of march. We were ordered to pivot from our location and take off after them. We finally had the lead, by accident. We came up from our streambed course and gave chase. The remaining Battalion units were far behind us, as they had maneuvered in a different direction.

It became a foot race between the NVA and us. Irritated, the Battalion Commander was bellowing his instructions over the radio while we were moving, wanting a status report every few minutes. We were almost on a dead run; our feet soggy from the steam patrols, most of our men had a slight case of trench foot, and we were moving much too fast, for good security, but we wanted to catch the fleeing enemy force if we could. The Commander kept bellowing on the radio telling us to speed it up, without any real knowledge about our progress. After several hours of chase, we were contacted by Division headquarters and complimented on our rapid movement and quick reaction to the situation. That probably did my nemesis in because we had apparently been detached from his unit and were now being directed by Division. That had to be the final straw, I never heard from him again.

Finally, we were told by Division that the NVA unit had reached the DMZ, congratulated us for our efforts in the chase and told to disengage. We would be picked up and returned to Dong Ha by the end of the day.

It was on this march I decided to end my career in the Marine Corps. There were probably several reasons for my decision, but at the moment I made up my mind, while in the chase, I was tired, dirty, mentally spent and disgusted with the situation and the harassment from the Battalion Commander. After the past several days of dealing with this pompous ass, I thought to myself, the hell with it, I don't need to be influenced or controlled by people like this. I thought, as a civilian I could tell a domineering boss to "kiss off", or I could leave any situation voluntarily if it didn't appeal to me.

As a military officer, you must "suck it up", take whatever is handed to you, tasks and superiors - and deal with them. Cry babies, complainers, and excuse makers, not withstanding, are not tolerated. Just do the job given you, and get on with life. Actually, this is a good philosophy, and I believe I had learned to accept it and to adhere to most of the principles of the Marine Corps. And I still do after all these years.

But at that moment in the field, on a march chasing the NVA, I decided I needed a change of lifestyle. One that would allow me more freedom of choice and opportunity for personal self-realization. That was it. I had made up my mind to resign my commission after my tour of duty was over. I would not waver from the decision, although I did experience some second thoughts for a period of time before leaving the Corps. It's interesting now, as I look back over the years, and write about this critical defining instance in my life. What I thought I was running away from in the military, ego centered bosses, and restricted opportunity for self-expression, I would encounter, over and over again, as a civilian in the business world.

There is truth in the adage: "The more things change, the more they are the same." In changing my life from one occupation to another, I found similar conditions and people characteristics, but I did have a little more flexibility in how I dealt with them. More importantly, with age and a different environment in which to learn, grow, and express myself, I gained the emotional maturity and intellectual reasoning capability, which I did not posses in those early years in the Marine Corps. These traits finally enabled me to be more understanding and less critical of both human and corporate limitations and to deal with my own inadequacies.

My decision to leave the Corps was not wrong, but I made it for the wrong reasons. I needed to grow in a different way, and only the influence from a different life would provide the stimulation for that to happen. The Marine Corps training and life style took me part of the way and embedded in me important values that would serve me well throughout my life. Had I remained a Marine, it's impossible to imagine what would have unfolded in that career choice without more emotional growth. I may have stumbled at some point and failed, but I had made my decision and I stuck with it. I tendered my letter of resignation a few months later.

We were picked up and taken to Dong Ha, where we had a couple of days to lick our wounds, sleep on a cot, dry out, treat our trench foot, and put the operation behind us. With some rest, hot chow, and a fresher spirit, we departed again for our home at the Cua Viet River base where we spent two weeks, before departing for Okinawa and a projected month and a half of rest and rehabilitation.

Most Battalions were taken out of action for a period of time and dispatched to Okinawa, to inject new manpower, conduct training, and generally put themselves together again before going back into combat. After months of battle and living in the field, both men and equipment were in need of repair. The Marine Corps base on Okinawa provided an important respite for the troops and the opportunity to replenish our equipment and recondition our weapons, which were in terrible condition from the fighting, constant use, and weather conditions.

The USS Princeton anchored off the coast, adjacent to our base at the Cua Viet. We boarded a landing craft with all our equipment after turning over command to another rifle company. The Princeton was an old World War II aircraft carrier, and had been converted into a helicopter transport and assault ship.

As the landing craft utility pulled away from the shore, I stood in the rear of the boat on an elevated gunwale, where the steering housing was located, talking with my Platoon Leaders. In my exuberance and anticipation of the next few weeks, I removed the ammo clip from my pistol and tossed it overboard. (We were suppose to empty our weapons and toss only the ammo overboard after we departed from the base.) No live rounds were to be taken on board ship for safety reasons. I threw my entire metal pistol clip away as a symbolic gesture to celebrate our cherished freedom from the war. I did not realize, however, my entire company was watching, and the next thing I knew they all tossed their metal ammo clips from their weapons overboard, and with a loud vocal, cheerful, shout.

I couldn't say a thing. I had set the example, and they had followed it. Actually, it served as a release from the past several months of anxiety and everybody was relieved and happy to be getting some hard-earned rest and liberty. I laughed and cheered, and wondered how we were going to account for the missing ammo clips when our equipment was inventoried in Okinawa. Finally, I decided to worry about that later and enjoy the moment.

We were on our way to the land of "Milk and Honey" for an extended stay. At least that was the way it was supposed to be.

But the NVA had other plans underway that would alter our stay in Okinawa and the lives of many of our men.

OKINAWA, A RESPITE

Our seagoing trip to Okinawa was a relaxing and comfortable, almost a vacation like experience, when compared to the past several months. We ate good, slept great, and showered frequently. It felt wonderful to be clean once again and to put the madness and responsibilities of the war out of our minds, at least for awhile.

Upon arrival in Okinawa, we were transported to Camp Schawb where we were to be housed for the next few weeks. The troops were located in nice barracks, and the officers were billeted in a dorm like facility, each with his own room. We had a *mamason* provided - an Okinawan woman to clean our rooms, wash our clothes, and generally perform menial household duties for our comfort and convenience. We paid them a small stipend for their service. It was worth every damn penny and was easy to be spoiled after living like an animal for the past several months.

The first order of the day was to put the troops on liberty. All of us needed some down time. Liberty call was to be given the next afternoon after our arrival, when all the gear and cleanup had been completed. I remember standing in front of the assembled company at their barracks, giving my little speech on proper decorum, knowing in my heart that everything I was telling them about behaving themselves was falling on deaf ears.

Realizing this, I closed out my little speech quickly, telling them to remember three things. First, if they weren't at formation the next morning, they would be considered AWOL (absent without leave) and subject to discipline, which meant they would be restricted to the base, probably the worst punishment possible at this point in time. Second, I advised them to stay in groups of twos and threes, so they could look after each other. Finally, I reminded them of the venereal disease potential on the island. Knowing what their prime objective might be, I advised the use of a condom in their endeavors. In those days we even provided them with a supply, before they went on liberty, to help mitigate a problem we couldn't control. With that said, I released the throbbing herd, hoping I would see them again in one piece.

Initially, our day time hours were spent working on our gear, and each night we gave the men an opportunity to go to their club, attend movies, or visit the local town for more "merriment. "

We also conducted some field training, firing weapons, and checking out new gear. The training was necessary, because we had many new transfers into the company. The men they replaced were rotated back to the states or other duty stations, having completed there time *in country*, normally thirteen months.

As I recall, over half of the men I had served with during the past several months went on to greener pastures - meaning they did not have to go back to South Vietnam. Consequently, the company going back into combat would be very inexperienced. A new Commander assumed leadership of the Battalion, Lt. Colonel Vest. He seemed like a good man, but I didn't have much time to get to know him, I was to be transferred within a few weeks.

One evening I happened into a local club, in the town adjacent to our base, and ran into a large contingent of troops from Mike Company, partying. Naturally, I joined them and we began telling war stories. It was here I learned from them that my initial speech at the air base landing strip in Dong Ha, prior to departing from the Qua Viet river base, had really hit home, and that they took it seriously.

You might recall, we had just finished an operation near Cam Lo and were on our way to the Cua Viet River Base. That was when I had gathered the men together for the first time, since taking command, and told them we were going to be a team, kick ass, take care of one another, do our job, and go home in one piece , and so on. Apparently, they bought it, and the rest is history. Maybe it was just the booze talking, I don't know, but their remarks made my day.

We enjoyed our respite in Okinawa, had a lot of fun, and generally put ourselves back together. I also learned I would probably be transferred in the near future as my time in command was coming to a close. Most officers spent about six to seven months in an Infantry Battalion, and I was approaching the limit.

I didn't really want it to end, but after a while, command and combat really wears a person down. I had experienced plenty of close calls, and I was beginning to get a little nervous about my future. Nevertheless, we still had a job to do and all of us went about doing it. We spent a lot of time training, primarily concentrating on getting the new transfers up to speed on tactics and the operating situation in Vietnam.

After only half of our projected time passed, we received some hasty orders telling us that our stay was being cut and we were going back *in country*. I had been out partying with some of my friends and stayed at Cadena Air Base, about thirty minutes from our base. I called in early the next morning to check with my First Sergeant, and to let him know where I was and when I expected to return. Speaking over the telephone, he very bluntly, but courteously, "Skipper, you better get your young ass in here ASAP, the old man is looking for you. He's mad as hell, and it appears we're moving out." With that greeting, I hopped a cab and headed to the base. Upon arrival, I checked in with my top Sergeant, then proceeded to the Battalion Commander's Office. He was pissed because I wasn't there when he called, and was a little uptight and excited about the new mission.

I was informed the fun and games were over and the Command group consisting of all the Battalion staff and Company Commanders were leaving early the next morning by aircraft. We were flying to Dong Ha for a briefing on a major operation that was to be conducted in and around the DMZ. The troops and other officers would follow by aircraft the following day.

Echoing a quote by Winston Churchill, "There was so much to do and so little time in which to do it," but we did it nonetheless, and we were on the plane as scheduled. No question about it - the fun and games were over. During our short absence the war had continued to intensify in the northern section of South Vietnam, particularly around the DMZ.

May 8 was the thirteenth anniversary of the fall of Dien Bien Phu, the last battle with the French and the end of their colonization of Vietnam, when they where defeated and literally thrown out of the country. The NVA were attempting an overthrow of the Marine base at Con Thien with a major push through the DMZ and into the northern region of South Vietnam. I had visited this base before, and it was only two miles from the Southern boundary of the DMZ, making up the northwest corner of the *Leatherneck square*. The enemy had begun massing troops in this sector and it was painfully obvious that they had come to fight and win. To meet this threat, a combined Marine and Army of Republic South Vietnam (ARVN) operation was planned to be launched around mid-May. Our Battalion was to be a part of this force.

THE DMZ

After less than thirty days in Okinawa, we were back in Dong Ha on May fifteenth, preparing for a major battle with a lot of inexperienced troops and officers. Upon arrival at Dong Ha, the command group spent the next two days in briefings and preparations to launch operation HICKORY, within the DMZ. The remainder of our Battalion arrived two days later by air and we assembled all of our forces and completed the transition to a combat readiness posture.

Our mission was to be heli-lifted from Dong Ha on the morning of May 18, into a landing zone inside the DMZ near the Ben Hai River, the boundary between North and South Vietnam. We were to act as a blocking force to prevent the enemy from escaping and to stop reinforcements from entering the region from North Vietnam.

In early May, the NVA had stepped up their ground attacks and artillery bombardment of our bases near the DMZ. Each time our forces engaged the enemy they fought tenaciously and then when our counter assaults began to overwhelm them, they would retreat back to the DMZ. At that time, Marine units were not allowed to enter the Southern boundary of the zone, consequently, the enemy could use this area as a safe haven or sanctuary from our attacking forces. In addition, the southern part of the zone was used as a staging area to launch their attacks on our bases.

As a result of the increased enemy activity, the policy was changed, and our troops were authorized to enter the southern half of the DMZ and conduct tactical operations against the NVA. Thus, our attack plans were now quickly formulated for the new situation.

This operation, the first of its kind since the start of the war, was to be a combined USMC and ARVN amphibious and helicopter borne assault, consisting of six Marine Battalions and five ARVN Battalions. The mission was to sweep south from the DMZ for approximately ten miles, destroying all enemy forces, installations and supplies. In essence, drive the NVA out of the area, while inflicting major damage to their army. The fire support available for this operation included all available artillery and air from both the Marines and Seventh Fleet, including seven destroyers, and two naval cruisers. This was a major operation and was scheduled to last for one week from May 18 to the 26th. Incidentally, I believe Ho Chi Minh's birthday was May 18, a fitting day to celebrate an operation of this size and importance.

The intelligence reports on the enemy positions and activities indicated that our Landing Zone (LZ) was adjacent to a fortified village just a few hundred meters south of the river. It was likely we would be landing in a "Hot" LZ, meaning we would be in contact with the enemy and under fire as we debarked the Choppers. I was the only experienced rifle Company Commander, so Mike Company was given the mission to land first and secure the LZ. As the leading assault Company we would, initially, carry the burden of the attack until the trailing units of our Battalion were landed for support.

As we bedded down that night after making final preparations, issuing ammo and briefing the Platoon Commanders, all I could think about was the possible casualty rate we would experience in our assault. I pessimistically assumed that it would be between 30-50%.

It was not a good night for me and probably a lot of other people, including the unseasoned troops who had recently joined our Battalion in Okinawa and had never before been in combat. About midnight, during the restless sleep hours, the sky seemed to collapse when we began receiving incoming rockets on our position.

Most of the Battalion was billeted close to the airstrip, from which we were to depart in the morning. Fortunately, our bivouac site was full of foxholes and trench lines. This provided some protection against the explosive power of the rockets. They cannot however, protect against a direct hit. Of one Marine that was killed in this attack we could find only his boot. We lost over thirty men that night, wounded and killed, from rockets.

The overall after effect of the rockets was not pretty and the shelling had a devastating mental effect on our men. It almost seemed the NVA knew we were coming after them. They seized the moment to welcome us back to South Vietnam by causing as much disruption and confusion to our forces as possible prior to the attack. It could have been just dumb luck on their part. No one knows for certain, but the coincidence and their timing were too accurate to be guesswork. We were operating with the South Vietnamese army, and one rarely knew where the allegiance of some of those soldiers rested. I know this is a disparaging comment about the army, but I believe it to be true.

This was just one of several times, when I was in Dong Ha, that enemy artillery or rockets were fired on the Base. The proximity of this busy facility and active airstrip to the DMZ and North Vietnam gunners, made it an ideal target. I have to believe it was under constant surveillance by the enemy. They simply grasped every opportunity to interrupt and destroy activity, troops, supplies, and equipment when their intelligence indicated that the timing was good, and our ability to locate them, return counter battery fire, or conduct air strikes were minimized. That made for good tactics - unfortunately against us.

On the morning of 18 May 1967, we boarded our Sea Knight troop carrying helicopters and headed northwest to our landing zone - about a thirty-minute flight. As we glided across the sky, my concern for our troop's safety intensified. I continued to mull over the potential casualty rate that could occur from this operation.

At a point I glanced at one of my young radio operators. Staring into his face, his eyes bug eyed wide, I wondered if I looked as frightened as he obviously was. I was scared, no question about it. I tried to cast out my fear, but the demons wouldn't go away. Everybody in my chopper, about twenty men, sat silent, fighting the same beasts, wondering what would happen to us when the choppers sat down, and we rushed from its belly of safety to meet whoever was waiting.

The preparation fires on the objective finally lifted, and the chopper headed into land. I kept trying to determine, in my mind, the course of action to take under the innumerable situations we might confront. There were no pat answers.

A helicopter assault concept was to debark the chopper as quickly as possible, move away from its circulating blades, find some cover for protection, and if someone is shooting at you, shoot back as quickly and with as much firepower as possible. Keep the men moving, establish a perimeter around the LZ, and protect it while the remaining units are landed. As more troops arrive, continue to extend the perimeter by widening the circle and seizing more terrain. Force the enemy away from the position. Provide space for the landing troops so everyone doesn't bunch up like a mob. Once the landing phase is complete, the landing units force the attack by fire and maneuver, maintaining the pressure on the enemy.

I had a set of headphones and was in voice communications with the pilot. Just before we began our decent to the ground, the supporting fire lifted, and he said he did not believe the site was "Hot" (no enemy or shooting.) Momentarily relieved, I prayed he was correct in his assessment as our chopper wheels touched down. I screamed, "Everybody out," trying to be heard above the rotors, and we lunged forward through the opening doors into the bright, hot, summer-like day. The LZ was an expansive open area, permitting at least four choppers to land simultaneously. This meant about eighty troops would be on the ground in minutes during the initial landing wave.

We quickly spread out. Each group moving toward their assigned quadrant of the perimeter - finding cover, establishing fields of fire, and waiting for all hell to break loose. Not a shot was fired by anybody. No sign of enemy activity anywhere close to the LZ. I think we were all stunned, since we expected the worst possible scenario. While the choppers continued to land, we expanded the LZ moving forward, occupying new positions, and providing room for the troops landing to our rear, in the center of the landing site.

Unless you've participated in a helicopter born assault or an amphibious landing, it would be difficult to appreciate or understand the tremendous amount of confusion and chaos that occurs. It was always amazing to me that these tactical operations ever worked. Somehow they do. The plan unfolds, but not necessarily as it was designed. Coordination and communication are critical, and under the very best of conditions is probably only marginally acceptable.

Our landing went fairly well, and nobody was shooting at us, which reduced the margin of error and confusion significantly. The entire Battalion finally landed, each unit occupying their pre-planned positions. Still no enemy activity.

We were really dumb struck at our good fortune and the lack of hostilities, as we had been so thoroughly briefed on the expected enemy strength and probable intense resistance to our landing.

The next phase of the operation for Mike Company, was to move from the LZ and conduct a search and destroy operation of the fortified village. It was about one thousand meters to our west.

We had also been told that the village was unoccupied by civilians, but we would probably encounter NVA troops. In addition, we would find a large number of well constructed, heavily dug-in bunkers. The report was only half correct.

Deploying the platoons, we commenced our mission moving within several hundred yards of the village. Our leading units reported they were observing a lot of movement in and around the bunkers, and from their distant perspective, the occupants were preparing to defend the village against attack. I ordered them to halt their advance and return to our position and called the fire direction center to request artillery fire on the fortified village. Why waste our men when we might be able to devastate their fortifications with our big guns and eliminate any will to resist?

We moved our company further to the rear, away from the firestorm that was about to occur. Then the shelling began. They shelled heavy and hard all over the position for several minutes and then lifted their fire. Immediately, two jets appeared on position carrying napalm bombs. We called them and they dove on the village, each dropping their canisters of burning hell.

After the melee was over and the fires died down, peering through our binoculars, we could still detect movement in the bunkers. No enemy were shooting in our direction, yet there was people movement. We ask the fire direction center if they had any other supporting arms available. "Yes," they responded, and we could have everything we want. Shortly, two old Corsairs, propeller planes appeared, carrying 750-pound bombs. In their slow, deliberate way, especially compared to the jets, they plunged toward the village and released their payloads, on target.

Immediately on the heels of the explosions, we launched our attack with, still, no shooting from the village. The lead platoons moved into the position quickly, then began searching the bunkers. Inside the numerous fortifications they discovered a large group of old men, women and children huddled together. Matter of fact, the troops gathered up one hundred and thirty five civilians out of the purportedly, unoccupied, enemy fortified complex. I couldn't believe it. They were assembled and marched off to the rear of our position for subsequent evacuation. However, the most amazing part of the whole event was that not one person had been injured from all of the artillery shells, bombs, and napalm that exploded on and around the position. Amazing.

Upon inspecting the village complex, after the civilians were removed, the reason was easily discernable. The bunkers were dug deeply in the ground and reinforced with thick logs several inches in diameter. Only a direct hit would have destroyed the structure, and even with that, the bottoms of the bunkers provided small caves for the people to crawl into for added protection.

There was one sour note. When one of our troops, in attempting to determine who was in a bunker, could get no response from his efforts to get them to come out, threw a hand grenade inside killing an old woman.

It was unfortunate. He had an interpreter with him, but in his haste and fear he acted too aggressively. On the other hand, this was early in the operation and he wasn't aware that many of the bunkers contained only civilians. After all, we were told, in all probability, we would encounter only enemy troops.

We had several news reporters trailing our unit and as we moved into the village, they accompanied the troops. Where the old woman was killed a reporter was on the spot witnessing the entire event. He later came to me complaining about the excessive hostility by the trooper. I could only respond that somehow, one hundred thirty five civilians had been spared a terrible death, and only one person was killed, accidentally, by a Marine who had never seen combat and was scared to death, but was only trying to do his job. He certainly had no intention of killing anyone who was not trying to kill him. That response didn't satisfy the reporter, but I had more to do than debate morality with him at that time and told him so.

The civilians were evacuated from our position and I never learned for certain who they represented. The fortified village was inside the southern boundary of the DMZ in South Vietnam, an area where loyalty was less clear. The people were probably local Vietnamese belonging to the south, but used by the NVA to support their logistical needs. The absence of young men was possibly a result of forced conscription by the NVA into their Army - or voluntary. We continued our search through the village and found four dead NVA soldiers on the edge of the village, who were obviously attempting to escape, when they were caught in the earlier shelling.

In one large bunker area we located an underground hospital facility, fully stocked with medical supplies, perhaps thirty tons of rice, and every type of medical instrument imaginable. We determined, because of the location in the DMZ and the supplies, the village was probably a field hospital for wounded North Vietnamese soldiers.

On the flank of the village we found a concealed, abundantly supplied ammo dump buried deep in the ground. It was covered and reinforced with large timbers. We estimated the ammo cache contained over ten tons of various types of explosives and ammunition.

Under normal conditions, all the rice and ammo would have been removed for subsequent use by the Army of Vietnam, (ARVN), or the rice would have been distributed to various villages, but the high temperatures, distance to landing sites, and unavailability of choppers due to other missions, necessitated that both the rice and ammo be destroyed. We burned the rice and blew up the dump, which produced a tremendous explosion and a huge cloud of black dust, that hovered over our position for several minutes.

Throughout the day the rest of the Battalion moved into their blocking position. Contact with the enemy was limited and we experienced only sporadic mortar fire on our positions. We located a trail leading from the village due north, toward the Ben Hai river. I dispatched a patrol to check it out to the river's edge, and in a kind of perverse humorous way, we made a sign on the back of a C-Ration cardboard box that read, "Fuck you, Ho Chi Minh, Mike Company, 3/4", and I ask the men to attach it to a tree, on a path, that crossed the river. We wanted to leave our calling card.

Mike Company personnel had been through some heavyweight emotional experiences that first twenty-four hours in country. Rockets and mortars dropped on us in Dong Ha, our first night back in South Vietnam followed by a helicopter assault that could have been a debacle if our LZ had been "Hot" - then the sweep of the fortified village, locating the large civilian contingent, discovery of the field hospital, rice and ammo dump. Both anxiety and fear had reached new levels in our minds by days end.

We settled in for the evening adjacent to the village and spent an uneventful night. However, a surprising turn of events awaited.

The next morning we were re-supplied by helicopters. Water was the most needed item with temperatures so extremely high. I think I must have consumed at least three quarts of water before we jumped off later that afternoon - we moved from our position, south into a hilly area overlooking the DMZ. Still no significant contact with the enemy occurred that second day, except for mortar fire.

But late in the afternoon, I received orders directing me to report to Phu Bai for duty with the Third Marine Division headquarters. I was being relieved of duties and transferred, much to my surprise at the timing, especially during an operation in the DMZ. I knew the transfer was forthcoming and had been alerted while in Okinawa that my time in command was coming to a close, but I had no idea it would occur while deployed on a major operation.

The new Company Commander, my replacement, reported into take over the next morning, and I was officially relieved at that time. This was routine procedure but it was rough leaving those guys in that situation. A little more time might have provided me with the opportunity to shake every man's hand, thank them for his support, and wish them good luck. I didn't have that luxury under the current situation. I spoke with my Platoon Commanders and staff NCO's, grabbed my pack, and headed down the hill to the landing zone to catch a chopper.

Walking along, I was accosted by half dozen men with their Platoon Commanders standing at attention in the middle of the trail. We didn't say much to each other. They handed me an NVA map case with the signatures of all the members of the First Platoon. Also inscribed on the front in bold black letters, "For the Best Skipper in the Corps". I loved all the guys of

Mike Company very much. They were like family to me. Incidentally, I still have the map case and it's stored with some of my war memorabilia. Interestingly, a couple of years after I returned home, I was looking through it and found concealed in a small indistinguishable pocket, a small note book, a letter from home, pictures, and some Vietnam money. I believe it had belonged to an NVA Sergeant. It would be interesting to know about him, his history and what became of him. I don't know how the men came about obtaining the map case. I hoped they "found" it in the village.

I saluted them, muttered something, and then got out of there as fast as I could. I didn't want them to see the tears welling up in my eyes. My last parting words with my head half turned from their view were, "You Bastards," then I was gone.

The emotion was nearly overwhelming, but perhaps that is the way things should happen. No long drawn out tearjerkers, dwelling on the past, because it was over, and a new future begins for everybody, everyday. It was my last command, of any kind in the Corps and I was now en route to the Third Marine Division headquarters at Phu Bai to assume my final duties as a Marine Corps Officer.

PHU BAI, AGAIN

I started my official duties in South Vietnam at the Phu Bai Base and I would finish them there, however, they would not be as exciting or demanding as those just completed. I reported in about the 23rd of May and was assigned as a staff officer to work in the Command and Operations center.

The facility was a heavily bunkered building filled with maps and communications equipment and staffed by numerous officers around the clock. Their job was to follow the actions of all the operating units within the Division concurrently. They monitored communications, responded to requests and sent out new directions from the Division Commander and his staff, while also keeping all of the key officers at Division fully informed - especially the Division Commander, Major General Bruno Hockmuth. This was the nerve center for everything that went on in the Northern I Corps area. I went immediately to work on one of the shifts in the command center, and began learning the responsibilities of my new job.

Interestingly, the operation we were following day and night was the one I had just left in the DMZ, and it would continue for five more days. All units were beginning to experience heavier contact each day, and my old Battalion was engaged in a significant battle on hill 174, about four miles southwest of Con Thien only a few miles from where I had left them.

Each day, I followed the action, writing summary reports, and plotting detail positions on the large situation map covering our entire wall, as each unit of the Battalion maneuvered against the enemy. On the 24th of May, Mike

Company, along with other units, attacked hill 174 and was "blown off the hill" by a heavy volume of enemy fire-power and mortars. They sustained many casualties. They attacked again on the 25th with the same results, sustaining an even heavier loss of men.

On the 26th, with another attack, they gained a foothold on the ridge and on the 27th took the crest. But the enemy had abandoned the position and retreated from the continuous bombardment and ground attacks. Mike Company had suffered major casualties while attacking Hill 174 during those four fateful days. They took more casualties than we had experienced in the past six months by a large margin - and I had missed the battle by a few days because of my transfer.

It was horrible reading the situation reports, and monitoring the tactical command radio nets on the action as it played out. Apparently, the NVA had established a superior well-prepared defensive position with rockets and mortars available in ample quantity, and the avenues of approach, into their position, were well covered by automatic weapons.

Even so, our combined arms supporting weapons bombed and shelled the hill for the entire four days while the battle raged. What went wrong? I can't say. I was told later, that bad tactical decisions were made and that the company was maneuvered into areas on the hill that exposed the men excessively to hostile fire. Also, some of the smaller units were not reinforced when under attack. I don't really know what happened or how decisions were made, I wasn't there, and who knows what course of action I might have chosen or what the ultimate outcome would have been. For all I know, had I been in command, Mike Company might have been totally obliterated, I'll never know. It was a sad time for me. In some crazy way I felt responsible because I wasn't there with them, at this critical time.

My time in the command operations center was relatively short. Some new Majors reported in and because of their seniority were assigned to the center. Consequently, I was transferred to another headquarters function. I was actually glad to move on. I didn't like working the different shifts around the clock, or being inside a subdued area eight to ten hours at a time with no fresh air or daylight.

I was moved to the Division G-3, operations and training shop and over the next few months would work on everything from tactical planning to training and special projects. I was asked to brief several Lt. Colonels on Quick Fine Techniques which, at the time, was a British Jungle Warfare method of aiming and sighting your rifle in reduced visibility, such as thick under-bush or at night in rapid fire. I had been exposed to this shooting method at their Jungle Warfare School in Malaysia, and had included the technique in our training program in Hawaii, and later in command of Mike Company.

It was a great method to help the shooter ensure he was at least aiming in the proper direction when firing his weapon on an unclear target. One of the techniques, very accurate for night ambushes especially, involved attaching a white string to the front and rear sights of the rifle running along the top of the barrel. The shooter would place the butt of the stock against his chest with his chin on the stock, and keeping both eyes open, sight down the string toward the target. This would ensure the barrel was pointed toward the intended target and the weapon was level. The rifle would then be fired in short bursts. It was amazing how accurate the shooter could be with this method.

Another approach was to hold the butt of the weapon in the center of the stomach with the body squared towards the target. Then, while keeping both eyes open, the fire is "walked" across the target.

The normal duties of a staff officer are not that exciting but can be demanding, as one spends long hours shuffling papers and completing reports. My routines did get interrupted a few times when I was dispatched to places like, Saigon, Okinawa, and Da Nang, for some Division coordinating purposes. These were great get-away excursions and usually offered the opportunity for hot meals, showers, and a fresh soft bed rather than the standard army cot.

However, one trip I was asked to make was not so comfortable or safe. General Hockmuth, who had taken over Command of the Division in April, learned that I had operated in the Qua Viet area with good success. He told me that he would like for me to visit with the current Commander, brief him on everything I knew about the area, the tactics we had employed, and accompany his units on some of their search and destroy operations.

From his briefing I learned that the enemy had regained control of some parts of the Qua Viet TAOR and were now, frequently mortaring the Marine base, inhibiting the re-supply function from the sea to Dong Ha. The river base was now occupied by an AMTRAC Battalion, about 30-40 amphibious vehicles. They were commanded by a Lt. Colonel who had been responsible for base security for some time. No infantry units were now located at the facility, and I assumed they were required inland to combat the continued infiltration of NVA into the region from the North. A set of written orders to validate my reason for travel and purpose, were given to me and I was told to be back in ten days. I was on my own as far as transportation was concerned. I was to do the best I could and finally told, simply, "let me hear from you when you return."

I took off the next morning with my 45 cal. pistol, poncho, a make shift dopp kit, extra socks, and headed to the Phu Bai

air strip where I hoped to hitch a ride, of some kind, to Dong
Ha. After some begging and pleading, I was assigned to a
chopper, and we landed at the base about thirty minutes later.
As we disembarked from the helicopter, we began taking
incoming - probably from across the DMZ in North Vietnam.

You might recall this incident described earlier when we
were all huddled inside a bunker, alongside the airstrip, while
the heavy guns pounded the base for about fifteen minutes.
This was to be my last visit to Dong Ha and my soft cover hat,
punctured by a shrapnel fragment, was my souvenir from that
trip.

Later, I was able to arrange boat transportation from Dong
Ha down the Qua Viet to the River Base. It had been about
four months since I had left the Qua Viet for Okinawa, but it
looked a lot different to me. The RMK Construction Company
was not longer in residence, and the physical location of the
base had been moved from the head of the river, down the
coast a few hundred yards. The docking facility was still in the
same location, as were the petroleum storage tanks. The area
seemed in disarray, obviously scarred by the frequent artillery
and mortar attacks.

I disembarked from the landing craft and walked down the
beach to the command center of the Amtrak Battalion. Inside,
I found the Commander, introduced myself and told him why I
was there.

"The Division Commander had sent me to share
information", I said. He had not been informed of my
intended visit, and as is very normal, did not seem interested
in having a young Captain tell him, a Lieutenant Colonel, with
years of experience, how he should run his organization or the
war.

Immediately, when he told me that no one had told him I
was coming, I knew this would not be easy, and my insights

were only obligingly received. However, I was welcomed to go on operations and offer my two bits of information. I was assigned a heavily fortified bunker, which was good, because we were shelled a few hours after I arrived. I was told this was SOP (Standing Operating Procedure) every day. The problem with the security of the base was simple, at least in my mind. The Amtrac Battalions had plenty of vehicles to run around in all day, but they did not have the training or the infantry mentality to patrol and search the area like a typical Marine rifle company, or as we had done.

They did not posses the expertise or mindset of a infantry unit. Nor did they possess creative action plans to keep the enemy off guard. I don't believe they were doing much in the form of nighttime ambushes, so, ownership of the ground belonged to the enemy during those hours.

When the pressure applied by our troops subsided, the NVA and VC increased their presence and authority. Nothing was permanent in South Vietnam, everything was always in a state of flux, and control of the ground would vacillate from one side to the other continuously.

I spent several days with the Battalion, did the best I could in sharing ideas and information, but decided shortly that it was time to head back to Phu Bai. I was able to catch a ride on a Navy patrol boat, the same kind that was dropping mortar rounds near our position at the Qua Viet several months earlier. They told me they could get me close to Dong Ha and I was welcomed aboard for the trip. These crafts were modified speed boats, manned by three or four men with an 81mm mortar mounted on the deck so they could fire on targets of opportunity while at sea, or traveling in a water inlet, wherever enemy troops were sighted. These men, I'm sure, were good sailors, but seemed a bit loose in their attitude and way of life. I had been on their boat all day. Night was approaching when they received new orders - I guess, to go on another mission. They told me they would have to drop me off somewhere so I wouldn't be in their way.

I found myself on a landlocked barge with three smiling, and reputedly, South Vietnam soldiers, who were the occupants. I really didn't quite know where I was or who I was with. I spent a few hours with the three musketeers, without understandable conversation - not knowing if they were friend or foe. I concluded they were hiding from their unit. Finally, I was able to flag down a motor boat driven by two Marines, and with much relief, was taken to a small Marine base used for in country R&R, located outside of Hue.

I grabbed a bed for the night and the next day caught a jeep headed to Phu Bai only about fifteen miles away. I had been gone ten days, had been shelled, rocketed, my chopper blown away, participated in a couple of search and destroy operations, spent a day with the Navy and dropped off without any idea as to my location, and now was at last returning from my assignment.

My original mission, I thought, was a failure, because no one seemed to care what I had to offer in the form of ideas or information on the Qua Viet. No criticism intended. Under the circumstances, there was no way I could have told the Commander how to fight his war. The intentions were good, the practicality unrealistic.

I reported in, gave my report and went back to the tedium of my staff responsibilities. But, I had experienced a helluva trip and the memories would be long lasting.

In early fall a different kind of opportunity developed when I was asked to participated in a track meet for the U. S. Armed forces to be run against the Vietnamese. Yes, the war was still going on, but someone high up in the chain of command thought it would be good public relations and a release from the drudgery of the war, to host a sports event for both the citizens of Hue and the Marines.

The sports activity, which also included a soccer game, was to be called "The Hue Olympics" and was to be conducted over a two day period in the old Imperial City of Hue a few miles from Phu Bai. As an appointed member of the Marine track team, for this event, I would run and train each evening on the dirt streets that crisscrossed our camp. I had two weeks to train for the meet and attempted to get my not-so-good body anymore in some kind of decent physical condition.

I was going to run the 100 and 220 yard dash, but found trying to run in jungle boots was not the easiest way to train for the sprints. Just prior to the meet, a friend of mine ,who was also scheduled to compete, located some low cut tennis shoes, which made training and running much easier.

On the day of the meet, we were driven to Hue and dropped off at the old stadium. What a sight to behold. It was located in the middle of the city. One side had collapsed into large rubble blocks from explosions that had occurred some time past. We wore our 45 cal. pistols most of the time for personal security, except when we were running. The Vietnamese officials for the meet put the lime stripes on the dirt track by hand, pouring it over a string that was stretched out in a straight line on the track. The lines were amazingly accurate.

The starter for each event would call the runners to the ready in his native language. Then holding a wooden block in each hand, he would clap them together for the starting signal. They did not use a starter pistol, as any gun shot sound might create consternation for the people attending the meet.

Competing in this environment was a bit challenging. As I prepared to run my events I took off my pistol and holster, behind the starting line, handed it to a friend to hold for me until the race was over. At the starting line, it was necessary to start in a halfback stance, rather than a typical sprinter's stance, so I could watch what I was supposed to do. The Vietnamese starter called out his instructions. There was a small sound when the wood blocks were clapped together. It was necessary to watch to make certain that you started the race with both the motion and the sound. It was crazy, but it worked.

I ran my sprint events, finishing first in one event and second in the other. These were only the trials (or preliminary heats) and those runners who qualified in their heats were scheduled to run the finals the next day. Therein was the problem, I had given everything I had in those two races, and I believe, I must have stretched and pulled every muscle that existed in my poor, tired, thirty year old legs. The next day, as I lay suffering from the previous day's exertion, General Hockmuth dropped into my hut, caught me in bed, and asked if I wasn't supposed to be running that day. I sheepishly responded, "Sir, I can't even walk today, much less run." He laughed and left. That was the end of my track career, the last foot race I would ever run. The "Hue Olympics" had provided the setting for an ignominious finish for my competitive athletic career.

General Hockmuth our Division Commander, was a fine man and leader, and I had tremendous respect for him. Unfortunately, he was killed some months later while flying in a helicopter which was shot down by ground fire. His career and life ended prematurely, like so many other people who suffered through the horrors of that war to become one of the KIA (Killed In Action) statistics in the Vietnam conflict. As a personal note, General Hockmuth, earlier, had presented me with a Bronze Star medal in ceremonies at Phu Bai.

My thirteen month tour was rapidly coming to an end and I began thinking about my future without the influence of the Marine Corp's "Shield and Anchor" (Marine Corps Symbol), in my new life. I was reading everything I could get my hands on and writing letters of inquiry to numerous companies about employment opportunities. I needed a job immediately upon leaving the Corps as I had a wife and two small "curtain climbers" to feed and little financial resources available to sustain our lives.

I considered graduate school although I had been out of college for over eight years. My business knowledge was limited and the only things I really knew well were military oriented. I didn't think my current skill level in guerrilla warfare, battle tactics, survival, and weapons knowledge would aid me much in a civilian occupation. I took the graduate record examination while in Vietnam but didn't obtain a score high enough for admission to many schools. I had been away from college too long and needed a lot of refresher courses, or so it appeared, from my test score.

I did attempt to enroll at Georgia State University, in Atlanta, a couple of years later, after I had been in the business world. The registrar told me I would need to take the exam again and I refused, arguing that my experience should count for something and that a test score should not be the only criteria used to evaluate a person's intellect and desire. A willingness to work hard, results form past efforts and the success obtained since leaving the Marines should count for something.

I lost the argument, did not retake the examination and went on with my business life. It didn't matter in the long run, although I'm confidant I would have benefited from the additional education. Interestingly, throughout my business career, I have been asked to lecture at several graduate schools - an unique turn of events from my earlier efforts.

In November, I was notified I had been selected for promotion to Major, even though I had submitted my letter of resignation.

The selection for promotion, to a field grade officer, was significant and had occurred with only seven and half years of service, which was early promotion at that time. In the past, it had taken anywhere from ten to twelve years as a Captain to obtain that rank. However, with the war, promotions were beginning to accelerate, due to the manpower increases and need for officers to fill the expanding responsibilities. Because of my termination date, I missed pinning the gold oak leaf insignia on my uniform, by about two months. I was extremely proud to have been selected, especially so early in my short career, and the promotion, had I remained in the Corps, would have advanced some interesting new opportunities and challenges in my life as a Marine Officer. I did receive a temporary promotion to Major, as a reserve officer, a year later after leaving the Corps.

My orders for transfer arrived in early November and directed that I depart Vietnam in mid December, for release from active duty in January. Those subsequent weeks in-country were not easy nor filled with optimism. I was second guessing the decision about my career move, had not scored well on the Graduate Record exam, and did not have a job opportunity arranged, all of which caused great consternation to my psyche, in addition to what existed routinely with the war.

Most Marines assigned to the Third Division were routed through the Phu Bai Headquarters for subsequent assignment to their units. I had the opportunity to visit with a number of contemporaries while en route to their assigned duty destinations. It was enjoyable getting reacquainted, in some cases it had been several years, and being brought up-to-date on their lives. The despair came later. In more cases than I care to remember, many of these fine young officers were to meet their ultimate fate in battle and never return home to their families. Casualty figures from the battles in process were a daily occurrence as situation reports were submitted regularly to the headquarters. Reviewing these, we would see the names of some of our friends who had only recently traveled through Phu Bai. It was a startling realization that the war was continuing to destroy the young manhood of American and sadden all of us, knowing that our friends and associates had been killed in the prime of life. Unfortunately, this terrible war and toll on American youth was to go on for many more years.

One evening, while having a libation with a friend of mine, as we sat in my hut sharing a bottle of booze, we talked about our future. He was a young, extremely intelligent, doctor from New York City and had served with my Battalion when we were up north in Dong Ha and Cam Lo. Discussing our next life, I inquired if he thought I could be successful in the civilian world. I respected his opinion and knew he had considerable experience as a civilian before joining the Naval Medical Corps.

He reflected for a moment and then told me, "Yes, I think you will be successful."

He believed I had what it took and should do well with my future endeavors. His remarks really made me feel good. After a bit, I sheepishly asked him why he thought I would be successful? What traits did he see in me to make him confident of my future efforts?

He smiled, had a taste of his drink and looking at me seriously, responded, "Because you're too damn stupid to know when to quit."

His remark, I thought at the time was a little harsh, but through the years, the haunting truth of his comment probably summarized the strongest trait I possessed. I've repeated his assessment to my friends several times over the years and many considered his evaluation to have been on target.

Another evaluation of my potential was given by a Lt. Colonel who worked in the S-3 operations shop and was my boss for a period of time. After some lengthy discussion about the future, when I was seeking his advice and counsel, he told me, "you could make a million dollars selling used cars."

He was serious and I tried to accept his evaluation as a used car salesman as a compliment. I guess I was always trying to convince somebody about something I thought important, regardless if it was or wasn't. Also, I had to talk my way out of trouble or make excuses for things I did throughout my entire stint in the Corps. I suppose I learned to express myself with a sincere concern, since most of the time I was probably trying to save "my ass", from some dumb decision or action I had taken.

Finally my time was up. I was no longer a short timer (Marines who have only a few weeks before being transferred) and I caught a chopper to Da Nang to catch my flight to the temporary stopover in Okinawa. About two hundred Marines, mostly enlisted, were on the flight.

In a most solemn manner, we boarded the plane, took our seats in deathly quiet, and awaited the take off. The plane coursed down the runway, picked up speed, and lifted into the air. The accent was rapid and breath taking, as it nosed nearly straight up for safety reasons. There was always a concern that low flying aircraft might attract ground fire, so upon take off pilots throttled their planes sharply upward immediately, as they lifted off the runway.

Once airborne, a tremendously loud roar erupted throughout the plane. The men began shouting joyfully. The tension had finally been relieved; they were going home. We had made it through the ordeal, alive, and were happy and ready to celebrate. One of the stewardesses told me later that every flight was the same. Almost in disbelief they were leaving, everybody would sit in stunned silence until they were safely in the air, and then suddenly, in unison, the entire group would shout their cheerful approval as their burden of the war was finally lifted.

We stopped in Okinawa, went through some processing, gathered any gear we had in storage and a couple of days later were flown to the States.

As I was going through the airport terminal in Los Angles to catch my flight to Atlanta, where I was to meet my wife, I was walking through a passage-way, dressed in my military uniform, when three hippies, I assumed they were hippies by their dress and long hair, welcomed me back to the USA by spitting on my uniform and calling me a killer of women and children. I could hardly contain myself, but I did. My war was over and I wanted only to relieve my pent-up emotions by being with my wife and children.

I'm certain I offered some verbal expletive to them for their "courtesy" and went on to catch my next flight. Unfortunately, their repulsive attitude was mild compared to the riots, hostility and demonstrations that would evolve over the next few years. The war waged on relentlessly, leading to what many would call the "low water mark" in the history of our country.

But, I was Home, in one piece, and that was the important thing at the time. Nearly eight years, as a Marine, were coming to a close and I now had the future to contemplate.

Yesterdays
Are Forever

"We saw not clearly nor understood,
But, yielding ourselves to the master-hand,
Each in his part as best he could,
We played it through as the
Author planned."

Alan Seeger

ATLANTA, GEORGIA,

A RETROSPECT

It is now April, 1999, thirty one and a half years since leaving the Marine Corps and returning from the war in South Vietnam. I've enjoyed a good life, am remarried to a wonderful woman, Elaine, and our combined family consists of five children and five grand children. I am in good health, been relatively successful in my civilian career and probably have only a limited amount of anguish remaining from the war. Overall, I continue to believe the training and wide ranging involvement experienced in the Marines, was a critical and necessary adjunct to both my personal and professional growth through the years. The decision to enter the Corps in 1960 was timely and essential to my maturation and emotional development. In other words, it forced me to grow-up, accept responsibility, be decisive, and discipline myself. I could not perceive the sacrifices and commitment I would need to make, in order to reach maturity and gain my much needed self confidence. I will always be grateful to the Marine Corps for the opportunities to learn the lessons of living and coping, sometimes forced to learn, many times, the hard way. Those yesterdays will forever remain a vital part of my life. They contain the events, challenges and opportunities that forged my Rite of Passage in the Marine Corps and subsequently, the transition into the person I am today.

My decision to leave the Corps was probably a good one, at that time. Although, had I stayed the course and maintained a positive attitude about the military way, I believe I would have been satisfied and happy. I have no idea how my career might have advanced, because of my tendency to be a little too "creative" and determined in those things I believed in strongly.

I was, and still am, a hard learner much like the child who must touch the burning stove to prove to myself that it is really hot.

The war was a major mistake, everybody knows that today. There is no revelation here. But, in those days, the sixties, we believed deeply in our country, our politicians were respected, and we approached life with a strong sense of patriotic values and adherence to the rules of the game. It was not in our mentality to challenge the system. No questions asked. We did as we were told and did it damn well. Our motto could have been taken from the poem, "The Charge of the Light Brigade"... "Ours is not to reason why, ours is but to do or die."

My Country right or wrong, my country, stood tall in the minds of many of us in the early sixties. But the war and resultant sociological change of attitudes, on many issues, changed our nation forever. Ultimately, for bad or good, I don't know what the final score will tally. I do know that wide divisions occurred in our population, and for many years the turmoil was nearly overwhelming.

We marched to war, because we were told it was the proper course to follow. We believed our country's mandate was to save the world, restore freedom for oppressed people, whenever, or wherever, it was challenged. I had to do my part and believed it was my responsibility as did many other young people. Later, we would realize the war was a fallacious attempt, perhaps promoted more for certain political ego aggrandizement than achievement of national objectives or stewardship for wronged peoples.

Our country lost nearly 60,000 people in that terrible Asian war. Another 300,000 were physically wounded, and there is no telling how many people still, today, carry mentally debilitating scars that will affect them and their families forever.

My time in the Marines was an enriching experience for the most part. I was doing what I wanted to do, and I believed I was serving my country as a patriot.

Many friends, associates, and family members were impressed that I had undertaken this memoir, which has now taken me two years to complete, after thinking about it for thirty-two. Some say they can't wait to read it, they are being polite. Some are less than interested; they are being honest.

For me it is an important work, a literary trial of sorts, that I had to commit to paper, if only to rediscover my early years and examine some of the underlying events that shaped my character and value system. The resulting catharsis has allowed me to touch and understand parts of my subconscious I had lost contact with over the years. Alert to the discovery, I made the dedication to give expression to these important times of my life, resulting in this book, which I hope will be meaningful for my family.

Revisiting my past, especially during those formative and molding years, has produced a positive effect on me. Besides, now being more aware of my past and the influences it created within me, I understand better how a person's decisions shape their destiny and ultimately, arrival at their destination. I've found that the past is indeed a prologue to the future and that Yesterdays will always live Forever in our hearts.